Queer Issues in Contemporary
Latin American Cinema

Queer Issues in Contemporary Latin American Cinema

DAVID WILLIAM FOSTER

University of Texas Press

Austin

Library of Congress Cataloging-in-Publication Data
Foster, David William.
Queer issues in contemporary Latin American
cinema / David William Foster.
     p.   cm.
Includes bibliographical references and index.
ISBN 0-292-70536-0 (cloth : alk. paper) —
ISBN 0-292-70537-9 (pbk. : alk. paper)
1. Homosexuality in motion pictures.   2. Motion
pictures—Latin America.   I. Title.
PN1995.9.H55 F67   2003
791.43′653—dc21   2003001850

Contents

Preface

This book is the fourth in a series dealing with Latin American film. *Contemporary Argentine Cinema* (1994) examined Argentine filmmaking since the return to constitutional democracy in 1983 and was therefore focused on films that dealt with issues of re-democratization in that country: the abuse of power, authoritarianism, sexual rights, women's issues, and the relationship between current events and national history.

Gender and Society in Contemporary Brazilian Cinema (1999) dealt with Brazilian films produced, with one exception, after the return to constitutional democracy in that country in 1985, although I was principally interested in framing the discussion in terms of gender. Hence the volume is organized in three large blocks: masculinist focuses, feminist focuses, and same-sex focuses. This organization was not so much to highlight the fact that Brazilian film deals with issues of gender, sexuality, and sexual transgression—it does so no more than the films of other nations, even if this constellation is part of national mythmaking for tourist purposes. Rather, I was interested in intersecting gender issues and filmmaking because there was not yet any monographic study on Latin American film from this perspective.

Feminist theory has seen the development, in part through its intellectual inspiration, first of queer studies, which question the gender categories held in place by the heteronormative patriarchy, and subsequently, masculinist studies, which both question the assumption of the universal categories of the masculine/nonmasculine binary (a primary contribution of feminism) and the normalization of the masculine (a primary contribution of queer studies). Specifically, I was interested in how the changes in Brazilian society were allegorized in primarily gendered narratives with the return to democracy, the critical analysis that redemocratization brought with it of the two decades of tyranny, and the empowerment of previously repressed and oppressed social groups (along one axis, women and queers). The allegories tended to focus on love stories—or at least stories in which gender is foregrounded—that had much to say about sociopolitical arrangements of social power and legitimacy. Concomitantly, I was interested in how gender—the foregrounding of a man's or a woman's body—could be particularly effective as a strategy of semiosis in a film.

Mexico City in Contemporary Mexican Cinema (2001) delineates the intersect of film and urban studies, in this case of Mexico City, the world's most populous megalopolis. Unlike Argentina and Brazil, Mexico did not experience neofascist tyranny, and therefore there is no sociohistorically significant dividing point for this study. However, the study takes advantage of the international attention paid to Mexican film in the 1990s and the fact that recent decades have shown, in the Mexican imaginary, a definitive shift toward the urban. Consequently, with a handful of exceptions, the films examined in the study are from the 1990s; all of them, if not direct interpretations of the urban experience, are set in Mexico City, and the city is in some way an integral part of each film's narrative. Even if the stories are not explicitly urban tales, the city intervenes in the experience of the film's protagonist; even if the physical attributes of the city are not specifically foregrounded, the story would make little sense if it were transposed to a provincial or rural setting.

These films underscore the extent to which so much of contemporary—one might say postmodern—Latin American reality has become urban: the migratory patterns in much of Latin America are toward the city; national identity means to a large extent having an urban consciousness; and the most significant filmmaking is set in the city. Alejandro González Iñárritu's *Amores perros* (2000), which became available in video after this study was completed and thus is not included in it, is a perfect example of what I am talking about. It is built around three tales of the city involving three social classes and interlocking, overlapping, and conflicting experiences in a precariously shared urban landscape. Gender is, of course, an issue of urban life, and the city is where both feminist and lesbigay movements have prospered. As a consequence, several of the films in this study continue the gender focus of *Gender and Society in Contemporary Brazilian Cinema*.

Queer Issues in Contemporary Latin American Filmmaking, the volume at hand, corresponds to the previous studies in a number of ways. In the first place, by dealing with specifically queer issues, it necessarily examines films both set in the city and in which the city plays a crucial role: this is particularly evident in Barbet Schroeder's *La Virgen de los Sicarios* (2000), in which the drug-related violence of Medellín, Colombia, at the height of the power of Pablo Escobar and the so-called Medellín cartel is integral to the same-sex relations narrated. Queer studies question patriarchal heteronormativity and the compact narrative of compulsory matrimony, compulsory heterosexuality, compulsory monogamy, and the unquestionable homologizing of romantic love, erotic desire, and individual fulfillment. In this sense queer studies are gender studies: while they may reach out to question other forms of social normativeness (for example, in the overall conception of the body, not just its sexualization), they are centered insistently on questions of sexuality. Sexuality (gender identities, gender roles, gender preferences, gender performances, erotic desires, sexual practices) as defined by compulsory heterosexuality (i.e., what we can call heterosexism) may be analyzed and questioned—deconstructed, in a word—while at the same time other configurations of sexuality may be explored and proposed.

The essays that appear here continue the practice of the other three titles in this informal series of selecting a limited range of texts in order to focus on each text in some depth. A few films are treated in a briefer fashion either because they are tangential to the direct representation of homoerotic desire (Víctor Saca's *En el paraíso no existe el dolor,* 1995) or because they are, I will argue, defective in their utilization of a reference to it (Marcos Zurinaga's *The Disappearance of García Lorca,* 1997). However, most films are examined in considerable detail. One might always wish to treat cultural products as deserving of in-depth analyses: if cultural production is socially significant, it deserves to be analyzed in detail to demonstrate this importance in terms of how its texts create and negotiate meaning. But it is even more imperative to discuss texts in detail when they are proposed as particularly pertinent to the intervention in highly contested debates such as those surrounding issues of gender identity, sexual preference, and erotic desire and their sociopolitical interfaces.

In order to devote myself to fairly detailed analyses of individualized texts, I have made no attempt to survey the entire canon of pertinent films. (I take note of the preliminary survey by Waugh.) In one understanding of queer studies, any cultural text—hence, any film—can be read from a queer perspective, can be queered. What this means is that it can be read against the grain of the unquestioned, and therefore untheorized, heterosexist presuppositions that ground the vast majority of our culture, and it means that the text can be shown to reveal internal contradictions, aporia, confused thinking, and strategic missteps in the exercise of patriarchal norms that make it interesting from the perspective of a spectator unwilling to abide by heteronormativity or gloss over its incoherences. (Sandy Quinn's study on "pink noir," which involves the queering of American noir films, usually considered exemplars of heterosexism, would be a good example of what I am referring to here.) Films examined here that match this parameter are Carlos Hugo Christensen's *A intrusa* (1979), María Luisa Bemberg's *De eso no se habla* (1993), and Jaime Humberto Hermosillo's *Doña Herlinda y su hijo* (1985).

In another understanding of queer studies, it will mean seeing how cultural products can be understood to promote principles of an antiheterosexist stance. This may mean defending and promoting the so-called lesbigay agenda (such as occurs in Francisco J. Lombardi's *No se lo digas a nadie*, 1998), as well as it might mean questioning that agenda in a move to destabilize any privileging of alternatives to the master narrative of privileged heteronormativity. *La Virgen de los Sicarios*, which drains any utopianism possible from same-sex relations, comes to mind here, as does Marcelo Piñeyro's *Plata quemada* (2000), in which a gay idyll in the end cannot separate itself from implacable political facts of life. Yet it can also mean poeticizing homoeroticism in the attempt to create alternative realms of erotic experience, as in Pablo César's *Afrodita* (1998), and the concept of alternative realms may more specifically involve the creation of protected spaces in a hostile world where homoeroticism, in something like a resemanticization of the closet, can be pursued with relative impunity: in increasing degrees of intensity, this is what takes place in Sérgio Amon's *Aqueles dois* (1985), *No se lo digas a nadie*, *En el paraíso no existe el dolor*, *A intrusa*, *De eso no se habla*, and *Doña Herlinda y su hijo*.

One of the major issues of this study is homophobia, widely understood as the irrational fear of homosexuals/lesbigays/queers. In reality, this is not a very useful definition, or at least it is a very limited one. I would argue, rather, that homophobia is a complex dynamic that functions to enforce the principles of heteronormativity and that any irrational fear associated with it is what homophobia as an instrument of heteronormativity is all about. In this sense, little intellectual effort is required: heteronormativity, to maintain its hold as a dominant social practice, marks off a wide swath of phenomena alleged to be threats to it. These phenomena are beliefs, behavior, or specific acts in themselves, or they are reflexes of them, signs that are read as indicative of a belief, behavior, or specific act such that the signs themselves do not constitute a challenge to heteronormativity in any direct sense but are taken to point to something that is. An alleged feminine swish of male hips is taken as a sign of sodomitic practices, and sodomy is a threat to heteronormativity because it is an improper sex act in that it represents a waste of reproductive seed. A crew cut on a woman is read to signal that such a woman refuses to assume the appropriate female role of reproductive sex with a man; moreover, her crew cut signals that she is usurping the role of the man with whom she should have reproductive sex instead of seeking to replace his subject position. And on and on.

In order to protect its turf—and it is a turf that evidently requires constant policing and whose principles, while they are taken to be so evidently "natural" and "universal," require enforcing with unflagging vigilance—heteronormativity generates a strategy of homophobia toward whatever or whoever would challenge it and endows that strategy with the power to hate, to execute that hatred with varying degrees of psychologically and emotionally violent terrorism, and—in one of its most singularly outstanding provisions—to function so as to interdict any debate of the legitimacy of heteronormativity, the strategy of homophobia, and the execution of the latter's power. In something like a perpetual-motion ideology machine, heteronormativity holds that any suggestion of the need to engage in debate regarding its supremacy is, prima facie, a sign of challenge to that supremacy, and in an efficient recursive fashion, that sign itself becomes susceptible to the defensive strategies of homophobia. In turn, any question of the legitimacy of homophobia as a way of enforcing heteronormativity is taken as a transparent sign of challenge to the latter and thus closes the loop.

What does require extensive intellectual investigation are all of the ways in which homophobia manifests itself along a continuum of terrorism and what the concrete consequences of its application are, both in terms of the everyday life of a society and in terms of its cultural production. I cannot undertake to do that here, although it is worth noting that it has barely begun to be done. We have ample documentation of acts of homophobic violence, although these tend to cluster at the end of the spectrum of physical terrorism. We have a certain amount of cultural production—typically in fiction—that tells the story of the emotional consequences of emotional terrorism. Let me choose as a paradigm, because of the iconic value of its title, Edmund White's *Boy's Own Story* (1982) or one of the great lesbian coming-of-age narratives, Jeanette Winterston's *Oranges Are Not the Only Fruit* (1985), both from the crest of the first major production of lesbigay literature in English. And we have now a good bibliography on the consequences of the homophobic silencing of cultural production, such as Lee Edelman's *Homographesis: Essays in Gay Literary and Cultural Theory* (1994); in film, Vito Russo's *Celluloid Closet: Homosexuality in the Movies* (1981, revised 1987; film documentary 1995 directed by Rob Epstein and Jeffrey Friedman); and in theater, Kaier Curtin's *We Can Always Call Them Bulgarians: The Emergence of Lesbians and Gay Men on the American Stage* (1987) and Nicholas De Jongh's *Not in Front of the Audience: Homosexuality on Stage* (1992). All of these works cut in two directions. On the one hand they examine the difficulty of writing/filming/staging lesbigay lives, while on the other they speak both to how those gay lives were told despite homophobic restrictions in the form of official, casual, and self-imposed censorship and how recent works have accomplished in large measure the destruction of the codes of silence.

Many of the works examined in this study deal with homophobia as an experience. That is, characters are subject to a generalized homophobia, if they are not the outright victims of its multiple procedures of specific violence. The grimmest film examined here in this regard is Arturo Ripstein's *El lugar sin límites* (1978), a title that evokes a common metaphor in Spanish for hell, which in this case is a direct evocation of the hell on earth that is the lot of the sexual outlaw whose life of constant humiliation at the hands of the agents of heteronormativity (agents who, nevertheless, are not above abusing him sexually because after all, he is a queer, a defective, feminized man) leads implacably to a murderous death. This is the dynamic of homophobia at its worst, and an examination of the film will provide ample opportunity to dwell on the internal contradictions of heteronormativity and the ways in which homophobia works to serve as a distraction from, a covering over of, those contradictions. Equally grim—perhaps even more so, since its context is the liberation from oppression and the creation of the New Man as a beneficent social agent in relation to the 1959 Cuban Revolution—is Néstor Almendros and Orlando Jiménez Leal's *Conducta impropia* (1984), one of the first major international documentaries to question the human rights abuses of the Cuban revolution (it was released originally as a French production, in French).[1] As this documentary reveals, the homophobic persecution of sexual dissidents (i.e., queers) as much turned the latter into the paradigmatic social outcasts as it made them part of a spectrum of abuse in which their alleged social dissidence was linked to other forms of social dissidence against which the Revolution must be

defended, while at the same time extending the master trope of homosexuality[2] to anyone who would question the Revolution: one must be
queer or protoqueer if one questions the Revolution.

Such a semantic chaining led to the sort of abuses that, with historical hindsight, are implicitly denounced in the internationally successful
Tomás Gutiérrez Alea and Juan Carlos Tabío's *Fresa y chocolate* (1993).
The film was touted as a plea for tolerance, while in reality this masked
the historical homophobia of the period in which it is set (the events of
the 1960s and 1970s documented in *Conducta impropia*) and the homophobia of the mid-1990s in which the film was made and although who
is tolerated and why are never quite fully explained (Santí prefers to
stress the various levels of reconciliation in the film). In the process, the
truly legitimate rights—artistic, affective, sexual—of the characters of
the film end up occluded by a paean to a presumed enlightened thaw
in Cuban society, at least as regards "homosexuals." By showing how
the film's elisions result from the homophobia still dominant in the 1990s
in Cuba rather than dismissing it as part of an intolerant past that has
been overcome in the rightful progress of the Revolution, my reading
attempts to understand how, when all is said and done, an erotic relationship between Diego and David is in fact figured in the film, even if
this means a sustained perverse understanding of the narrative and the
"intolerance" it purports to show.

Films like *The Disappearance of García Lorca* and *Plata quemada* constitute very different versions of homophobia, both with reference to each
other and in terms of what I have been saying here about homophobia.
In *Disappearance*, it is impossible to avoid the issue of homoeroticism, not
only because it was central to García Lorca's life, but because it is generally understood that his growing visibility as a queer at a time when
fascism and its own brand of homophobia were increasingly evident in
Spain and especially in his native Granada was an important factor in his
assassination in that city in 1936. By contrast to María Luisa Bemberg's
1990 *Yo la peor de todas* on the Mexican nun-poet Sor Juana Inés de la
Cruz, in which problematic issues of lesbianism in her work (see Bergmann; Paz) are converted into the principal motor of the film's narrative, *Disappearance*'s director, Marcos Zurinaga, struggles to convert the
centrality of Lorca's homoeroticism into a peripheral matter, making his
assassination more the consequence of accusations of a vague and generalized issue of social corruption—Lorca is viewed as a bad role model,
a Sophoclean corruptor of the young—rather than the specific consequence of the fact that the man was a queer in a city in which a strong

version of heteronormativity was viewed as a requisite against moral, social, political collapse on the eve of the Spanish Civil War. Moreover, the film is quite uncomfortable with the obsession of the fictional central character with the circumstances of Lorca's death, and it is necessary to prove his heterosexuality (as though that were ever possible) in order to avoid the audience's mistaking his interest in political history (with Lorca at the center of it) as a frenzied quest for gay heroes. This despite the way in which Jaime Manrique has, precisely, insisted that Lorca must be recognized as primus inter pares of gay heroes for Hispanic culture.

Plata quemada is rather a surprising film. Based on a novel by Ricardo Piglia in which the homosexual dimension of the relationship between two real-life bank thieves is considerably muted, Enrique Piñeyro's film version places their homoerotic relationship at the center of his film and, in my reading of it, shows how it becomes a tragic flaw of classical proportions that works to bring about their deaths. Yet, there is an appropriately framed anagnorisis in Piñeyro's version in which the two queer men, faced with certain death at the hands of police who are as homophobic as they are crooks themselves, reaffirm the deep relationship between them. Just as their society cannot transcend the homophobia that leads to their death (they are betrayed to the police by a woman abandoned by one of them to be with the other), Piñeyro himself is unable fully to face the consequences of the relationship his film sets out to represent. The erotic punches that are pulled in the film, the major final filming error that occurs, and the distractions of categorically displayed heterosexuality in the plot all work to suggest considerable disorientation, if not outright discomfort, in following through with what he has proposed to represent. And yet, as in the case of the perverse reading I propose for *Fresa y chocolate*, *Plata quemada* comes off as a very queer film indeed—especially in the context of the scant queer-marked filmmaking that has been forthcoming in Argentina (by contrast to narrative fiction and, quite notably, television), which has, at least in Buenos Aires, many reasons to tout an important shift toward gay rights.

Another issue that is treated in this study is the question of homosociality, particularly in its dimensions that segue into homoerotic relations. As Eve Kosofsky Sedgwick has pointed out in her important work *Between Men* and as Newfield has shown, homosociality is not homosexuality, at least with regard to American democracy. (For a brilliant contribution to Almodóvar criticism see Maddison's analysis of homosociality and heterosociality in *Todo sobre mi madre*, 1999.) Indeed, the two are mutually exclusive. Homosociality is understood to refer to the way in which patriarchal society forges bonds between men for the orderly transference and maintenance of masculinist power: these bonds not only allow for men to transmit power from one to another (along any number of social axes of class, caste, race, religion, profession, and the like), but also they allow for the process of inclusion of some men in power and exclusion of others from it, and they allow for the vigilant scrutiny of men to determine if they are abiding by the conditions of the patriarchy—that is, if they are worthy exponents of it.[5] It is here, of course, that homophobia comes in, since homophobia works against those men who do not abide by the heteronormative rules of the patriarchy, and it works both to punish and to exclude them, often by violent death. In homosociality, women are tokens of the exchange of power between men: appropriate and adequate heterosexual relations with women are taken as a guarantee of one's conformance with the patriarchy, and it is frequently through women that patriarchal power is transmitted—for example, from a powerful man to his son-in-law.

The bonds between men range over the sociocultural spectrum between what, popularly, we call the buddy system to, in a more formal and professional context, the old-boy network; clearly, one of the effects of homosociality, in its confrontation with feminism, is to co-opt some women such that they become token men in the perpetuation of the system. Such is the case, for example, with the figure of Mamá Grande in the title story of Gabriel García Márquez's collection *Los funerales de la Mamá Grande* (1962), and one might compare Mary Daly's concept of "token torturers" in various points in her *Gyn/ecology*. In order to maintain in place the heterosexist patriarchy, it is important that homosociality never yield to homosexuality, since this would disrupt the hierarchical equality between men, as in the homophobic understanding of homoeroticism, one of them would necessarily occupy the position of the "passive"—i.e., powerless—woman.

Yet as Sedgwick makes clear in *Between Men*, her analysis of nineteenth-century British fiction, and as others have gone on to point out in elaborating on this important issue, women often serve as channels of "erotic pulsion" between men who either cannot or will not, because of the constantly looming threat of homophobia, follow through on their mutual attraction. This is the function of Dorothy Lamour in her triangular relationship with Bing Crosby and Bob Hope in their "road" films (see Cohan, "Queering the Deal," and his *Masked Men*, 85–96). A film like Tony Scott's 1986 *Top Gun* is almost comically transparent in this regard, with the amorous relationship with the female civilian scientist Charlie(!) serving to distract attention from the bond between Tom Cruise's character, Maverick (ditto), and his dead buddy. One could immediately think of dozens of similar triangles in American filmmaking. Daniel Eisenberg has pointed out how the mythical Dulcinea in *Don Quijote* serves as a mediating function between the male pair of Don Quijote and Sancho Panza; theirs is only one of several examples of male-male bonding in Cervantes's fiction (Eisenberg, "Cervantes Saavedra," 48; Sahuquillo).

I will make this point about the often precarious nature of homosociality with reference to *Fresa y chocolate*, in which Nancy is interposed between Diego and David, and the sexual relationship between her and David ostensibly serves to show that the deep friendship that develops between Diego and David is strictly homosocial and not homoerotic—despite the clever sexual role reversal that closes the film through the exchange of symbolically charged ice cream flavors that provide the film with its title. Although less interesting as a cultural product, the Argentine Carlos Galettini's film *Convivencia* (1993), based on Oscar Viale's play by the same title, also flirts with crossing the line between homosociality and homosexuality. (A canonical text in this regard from Argentine literature is José Hernández's *Martín Fierro*, 1872/1876; see Geirola. Likewise canonical is Ricardo Güiraldes's *Don Segundo Sombra*, 1926; see Leland.) I need to be clear on this point: my critical assessment of *Convivencia* (or Viale's text on which the film is based) as a less interesting cultural product does not lie with the fact that homosociality rather than homosexuality is dealt with—that is, I am not dissatisfied with the film because it does not do what I think it should do with an opportunity to portray a gay relationship. Rather, my comments will deal with the way in which homoeroticism is barely contained in the film, and yet the film does not address why what is apparently presented as a homosocial bond, one of the many figured by Argentine cultural production, can barely contain a transformation into homoeroticism.

Since it is important to bear in mind that the patriarchy endorses homosociality but not homosexuality, it would be incorrect to say that there is a continuum between the two; they are, as I have asserted, mutually exclusive propositions in the structure of heterosexuality. Yet, the degree to which the ideology of patriarchal heteronormativity fails to address the reality of human passion means that the transformation of the heterosexual/homosexual axis from a disjunctive binary into a continuum means that when that transformation threatens to take place in a text, we can speak very precisely of the return of the repressed. I do not believe that Galettini has organized his film around repressed homosexuality/homoeroticism: if he has, he ends up doing very little that is politically honest with it. Viale, indeed, is so taken with the concept of homosociality that his 1979 play is complemented by a female version, *Convivencia femenina* (1986). Homosociality becomes, in *No se lo digas a nadie*, the smoke screen of a homoerotic relationship, whether viewed as a legitimate defense against homophobia in which, as one character says, "You can be anything in Peru but a queer," or whether viewed as another manifestation of patriarchal hypocrisy at the expense of women. Same-sex bonding between thieves becomes a disruptive — and ultimately tragic — same-sex desire in *Plata quemada*, which is exactly what heteronormativity predicts will happen, makes sure will happen, when the line between heterosexist homosociality and homosexuality is crossed.

The essays in this volume are marked in general by queer issues, which means that they are not specifically interested in lesbigay lives, at least those lived on the level of lesbian or gay or bisexual or any other non- or antipatriarchal identity. This reflects the nature of the filmic production in Latin America, where the identity issues of American filmmaking are virtually absent, which in turn reflects the fact that although there is a phenomenon of identity politics in some Latin American countries (at least in large metropolitan areas) built around sexual matters, a perspective dominates that I am here calling queer, even though the word does not exist in Spanish, has only a haphazard translation into Spanish (see Alzate), and is more often than not used as a clear and therefore problematic calque from English. The reader will immediately note that most of these films deal with male-centered narratives. This is not a consequence of my desire to privilege masculinist culture — for even male queers retain a large measure of masculinist privilege. Rather, it is because the films that have been made that focus on women, such as Bemberg's aforementioned *Yo la peor de todas*, tend to explore lesbian relationships and culture. I do not deny that lesbianism is, in the process of being whatever else it is, a queer challenge to the heteronormative patriarchy, but it is foremost about women's lives lived as lesbians or about lesbians transcending, as Wittig would have us understand, the patriarchal category of "woman." Clearly, this filmmaking deserves its own study, and therefore the only woman-centered narrative included here is Bemberg's *De eso no se habla*, which is not transparently about homoeroticism, but rather which I read as an allegory of the queer. As a

xviii   *Queer Issues in Contemporary Latin American Cinema*

consequence, discussion of it inaugurates this study—and also because I believe that Bemberg is the founding mother of a truly feminist, and also a truly queer, filmmaking in Latin America.

It will be obvious from my presentation of the issues of this study that my sources are contemporary queer studies such as exemplified by Sedgwick (in addition to *Between Men* and *Epistemology of the Closet*), Alexander Doty, Michael Warner, Jonathan Dollimore, and David M. Halperin. And obvious that I have drawn heavily on the example in queer film analysis from Richard Dyer and the pioneering work of Vito Russo, the second edition of whose *Celluloid Closet* includes some welcome references to Latin America (for an annotated registry of Spanish-language gay male films see Lechón Álvarez). This leads me to the question of theoretical imperialism. I hope it will be clear that I have not read these films in terms of any specific Anglo-American theorizing. Rather, coming from a background of international queer studies, I have used the latter perspectives to begin to talk about key texts that I identified for this project, documenting as necessary from research published in any language. If there is a preponderance of references to sources in English, it is not a consequence of any belief that the Anglo-American bibliography best informs a particular theoretical point, but rather because often it is (still) the only bibliography that is available. It is my hope, in the end, that the reader will perceive how I have not read these texts as entries into an international lesbigay/homoerotic/queer canon but as texts firmly grounded in specific issues of Latin American national societies and a continental (although primarily urban) understanding of sexuality. These are Latin American cultural productions, and I wish them to be understood primarily as such. If they also contribute to transnational debates about same-sex desire, patriarchal heteronormativity, homosociality, and homophobia, it is a consequence of the growing internationality of Latin American filmmaking in terms of the ambitions of directors and production companies, the wish to bring certain internationally debated issues to a national and continental grounding, the technical quality of many of the films being made, and—quite simply—the international recognition that so much Latin American filmmaking is now beginning to obtain.[4]

This study would not have been possible without the generous support of various programs at Arizona State University, which has contributed enormously to my scholarship over almost four decades, and the generosity of friends who aided me in obtaining some of the films

I examine here. My exceptionally fine research assistants over the several years of this project have included Eduardo Caro, Cecilia Rosales, Daniel Enrique Pérez, Cecilia Mafla Bustamante, María Martell, Álvaro Vergara-Mery, Kim Furumoto, Mikel Imaz, and Daniel Smith. Their assistance in reading these films has kept me from committing serious blunders of language and cultural content.

The essay on *El lugar sin límites* is forthcoming in *Violence, Bodies, and the Color of Fear*, edited by Arturo Aldama for Indiana University Press; the essay on *De eso no se habla* is forthcoming in a special issue of the *Revista canadiense de estudios hispánicos* devoted to María Luisa Bemberg; a Spanish version of the essay on *Fresa y chocolate* will appear in a special issue on contemporary Cuban culture.

Queer Issues in Contemporary
Latin American Cinema

This tale is dedicated to all people who have the courage to be different in order to be themselves.

DEDICATORY NOTE ADDED AFTER TITLE CREDITS
TO THE ENGLISH-SUBTITLED RELEASE OF *DE ESO
NO SE HABLA* (I DON'T WANT TO TALK ABOUT IT)

Charlotte's a metaphor for anybody that's different: a dwarf, black person, a young homosexual, even a big, fat ugly woman, who like anyone else has the right to a place in the sun.

MARÍA LUISA BEMBERG, QUOTED IN CALEB BACH,
"MARÍA LUISA BEMBERG TELLS THE UNTOLD," 27

Introit
Queer Difference

Approximately ten minutes into María Luisa Bemberg's *De eso no se habla* (1993), Leonor, the mother of the central character, Charlotte, awakens the boy who runs errands and helps out in the general store she owns and orders him to hitch her sulky, and she rides out into the countryside. There, ax in hand, Leonor approaches the home where she knows the parish priest is spending the night, asleep in the arms of his foreign Protestant concubine. She then proceeds methodically to smash the kitschy statues of dwarves that decorate the top of the wall marking the perimeter of the property; she proceeds to bury the statues in an overt act of closeting what they signify. Leonor returns home and makes a bonfire out of her daughter's books about little people: *Tom Thumb*, *Snow White and the Seven Dwarves*, and *Gulliver's Travels*. The violence of these acts, the fury on her face, the determination with which she wields the ax, and the intensity in her eyes as she contemplates the fire consuming her child's fairy tales all set the tone for the way in which she approaches difference in the face of Charlotte's manner of being in the world (Jenckes, in "Identity, Image, and Sound," 61, points out that Bemberg's key films all deal with issues of identity).

Charlotte is a dwarf, quite an unmistakable condition of difference, and the remainder of the film follows the various ways in which her mother denies this difference, defying those around her to mention the fact, and the way in which Charlotte herself deals with her mother's denial while at the same time charting, finally, her own life in terms of her body. Leonor's anger is that of someone faced with radical difference, a difference that must be denied because it cannot in any way be accommodated by the hegemonic structures of society. It requires little effort on the part of the spectator to understand what is going on here, with the result that Bemberg's film focuses directly and intently on the dynamics of the denial of difference, without having to do much semiotic work to convey to the audience the principle of difference involved. Bemberg cleverly sets her film in the period of the 1930s, at the time of the first fascist government in Argentina (*De eso no se habla* was filmed across the river from Buenos Aires in Colonia, Uruguay, a town that retains much of the architectural trappings of the period, from the modest one-story houses to the seignorial Belle Époque walk along the riverfront).

Bemberg's film career comes out of and is in many ways part of the process of cultural redemocratization that follows the neofascist tyranny of the previous two decades.[1] Here, she is clearly figuring a dominant principle of Argentine society as confirmed by the trenchant display text of the public militarization of the 1930s, to the effect that there are only limited responses to difference: that which is different may be eliminated, as was the practice of tyrannical regimes through the arrest, incarceration, torture, and eventual murder of those deemed different along a number of possible axes of nonconformance; that which is different may be denied (the option Leonor pursues, using the influence of her commercial prosperity to impose silence on others); or that which is different may be put on parade, obliged to display its difference, while at the same time being ridiculed and made an object of verbal and physical abuse for the difference that one is obliged to display (as in the infamous incident of the forced public display of forty-one Mexican transvestites in the early twentieth century; see Monsiváis, Irwin, González Rodríguez).

Obviously, the acceptance of difference, in the form of recognizing the legitimacy of that difference, is not an option. If persons of difference are fortunate, they may evade the society that denies the legitimacy of their difference, through either internal exile (e.g., the closet) or by becoming refugees; rarely can that difference be canceled out, and certainly never in the dwarfism that Charlotte manifests. The conforming authoritarianism of a society like Argentina's may have yielded considerable ground since the return to constitutional democracy among responses to the draconian measures to eliminate difference during the period of neofascist tyranny, as, for example, the 1996 municipal constitution of Buenos Aires, which specifically guarantees the rights of difference. Yet traditional social responses have been either politely to ignore difference or to penalize it aggressively through ridicule. The dynamic of ridicule is depicted in the Argentine workplace in Olivera Zapata's 1986 gay film, *Otra historia de amor* (Foster, *Contemporary Argentine Cinema*, 135–149), or, in Brazil, in Bruno Barreto's 1981 *O beijo no asfalto* (Foster, *Gender and Society in Contemporary Brazilian Cinema*, 129–138).

Leonor can reasonably be expected to be concerned about the difference of her child in order to protect her from ridicule. This much is implied when her neighbor, Señora Zamildio, on the occasion of Charlotte's second birthday party, attempts to console her and suggests that they bond in mutual commiseration on the basis of their children's respective physical handicaps—the neighbor's daughter is a deaf-mute. Leonor does everything but throw Señora Zamildio bodily out of her house, telling her that the two of them have nothing to share with each other. Charlotte's dwarfism is even more an evident difference than her playmate's deaf-mutism is, and Leonor knows full well that Charlotte will always be shunned and never chosen for marriage, even when she is not made a direct object of ridicule.

The first half of Bemberg's film is devoted to the dynamics of Leonor's denial of Charlotte's difference; the second half to Charlotte's expropriation of her right to difference, accompanied by Leonor's emotional collapse as a consequence of that expropriation. Leonor's denial is a complicated interplay of the manipulation of the closet and defiant display. On the one hand, she wishes to suppress any mention of Charlotte's dwarfism and the social difficulties it might bring to her. The destruction of the statues of dwarves that decorate the front wall of the property of the priest's lover is less the attempt to suppress any evidence that dwarfism exists in the world (something she can hardly do) than it is to announce publicly that she will not tolerate any such references in the microworld her prosperity allows her to manipulate.

On the morning following her destructive rage, Leonor speaks with the priest, who attempts to admonish her for inappropriate behavior while at the same time raising the subject of Charlotte's condition. Leonor cuts him short on both accounts, checking him in the first instance by threatening to reveal his tryst with the foreign Protestant and making it clear she will cut off donations to the church if Charlotte is mentioned again in any context that refers to her physical condition. One cannot help but sympathize with Leonor up to a point in this regard, since the overt identification of Charlotte's difference can only work to discriminate against her in a society in which difference is always a moral failing or a cruel joke of nature that serves to make the nondifferent feel superior for their conformance to the prevailing norm. But such sympathy only extends to a certain point, because it may contain the manifestations of ridicule and persecution that accompany difference, but it cannot revise the dynamic that legitimates such reactions to difference. Where this will become an important distinction is the way in which Leonor's denial fails to protect Charlotte—not from ridicule and persecution but from her own self-determined fulfillment as a human being. That is, Leonor's denial stifles Charlotte rather than protects her.

Other significant ways in which Leonor denies Charlotte's difference are found in her education and in her participation in San Juan de los Altares society. Leonor wishes to provide her daughter with a typical first-rate bourgeois education, at least such as would have been available in a provincial town in the Argentina of the 1930s. She has piano lessons, French lessons, drawing lessons, and, apparently, the proper array of standard bookish culture. Her name is an allusion to the prestige of French culture of the day, and she uses the language as a mark of social distinction—although it is always clear that she will never be allowed to travel in any way that will enable her to make use of this language or the other culture she is acquiring: her education will only serve to make her a superior social being in her milieu. Thus, in one way, Charlotte's education is a compensation for her difference; if she is perceived to be deficient physically, this can be balanced by a refuge in the world of learning, a learning, moreover, that takes place in the cloister—i.e., closet, both a safe space and a hidden space—of her doting mother's hearth. On the other hand, such an education is a denial of difference, for it means to provide the child with the polish appropriate to daughters of aspiring bourgeois families such as to guarantee their advantageous marriage and their comfortable installation in the controlling sector of hegemonic society.

This sort of double movement is typical of the texture of Bemberg's film: because of the visual nature of film, Charlotte's difference is always in immediate evidence, which only serves to heighten the irreality of Leonor's attempt to deny it. Where this double movement becomes painfully clear is when Ludovico D'Andrea, played by Marcello Mastroianni, appears on the scene. Ludovico is always a figure of difference. Like the German Protestant who is the priest's concubine, Ludovico introduces an element of exotic adventure in the staid life of San Juan de los Altares. The German woman is only a cheap sort of foreignness (not only is she German and a Protestant, although she has means, but she is merely a dumpy woman who can apparently get no better than the old reprobate of a priest to take her as a lover). Ludovico is a world trav-

Mastroianni
discussing a scene
with director Bemberg

eler, handsome and mysterious, the focal point of rumors about his past, what he is fleeing from, and why someone with his sophistication would end up in San Juan de los Altares. Ludovico is single, which is itself a form of unacceptable difference in the heterosexist ground zero of the film, and the fact that he frequents the town's brothel (also frequented by the mayor, the police chief, and other worthies) may confirm his sexual conformity, but not his social normality, since it is one thing to use the brothel to supplement conventional matrimony and quite something else to make it a substitute for the reproductive imperative, which is in part the source of rumors: why would a man like Ludovico not be properly married? None of this queers Ludovico in any significant way; rather, it only serves to enhance his exotic, but permissible, otherworldliness.

Where this otherworldliness comes into play is a topic of fascination for the town, for the customers at Leonor's general store, which he frequents, and particularly for Charlotte. Charlotte hangs on Ludovico's every word (something we see Leonor expressing some concern about, although she limits herself to shooing Mojamé, the errand boy, away from Ludovico with the order to resume his duties), and the look of intense curiosity on Charlotte's face shows that she sees in him someone who has lived the experiences she has only read about, going far beyond the safe realm of bourgeois exoticism. When Ludovico disappears, only to resurface with a whole new bag of anecdotes about his experiences, Charlotte's fascination with him is heightened. It is important to note that we see Charlotte listening to Ludovico while perched on top of the store's counter, her short stature very much in evidence as her feet dangle far from the ground: Charlotte's dwarfism is evident, but she is lost (i.e., closeted) in Ludovico's tales. If one were to wonder why Leonor allows

Mastroianni as the
sophisticated outsider

Ludovico's stage-center entertainment in her establishment, it may well be to provide yet one more distraction for Charlotte from the world around her; another reason is that Leonor herself is clearly entranced by Ludovico.

If Charlotte's education and its extension through the tales Ludovico has to tell are ways of protecting her from the world and constitute an overarching background for the entire film, the incident with Charlotte's horse is a very specific and therefore very eloquent example of the closet Leonor imposes on her daughter. Leonor wishes to give her daughter a horse as a present (elegant horseback riding is, of course, another re-fined bourgeois accomplishment). Leonor turns to Ludovico as a man of taste and asks him to obtain a horse for her. He accomplishes this as-signment, and the two ride out to the barn where the horse is being kept. When Leonor sees the horse, she goes into a fit similar to her foray to destroy the dwarf statues. Wielding a riding crop rather than an ax, she strikes the horse on the nose: it is one of the famous Argentine toy ponies, perfectly proportional to Charlotte's physical dimensions.

Leonor's rage stems from the fact that she assumed that Ludovico would obtain a regular-sized horse for Charlotte, and this is what she now makes clear. Ludovico then does obtain a larger animal for Char-lotte, and we subsequently see Charlotte expertly handling her tall mount, which becomes a real source of pleasure to her. However, she is obliged always to ride the horse within the confines of the barn, an-other form of the closet that ensures that Charlotte will not be exposed to ridicule or at least astonished stares, at the possibly grotesque sight of a woman of her dimensions astride the enormous animal (McGuirk, 367–368, makes interesting connections between Bemberg's film and Argen-

tine surrealism). The medium of film makes this juxtaposition especially
evident: what Leonor hides away from public gaze is clearly evident to
the spectator—the ethereal blue lighting of the barn's interior highlights
Charlotte's ecstatic pleasure in the limited riding she is allowed, but it
cannot hide the juxtaposition between her body and that of the horse.

Yet even though Leonor imposes the closet on Charlotte when she
thinks that something might call attention to her dwarfism, this does
not mean that Leonor keeps her completely sequestered from the world.
While the convent might traditionally have been an option in Charlotte's
case, Leonor has no desire to keep her out of the world entirely. Rather,
she promotes Charlotte in circumstances in which her dwarfism is not
likely to be particularly in evidence. Thus, when Leonor has soirees at
her home, Charlotte is welcome to participate as an accomplished display piece of her mother's refinement. Complementing the supposed ele-
gance of her home, Leonor's daughter chats urbanely with the invited
guests and entertains them with her musical talents by playing tangos
on the piano, accompanied by Ludovico's singing; she then retires to her
room to read what appears to be an adult book while the guests play
cards. This avoids her joining them and having to have special arrangements to accommodate her at the card table.

On another occasion, Leonor promotes Charlotte's availability to
participate in a church social with a selection of piano compositions,
deftly obliging the other members of the organizing committee to accept
her proposal, despite the timid but quickly squelched allusion to putting
her on display: her comrades must surely wonder why Leonor is suddenly willing to make a public spectacle of her daughter. However, it is
evident that Leonor wishes to organize a public display of her daughter's
talents—that is, of her nondifference or, better yet, of the difference of
her superiority to other children in the town or to anyone else who might
compete with her in playing the piano. And it becomes equally evident
that Leonor intends to make a public display of her daughter's talents in
such a way that those talents are showcased, but not her physical daughter as such. That is, since her daughter is, in terms of hegemonic values,
an incomplete or damaged human being, Leonor will put on display that
part of her, that metonym of her personhood, that is immune from the
harsh scrutiny directed at unacceptable difference. Specifically, she asks
her daughter to be seated at the piano when the curtain opens, to remain seated and move directly to her performance, and to not take a bow
when the performance is over but to wait for the curtain to close before
rising from the piano. Charlotte disobeys her mother.

Charlotte's marriage
to Ludovico

Charlotte's disobedience — she rises from the piano before her concert begins and stands directly before the audience to address them with a spoken program note about her concert — is the first in a series of events in which she will challenge successfully her mother's right to fragment her person with the goal of closeting her difference. Since Leonor is always lovely to her daughter, she has little choice but to swallow Charlotte's defiance of her wishes, especially since the concert audience does not react in any notable way to Charlotte's appearance and her explicit display of her "abnormal" body. This display is, however, only a foreshadowing of the much more blatant one that Charlotte will protagonize.

Perhaps the most stunning sequence in *De eso no se habla* concerns Charlotte's wedding to Ludovico. There are two subsequences, the church ceremony and the wedding banquet. Once again, Leonor walks a thin line between attempting to repress the visibility of Charlotte's difference and attempting to ensure that when she is visible, there can be no opportunity to make reference to that difference. Three details of the sequence are particularly telling.

Like a good mother of the bride, Leonor is determined that the conventional rituals of matrimony be executed with all due formality and without the slightest hitch. One of the characteristics of heterosexual matrimony in its most conventional guises is that when there is a hitch, it becomes magnified as something like an affront to normalcy, as somehow indicative that the parties involved are insufficiently attentive to the parameters of this most central of patriarchal confirmations. Thus, any problem with dress, with the church celebration, with the spirit of the party, with the reception, with the nuptial send-off is unflinchingly analyzed to detect any transgressive variation, any eloquent sign of noncompliance — which is, certainly, why "modern" weddings, especially lesbigay ones, may provoke so much critical commentary as so many disrespectful violations of the patriarchal paradigm (see Newman on Leonor as an agent of patriarchal authoritarianism). Leonor unquestionably wishes to adhere to the patriarchal paradigm, which is why the camera follows details of the event so closely, including details particular to the unique traditions of Hispanic matrimony of the day, such as the careful preparation of the wedding chamber (Charlotte and Ludovico are to return to his house): we see his maid carefully making up the bed with special linen and then centering on the bed a long-stem red rose, the symbol of Charlotte's institutionally legitimized deflowering, the stem the penis, the rose the vagina, and red the color of the confirming deflowering of the woman (the Spanish tradition, as heir to Arabic customs, displaces into symbol the material correlative of successful first-night intercourse in the form of the bloodied sheet publicly displayed the next morning from the window of the wedding chamber).

In her scrutiny of details, Leonor discovers that the wedding cake is topped off with a conventional decoration in the form of a sugar-candy bride and groom; obviously, both figures manifest real-life proportions. In a panic over the possibility that the "normal" figures will by implication call attention to the "abnormality" of the couple that Charlotte and Ludovico make (and one recalls that Mastroianni was a large and muscular man), Leonor grabs the figures from the cake and begins to eat them, head first. Since it is quite a mouthful and a large amount of sugar, she decides to hide (that is, closet) them by stuffing them down the bosom of her dress. This is a reverse concealment, because she is not hiding Charlotte's dwarfism directly but rather masking it by removing from view what can emphasize its existence—the figure of the bride who rises full length alongside the groom.

The next detail complements the ludicrousness of Leonor stuffing candied figures down her bodice with grotesque farce. Since Charlotte's father is dead, Leonor asks the town mayor to accompany Charlotte down the aisle. The mayor is an old reprobate, and at one point in the film we see him competing with Ludovico for the attentions of the same woman in the town brothel, that quintessential reduct of the heteronormative paradigm. The mayor is confined to a wheelchair because a stroke has left him unable to walk; he is also unable to speak clearly. He is wheeled around by someone who appears to be his son, who is apparently the only one who really understands the mayor's paralytic speech. Leonor wishes to have the mayor give her daughter away not because there is an allegiance of family relationship involved between the two of them—except, circumstantially, for the fact that by having the mayor give her daughter away, Leonor is also confirming her importance in town. Rather, the purpose in having the *alcalde* give her daughter away is because Leonor can have recourse to the one man in town whose stature is that of Charlotte's, as the wheelchair reduces him to her height.

Charlotte, once she has knelt alongside Ludovico at the altar, is not noticeably shorter than he is, although once they are married and withdraw from the altar, we see a posterior shot that clearly emphasizes their difference in height. Until Charlotte passes under the patriarchal tutelage of Ludovico, Leonor's use of the wheelchair-bound mayor as father of the bride is another of her strategies to allow her daughter to appear in public while masking her dwarfism. However, there is a major hitch in that the mayor has a heart attack and dies. Such a death of a member of the wedding party would always be a major foul-up that would cast a pall on the event, but in this case it threatens to disrupt specifically Leonor's scheme to have her daughter presented at the altar in a way that will not underscore her dwarfism. Leonor's solution is to leave the body propped up in the chair and to have his attendant, as he usually does, speak for his father, as though the man's mumble were inaudible; later he will be put on ice until the wedding reception is over. The only person who really catches on is Señora Zamildio, whom Leonor has insulted from the beginning of the film, and as the church recessional takes place and Leonor bursts out in hysterical laughter, Señora Zamildio slaps her to cut short her hysteria, thereby underscoring the ludicrousness of the entire event, as much Leonor's stratagems as the simulacrum of the whole heterosexist ritual.

The final part of the wedding sequence is the massive outdoor banquet. It is evident that Leonor hopes that Charlotte will remain seated, since the difference in stature between the newlyweds is so much less evident that way. But dance is also an integral part of Hispanic weddings, and it is also customary for the new couple to lead the dancing. Much to Leonor's horror, Ludovico takes Charlotte in his arms, much as one would a little girl, and displays his wife to the world in all her difference. There is no parody, no element of the grotesque in this scene (in juxtaposition to the burlesque of appalling difference — Jew versus Christian — in the "If You Only Knew Her Like I Do" number in Joe Masteroff's 1999 version of *Cabaret*); there is only Ludovico's extremely touching and totally loving presentation of the woman he loves to the world.

Ludovico's love for Charlotte, however, cannot remain untouched by the matter of queer difference. I have added the word "queer" here because although "queer" may not necessarily refer to sexuality, sexuality is what first comes to mind, since this is the field of the greatest measure of contestation with regard to difference, the point at which transgression becomes so particularly horrifying and therefore so particularly requiring of corrective violence. There are two dimensions of the dark side of sexuality—that is, what is considered to be abnormal and perverse—at work in the figure of Charlotte as it is juxtaposed to that of Ludovico. Before mentioning these, it is worth alluding to a possible third one, the titillation deriving from any chaste provincial and properly protected woman to a mysterious stranger. We never learn anything specific about Ludovico's past, and there is always a tone of sexual danger associated with him, enhanced by Mastroianni playing the debonair Latin lover to the hilt, including his fame and prowess at the local brothel and the lamentations of the madam and her girls over losing their most flamboyant customer (and they know that this will be a permanent loss, since true love, not the marriage of convenience that is the best source of the brothel's steady clients, is involved). But this would constitute little more than a soap-opera form of sexual excitement if it were all that is involved.

Where turbulent sexuality intrudes is because Charlotte is physically handicapped and because that handicap gives her the appearance of a little girl. It would be quite enough to evoke the sexual prurience surrounding the kinky allure of the handicapped, and some of the grossest sexual jokes involve having sex with a partner whose body deviates noticeably from either the conventional norm of "attractive" or at least duly normal, or from movie-star gorgeous—the body that is considered handicapped by blatant ugliness or by some sort of deformity that is felt to go even beyond the unacceptably ugly defies the standards of sexual evocation. Sexual erotics function in terms of specific fetishes and clusters of fetishes (the Lacanian desiring principle represented by the lower-case *a* in this theory's formulations). While such fetishes are culturally bound and vary along all sorts of social axes and over time, within any one culture at any one time, part of the dominant sexual ideology (e.g., "Sexo pero no mucho"—sex but not much—would have been a reigning principle for Leonor's generation and class) specifies certain primes of fetish and a certain hierarchy that involves marking boundaries between what are acceptable fetishes and what are unacceptable ones and which ones, while marginally acceptable, must remain in the realm of what is not publicly discussed.

Thus, an individual may discuss within a peer group certain dimensions of erotic desire while holding others in secret, perhaps always wondering if these secret desires shade off into the criminally or psychologically or morally perverse; one might even suspect or know that there are others in the peer group who share similar "tastes" (one will recall that, for the bourgeois Freud, it is these tastes that constitute the perverse fetish, which becomes a redundant configuration, even when the line for Freud between the "normal" and the "perverse" might have been more moveable, more flexible, than for his cohorts). The taste for the freak, however, is generally considered to be well over the line of what is normally acceptable, no matter how much one might recognize the sexual rights of all human bodies. But satisfying the sexual needs of the woman who is extremely ugly or too masculine (excessive body hair may be the operative consideration here) or too fat or under- or over-endowed—the list really goes on and on, and one could easily provide popular cultural references from Western culture in general or Hispanic culture specifically—is something best left for the other party: "You can have her, I don't want her, she's too fat for me" was a song lyric of my post–World War II youth. Bruce Caron comments on the importance of the function of the carnival sideshow and its relationship to issues of normality.[2] Although these comments are based on American culture, they serve well to characterize the function of the carnival sideshow in any society, such as that of Bemberg's film, in which there is a compelling criterion of normalcy:

> The carnival in its first fifty years was also the province of the bizarre. One essential quarter of this realm was the freak show. The freak show's spectacle of human diversity—from physical deformity to ethnographic titillation—fed a voyeuristic hunger in the assembled crowd of "townies" (otherwise known as "marks") raised on a daily diet of God-fearing normality. The naked misery on display, at once repelling and intriguing, generally reinforced the sense of superiority that even the generally poor, mainly rural, and mostly white townies might summon as their birthright. While some of the bodies on display achieved an odd measure of celebrity . . . most of the "freaks" in the shows simply had nowhere else to go. (Caron, in Brouws, 89; for a comprehensive study of sideshow freaks in the American carnival see Bogdan.)

It is important to note that Alejandra Podestá, who does a marvelous job playing Charlotte, is not conventionally pretty of face, aside from her dwarfism, and her attempts to dance flamenco to the music of Bizet's *Carmen* seem grotesque. When Charlotte chooses to enact the role of a gypsy woman, of the sexualized Other and a sort of female Don Juan, rather than performing according to the more classical—i.e., supposedly more decent and not blatantly sexual—culture as her mother would prefer, supplies one of many interludes in the film where a grotesqueness creeps into her figure that becomes the sexualized freak when she is the object of the dashingly handsome Ludovico's attentions. Deviant erotics are compounded when one sees Charlotte as a little girl. This is reinforced by the fact that Leonor wishes to maintain her as a little girl in her activities and in her dress. The matter of the horse is different, because the fully grown—and therefore fully sexualized—horse is meant by Leonor to impose normalcy, but, of course, it can only exaggerate it, and the simple fact is that Charlotte looks most like a little girl when she is astride the enormous steed, just as she does when she is perched on the counter of the general store, better to hear Ludovico's anecdotes, swinging her legs like a child. Anyone with an adequate knowledge of Hispanic culture will overlook the powerful representation by the horse of male sexuality in Federico García Lorca's play *La casa de Bernarda Alba* (written 1936); images of the horse appear throughout Lorca's writings, often with a sexual charge. To be sure, the horse is a widely recognized symbol of sexuality.

The issue of Charlotte as a figure of the child as sexual object is underscored by Leonor's horrendous error of interpretation regarding Ludovico's intentions. Ludovico requests an audience with her to announce his intentions to wed Charlotte; Leonor thinks it is to ask her own hand in marriage. She is emotionally devastated and becomes physically ill when she understands her error. Such an error may be a standard ploy in comedic plots, but here it assumes pathetic proportions less because Leonor is devastated to find she is not the object of Ludovico's intentions and even more so to the extent that such a proposal underscores the sexual maturity of the child she has always attempted strategically to infantilize. Parents generally have some problems with the discovery of the sexual desire evident in their children and in the perception of the sexual desire provoked in others, especially when it is expressed in terms of material erotics and not in the terms of evanescent greeting-card romance. However, in Leonor's case, Ludovico is in love with a little girl: he is the seducer of her child as a little girl and not as a grown adult.

It is to Leonor's credit, as elsewhere in the film, that she can come to terms with yet another instance in which Charlotte shatters the walls of the closet her mother wishes to confine her in, and the move to Ludovico's house clearly is a correlative of leaving the closet of sexual denial much beyond simply the symbolic exchange of the father's domain (with Leonor very much the phallic woman holding the place of the absent father) for that of the husband's. The film does not dwell, beyond Leonor's initial hysterical reaction (she behaves in a well-controlled fashion, but it is no less hysteria than if she had gone off screaming at hearing Ludovico's proposal), on any sexual innuendo on the part of the society of the film. The only other interpretive opening lies in the eloquent juxtaposition of the women of the brothel, with whom Ludovico is seen functioning quite appropriately, especially his virtual rape on the billiards table, ripped bodice and all, of the conventionally sexy madam (played by Bettina Blum) in a moment of frustration because of his sexual attraction to Charlotte; the madam laughs wildly at his erotic outburst.

However, my focus is more on the reaction of the spectator to the way in which Bemberg semiotically disposes Charlotte's marriage to Ludovico, especially in terms of the film's denouement. It is not an act of perversion on the part of the spectator to recall both our culture's conventional feelings about freaks and their relationship to a taboo range of erotic desire, such as the taboo relating to evoking the sexuality of children and allusion to the sexual seduction, Lolita-style, of the child. Ludovico is all delicacy and gentlemanliness with Charlotte, her mother, and the society he has chosen to inhabit. But the intense sexuality of Ludovico—both in terms of how he is evoked in the film and the sexual personae of Marcello Mastroianni the legendary actor—and the juxtapositions the film establishes between Charlotte and the madam, between Charlotte and her mother, between Ludovico and the mayor (both as sexual rival and then as the surrogate father-in-law) all lend a note of grotesquerie that a sense of the freakish sexuality between Charlotte and Ludovico can build on: just what will their wedding night be like?

All does not go well on their wedding night or on any subsequent night, and this segues into the brilliant denouement of the film, making this Bemberg's last and most cinematographically perfect text. Charlotte becomes listless and disinterested, and it quickly becomes evident that it is not because she misses her mother's love and protection. Quite the contrary. The walls of the closet are crumbling for Charlotte, and it is only a matter of time before she takes the final necessary step. And then the circus comes to town. It is Leonor who first learns of the arrival of the circus, and she attempts to get Ludovico to deny it a permit to perform (Ludovico has replaced his surrogate father-in-law as mayor); Ludovico, in a condescending gesture of worldliness in the face of what he sees as Leonor's provincialism, refuses to grant her wish, and Leonor now knows she is entirely defeated by the facts of life. This sequence is not without a dimension of irreality, because nowhere before has Leonor shown herself to be quite so prescient with regard to the meaning of the queer world. For the circus is the arrival, literally at her doorstep and that of Ludovico's, of the queer world to which Charlotte will necessarily have to come to belong if she is to survive emotionally.

Ludovico, acquiescing to Leonor's wishes, initially asks Charlotte not to go to see the circus, and she seems willing to abide by his request, although when he sees her moping over her dinner as the sounds of the circus are heard in the background, he urges her to go; she says that it is not important. But Ludovico—who throughout the movie has been a source for Charlotte of the exotic mysteries of the world—senses she is lying wide awake at his side, and he pretends to be asleep as she slips out of bed and disappears into the night. Thus, not only does Charlotte go to the circus, but she goes to join it, not just to be a regular spectator of it: the circus is spectacular display (and, in capitalist terms, a commodification) of physical, even what society considers to be freakish, difference. The film follows her disappearance into the night, assuming for the first time her point of view, as though her body were the camera. She approaches the circus master, who bids her a warm welcome, and she surveys the new world she has chosen, one in which, by her choice, her difference will be put on parade. As Ludovico discovers subsequently, she has gone off on her horse, riding it outside the barn for the first time.[3]

The penultimate scene of the movie is of Charlotte engaged in her definitive public display of otherness, but now integrated into one of society's great refuges of otherness, the rag-tag circus of freaks and scruffy animals (see Hotier on the circus as transgressive space). The animals are queer as the freaks are, for aside from whatever handicapping occurs to them as a result of mistreatment, underfeeding, and overwork, the whole idea of the circus is to present animals in the flesh that are as unfamiliar and threatening to the spectator as the bearded woman or the chicken man (see Johnson et al. for the representation of this dimension of the circus). And, too, one of the characteristics of the circus sideshow is to blur the boundaries between animals and humans, which queers the patriarchal boundaries between the species and the putatively natural hierarchies on which those boundaries are based.

Categories like carnival, circus, and sideshow are slippery ones, and each has undergone its own historical variations across various cultural and social coordinates. Yet, the sort of circus that figures in *De eso no se habla* is the typical nineteenth-century itinerant show that is an amorphous structure of whatever animals, human spectacles, and show acts are available from one road stop to the next; individuals drop out (hightail it out, are arrested, die), and other individuals take their place. Running off with the circus is virtually a universal Western motif, and it may well be an international one. Historical and theoretical bibliography is scant on these issues, but cultural production is rich and extensive, from American novels (Gresham; Dunn; Finney) to Argentine ones (Barletta; Gambaro) to Latin American ones (viz. Melquíades and his gypsy troop in García Márquez's *Cien años de soledad*). Also of note is the Chilean-Mexican Alejandro Jodorowsky's fascinating film *Santa sangre* (1989).

Precisely in the case of Bemberg's film, Charlotte runs off with the circus. She seems to know intuitively that these are her people and that she belongs with them. Thus, if the penultimate scene of the film centers on Charlotte assuming the position of the camera, such that we experience through her eyes the discovery of the circus (i.e., her body is no longer explicitly the site of difference because we cannot see it as long as we are seeing through her eyes), in the last scene we see her triumphantly leading the circus astride her immense mount, dressed in the typical mock military garb of the circus performer, something like a drum majorette. She disappears down the road with this band of performers whose basic camaraderie lies in their social marginality; presumably she will not be seen again in San Juan de los Altares.

The final sequence of the film, really two separate scenes that complement each other as a single sequence, involves what happens to Ludovico and Leonor. Ludovico presumably drowns himself in the river; his capsized boat is found, but his body is never located. Although the image of the oarsmanless boat is one of the last scenes in the movie (the last scene is that of the circus disappearing into the distance of the vast pampa), it is the complementary scene of Leonor shuttering herself away in her home forever. This scene, in which we see her at the window and then see her seal shut the shutters, is especially eloquent, because she is creating for herself the very sort of cloister/closet in which she was unable to contain Charlotte; she will now make herself a victim of the isolation she wished to impose on her daughter, and Leonor's stricken self-immuration can be read as something like a self-imposed life sentence to atone for having failed to learn the one major lesson queerness has to teach us: the price of attempting to "straighten out" difference inevitably results in an act of violence that is as harmful to the one who is nonstraight as it is to the person attempting to impose the straightening out of difference.

Although there is a subtext of sexual nonconformity in *De eso no se habla* (and one can speculate on what Charlotte's sexual life with the circus might be and that whatever it will be, to judge by the cultural models available, it is not likely consistent with the parameters of hetero-normativity), it is not the main point of the picture. Bemberg is amply known for issues of sexual nonconformity in most of her films, and so on this basis projecting onto *De eso no se habla* a measure of sexual nonconformity, if only by implication, is not critically untoward. But I do not wish to make sexual transgression the center of my argument here, because what is queer about *De eso no se habla* is not specifically anyone's sexual desire but rather the way in which the film decon-structs the straight norm of patriarchal heterosexism, of which Char-lotte's apparently happy wedding is the centerpiece of the film. Yet note that Ludovico, in a voice-over, specifically recognizes that marriage for Charlotte continues to leave unspoken the forbidden topic of her differ-ence. Many women marry to escape the home, but Charlotte does so in order to escape patriarchal society altogether—or at least its settled bourgeois simulacrum, since even the most outré forms of social margin-ality always reference back to the hegemonic patriarchy, and there is no definitive, effective evasion of it (which is why, perhaps, Ludovico, who is really in love with Charlotte in a respectably patriarchal way, commits suicide when he learns that he has both been used by Charlotte and seen by her as yet another agent of the patriarchy).

But more specifically, what gets queered in *De eso no se habla*—such as to create a queer perception on the part of the implied spectator—is the coherence of Leonor's complicity with the practice of the closet: she wishes to hide Charlotte's difference from view (i.e., to deny the ac-knowledged perception of difference on the part of others), while at the same time she wishes to display Charlotte's difference as having been canceled out by other attributes, such as her social graces, her cultural talents, and her fulfillment of the ceremony of wedded bliss. Charlotte cannot be both simultaneously hidden as different and displayed as tran-scending difference, and if Charlotte is able to transcend the violence of her mother's closet, Leonor is not, which is why she has no choice but to occupy the closet she wished to construct for her daughter.[4]

Bemberg's film is moving in its depiction of Charlotte's determina-tion to evade the closet, and it is terrible in the depiction of the violence Leonor brings to herself in creating that closet.

One final note: the film is narrated in retrospect by the errand boy, an outsider within the film (he is of Arabic descent, hence his mangled name Mojamé). The narration is done by Alfredo Alcón, one of Argentina's great stage actors and its most famously gay one—although unacknowledgedly so.[5] Bemberg may have gotten his collaboration in her stunning figuring of the dynamic of the closet, but in real life, the closet is still very much a part of Argentine life.

No es la conducta erótica con otro varón lo que hace al individuo "homosexual", según este discurso [vigente en México], sino el gusto de hacerlo, el hecho de que se busque y encuentre placer. [Erotic conduct with another man is not what makes the individual "homosexual," in the prevailing discourse in Mexico, but the pleasure taken in that conduct, that its pleasure is sought and enjoyed.]

GUILLERMO NÚÑEZ NORIEGA, *SEXO ENTRE VARONES*, 91

Homosexuality In and Out of the Closet

It is a generally accepted principle in queer studies that no adequate definition of heterosexuality would be possible without the category of the "homosexual" (Dollimore; Katz). In conformance with basic principles of semiotics, no sign can exist without defining what it is not, and what it is not is as important as what it is. In the distinctive feature analysis that is crucial to semiotics, the interplay of negative and positive valences is what conforms the unique unit that is any specific sign. In semiotics, no one sign is dominant, and all are held together in a structure by the interrelationship of their contrasting valences. Some valences, or combinations of some valences, may be statistically more frequent than others, and some valences can only combine with each other in specific ways; furthermore, some valences may be statistically more pertinent than others.

In a social semiotic, however, valences acquire ideological charges, and thus some valences may in fact be more dominant than others. Ideology, it would seem, can work to problematize the combinations of valences, and it is not always clear that valences that emerge as hegemonic and those that are kept in a position of subalternity conform necessarily to a metatheory of semiotic possibilities. Nor is it always clear that, metatheoretically, there is a stable coherence regarding the conformation of the signs of a social semiotic (see Greimas for a model of sociosemiotic analysis).

This is particularly evident in the case of the social sign of "heterosexuality" and its associated sign of "homosexuality." While the heteronormative patriarchy proposes a fully coherent and transparent sign of heterosexuality and matches it with an implied fully coherent and transparent sign of homosexuality, it is far from evident that there is any reliable stability as to what these two terms mean. I am not referring to the way in which meaning for these terms might vary widely with respect to historical context—that is, that they are not universal signifiers, even though they are often proposed by both heteronormativists and gay activists to be that precisely. Rather, within the coordinates of any one specifically identifiable society, there may be considerable confusion as to what these terms can possibly signify. It is both a question of their mutual interdependence and their inherent instability of distributed meaning between one and another such that, unlike elementary signs like "male" and "female" (which, to be sure, are not without their own problems of analysis), heterosexual and homosexual are engaged in a constant process of redistributed valences that renders them highly suspect as signs of meaning, leaving them more as opaque symbols— rallying cries, if you will—than analyzable units of meaning.

Queer studies are fundamentally dedicated to charting the implications of what I have described so skeletally. Two of the axioms that drive such a field of studies are (1) that homosexuality cannot be viewed as deviance from or a degradation of heterosexuality, but that the two terms— in reality, two clusters of terms—only make sense when viewed as asymmetrical converses of each other; and (2) that the principles on which a division of meaning between the two is constructed (i.e., the way in which their respective differentiated valences are proposed) reveals a considerable degree of squishiness, such that they can only be useful in a social discourse untroubled by bad faith and oblivious to incoherences of meaning. That internal contradictions or incoherence may indeed be a circumstance affecting all of the macrosignifiers of social meaning, such as race, class, gender, ethnicity, and the like, is what has led queer studies to be interested in larger issues concerning the construction of social meaning than just that of sexual preference (Warner in his introduction to *Fear of a Queer Planet* explores the queer studies interest in sociosemiotic incoherence of heteronormativity). It is for this reason that Richard Dyer, in a work on "whiteness" and why it is an unmarked category of Western cultural production, can relate the marked/unmarked binary to an array of such categories in our society that queer studies proposes to interrogate:

> [T]he man/woman binarism is a sexist production. Each consists of two terms, the first of which is unmarked and unproblematized—it des-

ignates "the category to which everyone is assumed to belong" (unless someone is specifically marked as different) . . . The marked (or queer) term ultimately functions not as a means of denominating a real or determinate class of persons but as a means of delimiting and defining— by negative and opposition—the unmarked term . . . Heterosexuality . . . *depends* on homosexuality to lend it substance, and to enable it to acquire by default its status *as* a default, as a *lack of difference* or an *absence of abnormality.* (44)

The problem with Dyer's formulation, as accurate as it may be both in reference to the interrogation of the homologies of binarisms that informs queer studies and the way in which heteronormative patriarchal thought cannot do without those binarisms, is that it fails to take the next step of questioning the coherence of the logic of such thought. The category of the dreaded Other that patriarchal thought finds so necessary to hold firmly to its own carefully delimited sphere of sociosemiotic meaning—a dreaded Other that postcolonial thought reinscribes as first the legitimated Other and then as a fully independent category of sociosemiotic meaning—is virtually a grab bag of any and every sign that exceeds such a delimited sphere. This is particularly obvious in the case of a concept such as "homosexual," since with each use it is necessary to attempt to clarify what is meant by it because the only stable meaning inherent to it is something like "not convincing as a transparent straight": what always remains squishy is how the individual is not convincing.

As such, it cannot simply be an easily perceivable binary of "this" and, if not "this," then "that": that is, it is more than the valence markings of plus or minus that underpins semiotic analysis on its most basic of levels, as in the case of structural or generative phonology. Rather, the categories that lie on either side of the binary divide must constantly be strategically constructed, because it is not always self-evident what is "white," what is "male," what is "straight" (at least not to the degree it is clear what is voiced or unvoiced in phonology—and then, even so, this is not a binary that is all that irreducibly self-evident). And it is in this strategic construction, wherein the limits between what lies on each side of the binary divide, between what lies inside or outside of the category that is privileged as the norm or the normal, where incoherences, ambiguities, internal contradictions, and, quite simply, absurdities of meaning can be perceived to occur. Daily life in a society may be a parallel activity whereby such strategic constructions are constantly taking place at the same time that members of the society are engaging in a tacit agreement to ignore the lapses which occur in such constructions that might not resist too close an interrogation of the conceptual bases of those same constructions. Yet, when the binary discourse breaks down and when deadly violence is the consequence of that breakdown, it becomes necessary to interrogate those constructions without turning a blind eye to their fundamental incoherences.

EL LUGAR SIN LÍMITES

Arturo Ripstein's 1978 film *El lugar sin límites* (a metaphor in Spanish for hell) is just such a site of interrogation. The film, based on the 1966 novel of the same name by the Chilean José Donoso, was released in English as *Place Without Limits.* Ripstein is unquestionably one of Mexico's top five current filmmakers (for an overview of his career see Noriega and Ricci's "Retrospective"). In telling the story of La Manuela, a transvestite prostitute who is killed by one of her preferred customers for having gone too far in insinuating a questioning of his masculinity as regards his preference for men dressed as women over supposedly real women, Ripstein pursues the incoherence of the construction of heterosexuality in terms of three separate narrative strands (concerning the codes of masculinity in the film see Mora). The first narrative concerns the circumstances of La Manuela's death at the hands of Pancho and why after seeming to find in La Manuela a subtle agent of sexual satisfaction Pancho feels compelled to kill her. The second narrative concerns the circumstances of how La Manuela and her colleague La Japonesa have come to be the owners of the brothel where the action of the film takes place and how they come to be the parents of a La Japonesita, now a woman in her twenties. The third narrative involves the role of Don Alejo, a local bigwig who is both La Manuela's and La Japonesa's sponsor and, in an extended sense, La Japonesita's godfather, and yet he is a nonparticipant bystander in La Manuela's death despite the inevitability of the chain of events that get set in motion and that he might have been able to halt. (Although Urbistondo does not speak of the patriarchy in feminist/queer terms, his seeing of Alejo as a metaphor for God captures the essence of the character's social role.)

La Manuela, as she is played by Roberto Cobo, is pretty much a brothel stereotype. (Cobo's first major role was as El Jaibo in Luis Buñuel's 1950 *Los olvidados,* and his career has since involved transvestism in various ways; his most recent cameo role is as a mature Tijuana madam in Alejandro Springall's 1997 *Santitos.*) Notably unat-

La Japonesa's brothel

tractive physically and now around fifty but quickly approaching sixty, La Manuela seeks to portray a fiery flamenco dancer whose red mantilla is her distinctive trademark. La Manuela's routine is part of the entertainment at the brothel she and La Japonesa have long inhabited and which their daughter, La Japonesita, administers. The young woman's administration involves the frequent abuse of her father, perhaps as much out of resentment for the circumstances of her birth (more on which below) as for any homophobia she may experience. The space of the brothel, after all, is generally conceived of as a privileged arena of patriarchal heterosexuality, inasmuch as it is organized around women whose role is to provide sexual services to men. If it could be argued, as campaigns of public decency often do, that brothels are a threat to the patriarchal family, the response is that, quite the contrary, they afford a beneficial sexual outlet to men. These may be men who occupy positions of power, and their supposedly concomitant sexual prowess makes it convenient for them to seek with prostitutes a frequency of sexual contact and a range of sexual practices such that their respectable wives are left to the tranquil administration of home and family. Moreover, the brothel provides a public space — public, that is, within the closed circle of men as worldly figures of patriarchal agency — in which the customers confirm in the presence of each other, if not directly then at least metonymically, their heteronormative sexual identity and performativity: metonymically in the sense that consorting with prostitutes and engaging in the various rites of seduction are metonyms of the subsequent, if customarily invisible, sexual compliance with a proper masculinity.

Brothels also play an important social role for men who are socially inferior to those who are the preferred customers and who are even likely to be the owners of said establishments. This is so because, while it is expected that these other men will also be fulfilling their patriarchal responsibilities with women of their own class, it is assumed that they too, as proper men, are possessed of a sexuality in excess of what they can legitimately satisfy with their legal wives: whores pick up where the sexual responsibilities of decent women leave off. It is inconvenient for society for men whose sexuality may, because of their class origins, be lawless in a way in which it is assumed that of highly placed men is not, to be engaged in random sexuality with women in general and even perhaps with the daughters of the powerful (who would likely consider it rape punishable by death). Thus, prostitutes provide the necessary escape valve. In large cities, there is a social categorization of brothels, but in Latin American small towns, brothels are often frequented by men from a range of social classes. This may not make them the most democratic institution in town, but rather provides yet one more realm for the display of class privilege. There can be little doubt as to who gets the pick of the women, who can demand what of the women (and pay for it), and who can determine the parameters of sociability within the highly charged social microcosm of the brothel (concerning brothel life in Mexico, one might begin with González Rodríguez).

It would appear from the foregoing that the space of the brothel is a carefully and strictly regulated realm for the enforcement of heteronormativity and along with it other controlling structures of the patriarchy, such as social hierarchy of men and the rigid disjunction among men as sexually served by women; concomitantly, women who administer brothels are enforcers of these circumstances. Yet, homoeroticism appears in the space of the brothel in three ways. In the first instance, it appears as the hidden ingredient in all forms of homosociality (this is a point Sedgwick makes repeatedly in her groundbreaking work *Between Men*). Homosociality enforces heteronormativity via the pacts that are forged and maintained between men for purposes of masculine social control, with the clear understanding that those pacts could not adequately function, at least not in what we understand to be the ground zero of the Western patriarchy. They would be perturbed by the existence of sexual desire between men: the line between homosociality and homoeroticism is potentially unstable, such that there are ample opportunities to suspect that sexual desire may indeed circulate among men bound by a pact of homosociality. All this explains those nagging doubts about locker-room antics, fraternity hazing, barroom buddyism, and the beau geste of brothers in arms—or in sports (see Pronger; with regard to homoeroticism and Latin American soccer see Sebreli).

The sort of latent homoeroticism that is the hidden face of homosociality—hidden because it can never be acknowledged and therefore never acted upon — is not unreasonably accompanied by the presence in the brothel of men who have to one degree or another recognized consciously their own same-sex desires such that what they are able to witness in the brothel, if not obtain there, is a display of male sexuality that may satisfy in one way or another their own desire. Whether these men also engage the services of prostitutes as functioning bisexuals or self-enforcing heterosexuals or whether the time they spend with the women is only for purposes of "talking," they can usually be certain that they will not be compromised, since many a prostitute is relieved to take a man's money and not have to do much for it other than talk with him. In both of these senses, homoeroticism is the never-absent dimension of all sexuality, both to the extent that absolute heterosexuality is probably not much of a human fact, which is why heterosexism makes so much of its privilege, and in the way that homoeroticism, no matter how loudly denounced, can never adequately be banished from even the most strictly enforced social realm: even if you round "them" up and shoot them, you still have no way of knowing if you have really ever gotten all of them.

The second instance of homoeroticism in the brothel concerns the relationships between brothel personnel which occur along a number of axes of power and involve madams, prostitutes, and female staff. These are all lesbian relationships in one configuration or another: male staff may be involved in heterosexual relations or wish to be involved in heterosexual relations, but there is less cultural production and commentary to this effect (one can think of the unrequited love toward the prostitute Santa harbored by the blind piano player of the house where she works in Federico Gamboa's 1903 homonymous novel). Since lesbianism is defined in ways that are radically different from those of a female-marked version of gay male sexuality, it may not always be readily apparent to the male scrutiny of relationships between women, a scrutiny that is likely to insist on genital sex as the confirming sign of same-sex sexuality. Yet, the way in which the brothel, despite inevitable feuds, rivalries, and jealousies between its occupants, is a female homosocial space displays the same sort of segueing from heterosexuality to homoeroticism characteristic of male homosociality and, moreover, promotes lesbian relationships when viewed from the perspective of Adrienne Rich's lesbian continuum and the proposition that far more than being defined by genital sexuality, lesbianism is primarily present whenever women define their lived experience in terms of other women.

In that the brothel figures, however deficiently, as a lesbian commune and that despite forces brought to bear to divide the women (i.e., conflicts may be promoted as forms of controlling them) they may sense the need to band together against their exploiter (remembering that madams are agents of brothel owners and the system of exploitation in general), a sort of sisterhood develops that can be read as a form of lesbianism.[1]

Finally, the third way in which homoeroticism is present in the brothel concerns the extent to which a brothel may actually cater to same-sex preferences by having one or more male prostitutes available or by tolerating sexual contact between the male clients and male employees, probably typically young boys who serve as factotums.

All of these elements may not be present in the universe of Ripstein's film, but they are part of the brothel culture the film evokes, since the film takes place entirely within the confines of La Japonesa and La Manuela's house. But the real issue with regard to *El lugar sin límites* is how the realm of the brothel defies the heteronormative principles on which the foregoing discussion continues to be based, assuming as it does that there is a difference in what is systematically maintained between men and women, between the straight and the queer. This is, however, not true in the universe of the film, because La Manuela is a female impostor who, to be sure, considers herself a woman and wishes for everyone to endorse her alignment with the feminine.

However, there can be little doubt that it is common knowledge that La Manuela is a cross-dressed man and that the attention she garners is for her condition as a cross-dresser. Cross-dressing does not in and of itself constitute an example of same-sex preference, although it is unquestionably queer to the extent that it disrupts the controlling principles of heteronormativity that proscribe any blending of sexual identity (Garber). However, when cross-dressing accompanies a sense of the individual's having been mistakenly gendered, that one is in fact a woman trapped in a man's body or vice versa and that one's goal is to be reconstituted as belonging to the sex other than the one to which one has been assigned, then it is likely that, while the gender binary is disrupted by the concept of incorrect sexual assignment and its manifestation in cross-dressing (complete surgical and pharmacological transgendering not being an option available to someone of La Manuela's world), this queering is going to involve same-sex preference. If same-sex preference does not occur from the point of view of the person doing the cross-dressing (who clings to the conviction of belonging to the other sex), it does from the point of view of the person desiring the cross-dressed body, since what is being desired is a body that does not adhere to the rigorous categorizations of the heteronormative binary.

It is often claimed that the desire of a "real" man for a man cross-dressed as a woman is inexplicable: if such a man wants a woman, there are plenty of "real" women available (for a sociological analysis of trans-vestite prostitution in Mexico see Prieur). Let us leave aside for the moment whether such "real" women are so readily available, especially in the social universe of Ripstein's film, as we bear in mind that houses of prostitution exist in large measure because women are not always so readily available and that, indeed, one fundamentalist religious version of the patriarchy is to ensure that women are never available for sex outside matrimony. But to what degree are there men whose desire is for women who are in reality men cross-dressed as women? That is, their desire is precisely for a body that in some complex way suspends the heteronormative binary by constructing a calculus of desire that involves the fetish of both the male and the female, as opposed to the fetish of the categorical same sex, i.e., gay or lesbian, or the fetish of the categorical opposite sex, i.e., straight (my discussion here is inspired by Butler's widely cited theorizing of the performance of sexual identity). Such queer desire constitutes the center of the plot of Ripstein's film, both its existence and the impossibility of calling attention to its existence. That is, La Manuela sees in Pancho a suitable client; perhaps as a woman rather than as a prostitute, she may even entertain a measure of sexual desire for him. La Manuela engages in a game of seduction of Pancho as she dances flamenco for him, wrapped in her trademark red mantilla: the suggestion of the appropriateness of the relationship between the two of them is that Pancho's truck is also fire-engine red. Throughout the sexually charged sequence of La Manuela's dance, Pancho cannot take his eyes off of La Manuela, which only encourages her stratagems of seduction.

However, the tension comes to a head when La Manuela makes a direct play for Pancho, and the latter's brother-in-law begins to tease Pancho about preferring the attentions of a transvestite fag. There is, so the narrative logic of the film would have us believe, no option available to Pancho but to kill La Manuela, and her death affirms his masculinity in the sense that it is an appropriate revenge for La Manuela's apparent assumption that Pancho would find her to be a desirable sexual partner. It also removes permanently from his world someone who might continue to display to that world the possibility that Pancho might find La Manuela to be a desirable sexual partner. It is important to note that the way in which Pancho displays transgressively that La Manuela is a desirable sexual partner is not in having sexual relations with La Manuela nor

The seduction
of Pancho

in penetrating her, but in allowing himself to be kissed by her. This explicit marker of romantic love is what makes Pancho a target of ridicule.

These two reasons are adequate within the macho logic that drives Pancho in his retaliatory rage, although we don't know to what extent it is the consequence of homosexual panic at actually finding La Manuela sexually desirable and to what extent it is propelled by the need to confirm to his peers that he is a "real" man who does not need the services of someone like La Manuela (Palaversich places Donoso's original novel in the context of Latin American sexuality and heteronormative violence and discusses homosexual panic in the novel, which Ripstein transfers intact to the film). Pancho's murderous rage leads one to wonder if there is more involved. What would the attraction be to an apparently straight man of another man cross-dressed as a woman? Or, more specifically, what fetishes provoke sexual desire in the former in the sexual theater being described here? How does a straight man make sexual use of another man cross-dressed as a woman?

Although these questions might seem to be answered rather straightforwardly on the basis of sexual practices customarily attributed to the passive role in standard erotic enactments, it is interesting to note that in some research done on transvestite prostitution there emerges the claim that male clients frequently insist on playing the so-called passive role while the transvestite prostitute is to play the so-called active role in such standard erotic enactments (concerning this dynamic see Schifter). Thus, not only is someone like Pancho possibly identifiable as a "real" man who prefers the company of transvestites, but furthermore he may be one of those clients who wishes the transvestite to play the active role of the "real" man. Ripstein's film does not insinuate such a dynamic, but it is important to understand the social semiotic his film is tapping into. In the arena of sexuality, everything is possible, yet only certain things may be acknowledged publicly: there are desires that one cannot acknowledge to exist and that one cannot acknowledge practicing or wishing to practice; moreover, one cannot tolerate having attributed to him (because we are here speaking of the need for the male to defend his masculinist privilege by not allowing any detraction from his masculinity out of fear of losing that privilege) desires and practices that belong to the realm of the unacknowledgeable.

There is certainly no hint in the film that Pancho might wish to play the passive partner in any sexual relations with La Manuela, just as it is not completely clear initially that he is even attracted to La Manuela at all, although he does become visibly excited when she dances flamenco for him and despite the attributions of his companions. The details of La Manuela's relationship with La Japonesa certainly demonstrate that La Japonesa is not incapable of penetrative sexual activity; more on this below. But what can be confirmed from what is explicitly displayed in the film is that while La Manuela may view herself to be a woman and therefore not to be engaged in same-sex desire in her approach to Pancho, Pancho and his companions know very well that La Manuela is what is conventionally called a man and that therefore any sex with her would transgress the heteronormative paradigm. There is an important aside to be made here: Gonzalo Vega, who plays the part of Pancho, has long been a heartthrob of women in Mexico for his work in film and television; presumably, he has also been a heartthrob of gay males. Yet it is a fairly common assumption that Gonzalo Vega is gay, although this is not publicly acknowledged to be so. It is inevitable that spectators in the know will read his part in terms of Vega's personal life. This may always be so in cultural production but seems to be especially so in the case of film and television, which is why historically actors and actresses have so jealously controlled information about their personal lives, as in the case of the now paradigmatic closeted Hollywood actor Rock Hudson. However, the "real-life" gayness of the body playing Pancho cannot help but afford some pathetic rhetorical highlights to the homosexual panic and homophobic rage that lead him to murder La Manuela (see Ehrenstein regarding the relationship between the sexuality of movie stars and the roles they play).

Where all of this becomes incoherent is in the La Manuela-Pancho formula that both maintains heteronormativity and queers it. This happens because, as has been stated, La Manuela would appear to sustain a conventional female-male binary in her seduction of Pancho. Yet Pancho's reaction, the reaction of his companion, and his eventual killing of La Manuela are all based on the understanding that La Manuela is a man posing as a woman and is therefore challenging implicitly the validity of the rigid binary divide. The fact that the film sees none of this as fantastic, that the audience is asked to see what happens as completely logical, if pathetically unfortunate — Pancho kills someone for creating an insinuation that he is less than a "real" man — is only possible because of the incoherence that is at the heart of heteronormativity. The rigid gender binary and queer transgressions, along with fatal violence because of the transgressions and in order to maintain appearances, would seem to be integral parts of the world as it is supposed to be.

The second crucial incoherence in *El lugar sin límites* is what perhaps could be called outrageous in Ripstein's film and the José Donoso novel on which it is based (see Foster, *Gay and Lesbian Themes*, 87–93): the way in which La Manuela and La Japonesa successfully meet the challenge made to them by Don Alejo, the town's primary power figure, to have sex with each other — they successfully engage in sex under his gaze, and he deeds the brothel to La Japonesa; in time, it is the issue of that single sex act, La Japonesita, who at the time of the narrative is engaged in administering the brothel. Don Alejo's cruel challenge could be read as a transitory decision to impose heteronormativity on the inhabitants of his brothel — that is, to straighten out La Manuela as well as La Japonesa, who is untroubled by the former's self-attributed female identity. While he is successful in getting La Manuela to perform "like a man," at least for this once, Don Alejo is unaware that his challenge is only serving to further queer La Manuela, who performs the penetrative role, but as a woman. In fact, in order to encourage her, La Japonesa tells La Manuela, "Piensa que yo soy la macha y tú la hembrita." That is, La Japonesa encourages La Manuela into a penetrative role by suggesting that she fantasize that she is in fact being penetrated by La Japonesa. Moreover, in making the bet with Don Alejo in order to obtain the deed to the brothel, La Japonesa tells him: "No es el primer maricón que puede engendrar, sólo hay que meterle un dedo por allá para que funcione." Thus although she reinscribes La Manuela for Don Alejo into a masculine penetrative role, at the same time she suggests to him that La Manuela will be aroused enough to penetrate by virtue of having been penetrated by her, a woman, in the way in which, as common knowledge would have it, gay men are used sexually by other men. The fact that heterosexual sex may in fact involve the arousal of the man by the woman in this fashion is not part of that common knowledge, because it would suggest that all men, straight or queer, are aroused by anal penetration, which would in turn constitute a double defiance of the logic of the rigid gender binary: women don't penetrate and men are not penetrated. Thus, Don Alejo's challenge is a reinscription of heteronormative logic: a man and a woman having procreative sex together, confirmed eloquently by the fact that La Japonesa and La Manuela have a child as the result of this event. And it is a further queering of that logic: La Japonesa and La Manuela can only have straight sex through a gender role reversal that involves an act customarily thought to be a paradigm of gay sexuality. Moreover, La Japonesa is played by Lucha Villa, a woman who, although she is not identified as a gay in the way in which Gonzalo Vega is, is someone whose imposing body is also associated with unconventional sexual roles to the extent that she often appears less as a conventionally feminine woman and more as a cross-dressing man.

The third element of incoherence in the film involves Don Alejo's non-reaction to the murder of La Manuela. It is not that Don Alejo should come to the defense of La Manuela as a human being, but after all, La Manuela is an integral part of the town's economy. Don Alejo may have deeded ownership of the brothel to La Manuela and La Japonesa, but it is clear throughout the film that as the major power broker in town, he has a vested interest in its functioning. However, Don Alejo also has a vested interest in the power of the patriarchy, which means that he has little choice but to invest in the proper functioning of the system of compulsory sexuality, in both its public face (bourgeois decency) and its hidden one (the brothel as an essentially legitimate escape valve for that system). To put it differently, Don Alejo, although he could well hold Pancho to an accounting for the loss of chattel, has little choice but to collaborate with the system of heteronormativity, since a large measure of his real power derives from the symbolic power of the established sexual system, which is why brothels are so integral a part of the power structure and so often a point of congregation of the powerful, as can be seen over and over again in Latin American cultural production.[2]

In this sense, then, Don Alejo is trapped between conflicting interests or between conflicting compelling needs, and his response is a look of bewilderment as he contemplates La Manuela's twisted body (Pancho kills her by running her down with his truck and then punching and kicking her to death: the red of his truck merges with the red of La Manuela's mantilla and her blood). Interestingly enough, Ripstein follows through on his use of principal actors, because the public personae of Roberto Cobo and Gonzalo Vega as gay men underscore the horror of being obliged to collaborate with murder as an acceptable way of enforcing the patriarchy, not just in punishing deviance, but in confirming a particular code of sexuality that at the same time demands deviancy in order to effect that confirmation. If violence without recourse is the lot of La Manuela—whose alleged deviance and consequent murder constitute a historical necessity that she cannot escape—witnessing violence without recourse is Don Alejo's. By extension, it is the spectator's lot to duplicate Don Alejo's gaze. Whether spectators will accept the legitimacy of Pancho's revenge or understand how hellish the system of heteronormative sexuality is that is being defended but of which Ripstein's film offers such an eloquently staged critique, is another matter.

AQUELES DOIS

As John Corvino has pointed out, the principal defense that can be made for homoeroticism is that it serves to make certain people who practice it happy, and that, in turn, is good for a healthy society. If one can find no principled reason to invalidate homoerotic relations (and Corvino carefully reviews the reasons that have been put forth on religious, moral, psychological, and social grounds and finds them lacking and unpersuasive), one is not subsequently compelled to find a reason to defend homoerotic relations (i.e., something does not have to be socially redeeming; to be permitted it is sufficient that it not be a clear and present danger to society). However, if one is constrained to seek a reason to defend homoerotic relations beyond the demonstration that they harm no one—not those involved in them nor third parties (except for the way that all love is potentially harmful, at least psychologically)—then such a defense is to be found in the sheer joy that satisfactory sexual relations bring to any individual, straight or otherwise.

The Catholic Church, at least since the late 1960s, has recognized that sex, beyond simply serving the crucial function as a stimulus to procreation, also serves in no less a crucial way to cement the bonds of love and mutual responsibility between individuals. Of course, the Church is interested only in monogamous, heterosexual (and canonically Catholic) marriages, but it is a proposition that overlaps with the larger proposition so integral to the culture of the twentieth century, that good sex makes for good people.

Thus, one strategy for the legitimation of homoerotic rights must be the promotion of the social value of happiness as deriving from sexually happy individuals. In the process, it becomes necessary to denounce the misery—individual and therefore also collective—that derives from the denial of appropriately viable sexual relations. Moreover, it becomes important to analyze and denounce the structures of homophobia which impede the process of recognizing the social value of happy queers— and, concomitantly, the social liability of miserable queers. Moreover, homophobia directly threatens the aspirations to happiness of queers (who find important support in the United States for their efforts to be happy thanks to the Declaration of Independence and its reference to "unalienable Rights," among which are "Life, Liberty, and the pursuit of Happiness," and the Preamble to the Constitution, which has as a goal the promotion of the general welfare) by both denying their human dignity and promoting psychological and physical violence against them. Homophobia also "poisons the waters" of society by working to close off all debate over the legitimacy of queers: even to seek to open such a debate is to make one liable to the effects of homophobia, which includes minimally accusing one of being queer by definition and, in due course, exposing one to the psychological and physical violence homophobia incites and naturalizes.

The title of Sérgio Amon's 1985 *Aqueles dois*,[3] based on Caio Fernando Abreu's short story of the same name, invokes homophobia. The phrase *aqueles dois*, "those two," which also appears in the film in the form *esses dois*, "these two," an even more prejudicial use of pejorative deixis, functions to evoke a set of individuals whose conduct or being is socially and morally reprehensible. Indeed, such formulations imply a Möbius strip along which being and doing are imbricated and inseparable such that, as in this case, if one is queer, one engages in nefandous sex; if one is perceived to engage in nefandous sex, one is a queer; if one is perceived to have the potential to engage in nefandous sex, because of any constellation of signs that can be read as signaling such a potentiality, then one is equally queer; and if one is even alleged to be queer, one must necessarily be queer, because why else would anyone do something that would promote the deadly transgressive interpretation? (See Moreno, 134–135, for a contextualization of Amon's film in Brazilian filmmaking on queer issues.)

No one in Amon's film ever sees Saúl and Raúl engage in sex, and this includes the viewer: physical relations between them (beyond hugging, such as when Saúl goes to console Raúl for the death of his father) are hardly demonstrative, and it is only on New Year's Eve, after drinking and listening to the revelry in the street, that there is a quickly abandoned scene in which, after Saúl asks Raúl in the semi-dark if he has ever had relations with a man, we see Raúl, wearing only underwear, rise to go to Saúl. Indeed, the physical "proof" of their relationship appears to lie with two pieces of circumstantial evidence. One is a photograph that Saúl accidentally drops in which he and Raúl, both smiling into the camera of a plaza photographer, each has an arm over the other's shoulder. The second is when the lovesick Clara, who has been avidly pursuing Raúl in the office in which all three work, goes to a fortune-teller. The cards reveal that another man is standing between Clara and Raúl. Clara at first thinks that it is her husband, from whom she is separated. But the fortune-teller says no, that's not the card that has come up, and Clara, quickly recalling the way in which other men in the office have mocked Saúl and Raúl, immediately puts two and two together. The fortune-teller offers to perform a *trabalho*, literally a work or job, in this context an elaborate ritual of magic intended to have a specific effect, which in this case would be to force Raúl to respond to Clara's amorous advances. Clara wisely snaps her purse shut with the crisp observation that "that" is an illness with no cure; subsequently, we see her acting coldly toward both men, and it is to be assumed that she did not keep the results of her visit to the fortune-teller to herself.

What is going on here, then, is a dense interpretive undertaking designed to demonstrate that the two men are queers and that, for the sake of the health and well-being of the "large family," as the firm's owner alleges it to be, the two men must be fired; after playing for them an anonymous denunciation left on his answering machine,[4] Dr. André dismisses them, claiming that he is uninterested in who left the message (that is, the discourse of homophobia is unquestionable, irreproachable, unimpeachable) and only in its content. Thus the allegation is by definition self-confirming: the simple act of making such an allegation ensures its truth, and the impregnable fortress of homophobia renders it a discourse that is unquestionable, irreproachable, and unimpeachable.

In terms of a praxis of masculinity, the message is clear: a man cannot do or be anything that will put into effect the implacable machinations of the homophobic chain reaction, which is a metonymic dynamic whereby any sign can promote a totalizing enterprise of interpretation that results in the conclusion that the individual under scrutiny is queer. Since no man (or woman, although the heteronormativity of a masculinist society may subject men to greater scrutiny than women) can ever prove definitively that he is straight, one's daily life must be structured in such a way to (hope to) prove that he is not queer—or at best to forestall any attempt to begin to read him as queer, since, once set in motion, homophobia can rarely be checked. Indeed it often becomes a self-fulfilling prophecy, as Bruno Barreto so brilliantly demonstrated in his 1981 film *O beijo no asfalto*, perhaps one of the finest treatments, in both the film and in its original 1960 dramatic version by Nelson Rodrigues (see Foster, *Gender and Society*, 129–138).

The incitement of this chain reaction in *Aqueles dois* assumes many dimensions. The most obvious one is the simple fact that there are more candidates for any one position than there are positions available. Just as one of the functions of racism, sexism, classism, and the like is to narrow competition for those who exercise them because they feel that they are members of the hegemonic minority, whether in the workplace or in other quarters, homophobia often serves to engineer the dismissal of others in order for one to succeed through less competition; a corollary of this is the belief that "they" stick together, defending their own and thus increasing the competition for members of the majority, and therefore their elimination is justified to "make things fairer for us regular types."

One of the interesting aspects of *Aqueles dois* is that, at least on the basis of conventional stereotyping, a number of gays work for Dr. André. One is a young man, Mário, who is hired at the same time Raúl and Saúl are (six apply for positions, and three are hired for the positions available). Although Mário never figures prominently in the film, his effeminacy provides an immediate place-holder for homophobia. But there is bigger game in the persons of two coworkers who appear to have created a relationship between themselves and thus are a greater threat than the perhaps easily intimidated Mário might be because he is more obvious in his queerness. Then there is Ferreira, tellingly addressed in the diminutive as Ferreirinha. In Portuguese the use of such diminutives, particularly with surnames, is one discursive strategy for identifying someone as queer without saying so in so many words: the diminutive of affection in the language (which is more truly so when effected with the first name, the default name for most Brazilians) is appropriated as a homophobic slur, as an insinuation that the person being so named is queer.

Ferreira is an older man who has been with the firm for many years; like Mário, he too evinces the signs of effeminacy, which are read as more offensive and transparent because of his age and his obvious bachelorhood. Saúl comments to Raúl that it is unfortunate that Ferreira has no other life than the firm and that undoubtedly this is not the life he would have chosen for himself (i.e., to make the firm the center of his life rather than, I understand, an erotic relationship, which homophobia has forbidden him). Ferreira makes a mistake in handling the affairs of a client particularly valued by Dr. André, who has no qualms about humiliating him in public. He is consoled by the one office worker, Norma, who appears ready to defend the human dignity of her coworkers; it is she who provides a counterdiscourse to Dr. André's assertion that the firm is one big family by saying that it is a vipers' nest where everyone is out for himself alone.

Another sign of homophobia in the universe of the film is the identification of the presumed similarity between the two men. They are physically different, with different life experiences. Raúl is separated from his wife, is a bit older, and is balding and bearded; Saúl, who was engaged in a long-term, never-finalized relationship with a woman whom he claims to have been the passion of his life, is smooth-faced and boyish, with perhaps what one might call (with positive or negative inflection) a "sensitive" look about him. The similarity of their names is the director's wink toward the audience that, after all, they are two peas in a pod, so to speak. Although neither has a history of homoerotic relations—and indeed it is not completely clear in the film that they will be in any definitive way bonded by homoerotic relations, at least not in the fullest sense of the term as understood both by homophobia and gay liberation—there is a chemistry between them that should, in any reasonable understanding of the word, pass for love: they find they have mutual interests that lead to animated conversations, such that they enjoy each other's company; they have emotional needs that resonate with each other; and Saúl's verbal play to Raúl on New Year's Eve, asking him if he has ever made love to another man (an advance that Raúl appears to respond to willingly), at least suggests the possibility of a satisfactory physical sexuality.

Yet if the similarity of their names suggests that they must inevitably come together in a synergetic relationship, it also underlies the conjoining of the two of them in a homophobic denunciation. The anonymous message left on Dr. André's answering machine speaks of "those two

Close office mates

guys with similar names," as though the similarity of their names were proof of their queerness. American popular culture seems to hold that certain names are queer in essence, a variant of the Isidorian formula whereby names are the consequence of things; some gays change their names to forms that have already been recognized to be part of gay culture: Ken, Kurt, Bobby, Billy, Joey, for example, recur in gay texts. I suspect this is not the case in Brazilian culture, with the exception of certain preferred "stage names" that may be used by transvestites and drag queens. However, the process of homophobia in the film implies that "those two" are a "natural pair" on the basis of the similarity of their names, as though it were inevitable that they would turn out to be queers together on the basis of their names. Hired at the same time, working side by side in the same office, chatting each other up, eating together, and being photographed in symmetrical poses all reinforce, in the homophobic culture of their persecutors, their twinness as constituted primarily by their names.

Although their persecutors see them together in a symmetrical pose in a photograph that Saúl accidentally drops in the elevator (it is part of a portfolio of materials, including his own drawings, that he is taking to show Raúl), another crucial scopic incident in the film involves the love-struck Clara. Clara tries in vain to engage Raúl in a relationship, using what she understands is a friendship (nonhomoerotic, of course) between him and Saúl to get to Raúl, inviting him to a party at her house, going to his apartment to demand, rather to his surprise, that he "clarify" the relationship between them (in so doing, she unwittingly forces Raúl to miss a movie date with Saúl), and availing herself of her friend's wise recommendations as to how to win him. During this process and before she follows her friend's advice to seek the ministrations of a fortune-teller, we see her studying Raúl and Saúl engaged in a conversation of close physical proximity over lunch. As she passes the outside of the lunchroom, she sees the two men together and stops cold to study them together before she reluctantly continues on her way. It will be this discovery of their closeness that will perhaps make it click in her mind that they are queer lovers when the fortune-teller shows her how the cards identify another man who is not her husband standing between her and Raúl.

Homophobia relies heavily on scopic evidence: one is seen as being and doing whatever it is that triggers the semiotic chain reaction of homophobic interpretation, and homophobia is unusually generous in what it allows to count as evidence. Thus, where for the spectator the two men are simply engaged in close conversation, Clara appears to have the sort of pang of jealousy usually inspired by discovering the object of one's affections in the company of someone else when that person is desired to be in one's own company: the more apparently intimate the relationship with the other, the greater the degree of jealousy. Clara's jealousy, discernible by the look on her face, is not here immediately homophobic, but it is evident that she is disturbed by seeing the two men together when one would assume that she would only be disturbed if she saw Raúl in close conversation with another woman. Clara has a second scopic opportunity in the film, this time one that is clearly underpinned by the homophobic anger of the woman spurned for another man. When Raúl's father becomes ill and he must take a leave of absence to visit him in a provincial town, he calls for Saúl to join him for moral support; their meeting, in which Raúl informs Saúl of his father's death, is the first time we see them embrace in a fervent emotional display. When Saúl is called to the phone at Clara's desk to take the call from Raúl, we see her stare at Saúl in frank and stony hostility. She now "knows" about them, and this call for help from Raúl confirms the extent of the queer relationship between them.

Finally, homophobia, in order to function efficiently, must seek the confirmation of its propriety through social consensus: others must agree with the homophobic persecutors that their perceptions are correct, and they must agree with them as regards the appropriateness of the punishment to be meted out. Thus, the men's coworker initiates the discourse of denunciation whereby others are informed of his "discovery" and are asked to agree with him that for the health and well-being of the workplace, the threatening workers must go. Norma's question as to what difference their relationship makes to others falls on deaf ears, and various office mates support the persecutor's assertions with complicitous silence (in such a situation, someone like Ferreira has no choice but to be the most complicitous, since he would hardly want to attract the aggressions of homophobia, which always seek to justify themselves by expanding their circle of inclusion), and the result is that the persecutor has every reason to believe that his denunciation is endorsed by the right-thinking men and women of the office. It is cold comfort that the persecutor's decision is to denounce the two men via an anonymous phone message rather than, as is more often the case, by taking up bricks and bats. But it must be understood that the summary severance (which is therefore an unethical if not illegal bypassing of due process) from one's source of livelihood (and more so in the tight employment market suggested by the film) is virtually as violent as direct physical assault.

Yet the conclusion of the film provides an interesting, rather utopian twist on the inevitable consequences of Dr. André's firing of the two men. Suspending disbelief as regards the economic viability of the two men's situation following their discharge, the film describes the high state of happiness in which they spent the month of January despite the searing summer weather that melted the streets around them. Like conquering heroes and perhaps as an intertextual allusion to skipping off to happiness on the yellow brick road of Oz, we see them come joyfully into view over the rise of a hill amid street traffic. The voice-over of the film notes that while they spent a deliriously happy month of January together, the office they left behind was plunged into an unhappiness from which it could not recover.

The context of happiness is reinforced by the fact that their dismissal takes place at the end of the year, after the two important happy holidays of year's end, Christmas and New Year. We see the office workers decorating the office for Christmas and serenading each other with snatches of seasonal carols, and the supposed first sexual encounter between the two men takes place against the backdrop of the festivities of New Year's Eve, *reveillon*, second only to *carnaval* among the most important festive occasions on the Brazilian social calendar (for an interesting film built around the importance of the New Year's celebration in Brazil see Walter Salles and Daniela Thomas's 1998 film *O primeiro dia*). But this is also the context in which the denunciation against Raúl and Saúl is submitted to Dr. André and in which he understands the pragmatic advantage in dismissing them.

Homophobia would have us understand that its virtue lies in ridding the world of the pernicious and contagious evil of sexual deviation in order to ensure the healthy prosperity of heteronormativity. In addition to the proposition that sexual deviance is a moral blight, its persecution is wont to be defended as absolutely necessary to avoid the deleterious effects of merely being in the presence of queers. Of course, homophobia never is called upon to specify what those deleterious effects are, and it is true to form that when such formulations are made against "those two," no specifics are forthcoming as to why it is necessary to get rid of them. What is particularly effective about Amon's film is the implied message that what is wrong with them is that they are, quite simply, happy together.[5]

It is a moot point whether what homophobia cannot stand is happy queer people. But it is an important postulate of heterosexism that queers cannot, by definition—i.e., because of their violation of the taboos of nature—be happy, be gay in the true sense of the word; therefore, the presence of happy queers is a transparent insult to, because it is a direct defiance of, the grounding principles of heteronormativity. In the context of Dr. André's establishment, the special happiness of Raúl and Saúl contravenes the proposition that the office is one happy family, underscoring as it does the unhappiness of their coworkers. It is an unhappiness that is the consequence of the viperish divisiveness that exists among the workers and that closes over all of them as an unremitting pall when the discordant happiness of the two offending men is removed. Put another way, the difference of their happiness points up the unhappiness of their coworkers, and it is vital, even if it means gross injustice toward Raúl and Saúl, for Dr. André to restore the undifferentiated unhappiness of his staff: their sour visages, their frightened looks, their angry stares, their furtive and accusing glances.

It is highly questionable to what extent Raúl and Saúl will be able to maintain their happiness in the face of the grim social reality of their world, whether it is within the confines of Dr. André's firm or out on the streets of Porto Alegre, where the film was made. Yet, I would insist that *Aqueles dois* is less a film about homoerotic love than it is about homophobia, whether in the workplace or in society in general; as cultural production has often shown, the workplace is only one icon of society in general. The workplace is a privileged site if only because of the significant portion of one's day spent there; for an excellent Brazilian gender-marked film about the workplace as social icon see Suzana Amaral's 1985 *A hora da estrela* (see Foster, *Gender and Society*, 70–82).

Aqueles dois is less a film about homoeroticism because the relationship of the two men as lovers is only represented obliquely, and it is more about homophobia because it is this dynamic that is directly detailed in the film. We see more about the consequences in generating homophobia in others of Raúl and Saúl's relationship than we see of the love between them — not at least when one considers how gay films have found it important to insist on detailing the coming together of same-sex bodies. Actual physical love is both a strategy for the naturalization of homoerotic sexuality and a way to dispel heterosexist assumptions about homoeroticism: this takes the form of demonstrating emphatically that such love is more than a grotesque mockery of a superior heterosexuality by placing in evidence the significant differences of same-sex love and the happiness that it brings to its practitioners, to match equally the conventionally assumed happiness that accrues to heterosexual love. *Aqueles dois* provides none of this, not even the representation of the most fleeting of kisses between the two men, although there is a fleeting fantasy scene of the two of them dancing together.

This fantasy is part of a sequence in which Saúl and Raúl are at a party: Clara seems to have managed to get Raúl to accept an invitation, even if it means inviting Saúl (as well as other office mates) too. Raúl and Clara dance together briefly, and Clara attempts to kiss Raúl, but he spurns her advances. When he and Saúl leave the party at the same time, they end up sharing a bottle of beer seated on a curb in front of a bridal store (perhaps the two men will come to "wed" each other). They pass the bottle back and forth between them in the sort of shared physical camaraderie in which the homosocial begins to slide into the homoerotic, and what one suspects is the phallic symbology (in a film that cannot represent actual physical intimacy) of the beer bottle is emphasized by the way in which Raúl sits on the curb with the bottle protruding from between his legs. Later, when Saúl awakens in his own bed, his hand is touching a beer bottle. The dance fantasy occurs when the two are in a park together, and they appear to share an imagined scene in which Raúl asks a woman seated on a bench to dance with him. Other dancers appear, and the representation of dancers in multiple dimensions dissolves into the two men dancing together. Bridal store, beer bottle, joined dancing all function here as displaced images of the growing erotic involvement between the two men.

Since men do have greater body contact in Brazil than in the United States, photographs in the public plaza with arms around each other's shoulders, the close-in proxemics of an earnest conversation, or the hearty exchange of a manly embrace hardly qualify as markers of same-sex desire or activity, no matter how meaningful they become in an accumulated fashion (i.e., once again, the chain reaction of homophobia) to the jilted Clara and the jealous coworkers of Amon's film.

It appears that *Aqueles dois*, to judge by the criticism posted for the film at the website of the Casa de Cinema de Porto Alegre, provoked some confusion as to its intentions. Some critics praised the eloquence with which the film represented the alienation of the big city and the dehumanized workplaces it often engenders. This is fair enough, because the film does abound in images, enhanced by a mechanistic repetition that evokes Fritz Lang's groundbreaking 1927 expressionistic masterpiece *Metropolis*, of the deadening meaninglessness of office work, which is in turn placed into the context of the cacophony and depersonalized massiveness of the big city and its built space. These mechanized images underscore how the office worker is a nobody lost among desks, equipment, buildings, streets, and streams of people and vehicles. The overwhelming effect of such dehumanization and depersonalization is a generalized spiritual malaise whereby the individual is miserable and unfulfilled, is simply unhappy. This unhappiness is a uniform condition that, in such formulations about the workplace as this film would tend to suggest, is necessary in order to keep the whole machinery (which is the controlling expressionistic image of Lang's film) plodding along. In this sense, the unhappiness that closes over Dr. André's office with the departure of Raúl and Saúl is not because of any regretful perception on their coworkers' part for the shoddy way in which they have treated the two men or on Dr. André's part for firing them. Rather, it is a return to normality, with the destabilizing element of their happiness (which, in all truthfulness, is not that publicly evident as they go about their work in the office) having been removed. That such normality is restored thanks to the exertion of homophobic heterosexism is simply the dominant irony of the film.

Yet the reviews of the film that focus on it as principally a metaphor of the deadening routine of the workplace miss the way in which part of that routine involves the dynamic of homophobia and the way in which it functions to eliminate a sexuality that must be condemned precisely because it makes its participants happy and, in so doing, highlights the unhappiness of others. By this I do not mean to say that *Aqueles dois* defends the greater efficacy of same-sex love to make people happy, but only that it shows how any happiness generated by it must be destroyed by the unhappiness—at least as modeled in this film—of heterosexist society in general, an unhappiness that is featured in the counterpoint of Clara's ludicrous participation in the soap opera of heterosexual conquest. By the same token, this is not to say that same-sex relations do not involve their own soap operas or their own variations on the heterosexual soap opera; it is just that this dimension of same-sex love is not a part of the relationship portrayed in the film (on the soap opera of homoerotic love in some recent Argentine films see Foster, *Contemporary Argentine Cinema,* 135–149).

The reviews incorporated into the documentary site mentioned above are never able to come to terms with the representation of homophobia in the film, which perhaps signals the way in which such homophobia is so naturalized in our society that it is difficult for some to be surprised by its presence or to be particularly concerned about its inexorable machinations; this lack of remark becomes, in turn, another way in which homophobia works. At the same time, some reviews mention the precipitous denouement of the film. This is somewhat ironic in that, as my remarks have indicated, what is truly incomplete about the film is the representation of actual same-sex eroticism—or at least its representation in ways that would express the genital sexuality that our society demands as the mark of "real" sex, even though it is important to promote the validity of nongenital varieties of sexuality as equally fulfilling and as equally determining of a specific sexual identity as genital sexuality is held to be.

If the ending of the film is precipitous, it is because the machinations of homophobia are so inexorable. Once Raúl and Saúl have been identified as queers and once their persecutor has ensured that he can get others to invest in his interpretation of their relationship, it is a simple step to effect a denunciation that can have no other effect than to bring about their dismissal: the violence of the denunciation, it is guaranteed, will be compounded by the violence of a summary and uncontestable firing. Unless their persecutor were to value his homophobic interpretation as a license to torment them relentlessly and with impunity as a part of the daily commerce of the workplace, there is no compelling reason for homophobia not to move toward its unchecked execution, which comes in the form of the denunciation of the two men in the anonymous message left on Dr. André's answering machine. It is worth noting that this answering machine is the latest in the mechanical gadgets of his emporium, with its own particular disembodiment of the human voice, the disembodiment of the telephoned voice to the next power. Significantly, Dr. André insists that whom the voice belongs to is unimportant, only the message matters—the discourse of homophobia as a deus ex machina.

In this way, the film underscores the precipitousness not of the film's narrative rhythm but rather of the discourse of homophobia: it works with swift and deadly marksmanship, and there is no appealing its pro-nouncements. At various points throughout the film, Saúl engages in a flashback in which he sees the twisted body of a victim of violence lying in a bed in a wrecked room. It is difficult to discern if this is how Saúl fears that he will end up, since most queer persons are repeatedly assured explicitly and by insinuation that a violent end awaits them in this world as much as eternal condemnation in the next, or if it is a scene he has actu-ally witnessed somewhere along the way. In a more "realistic" ending to *Aqueles dois*, some form of physical violence would not be out of place, even if what it meant was that the two end up destitute on the streets, since once you are fired for being queer, it is conceivable that you will not easily get significant employment again. But it could also mean that either one or both of the men will be attacked by the gay-bashers who are the strong-arm enforcers of heterosexism or that either one or both will end up committing suicide because of the dead-end consequences of having been branded with the mark of the queer. That none of this occurs at the end of Amon's film is notable indeed, given prevailing so-cial realities in Brazil and elsewhere in Latin America (not to mention in the United States). And it is for this reason that it is even more notable that the film ends with what is the absolutely unacceptable proposition for homophobic heterosexism: two queers happy in love with each other.

CONVIVENCIA

It is well established that homosociality is not to be confused with the homosexual or the homoerotic, beginning at least with the fact that the former is a constitutive principle of the heterosexist patriarchy. Homosociality produces solidarity among men in order to ensure the defense of masculinist society in which women play a sec-ondary role: when sororal bonds between women might at times veer toward a position of resistance, dissidence, and opposition, taking on features of a social configuration independent of and antagonistic to the patriarchy, they become subject to appropriate sanctions so that things return to "normalcy" (as in the model provided by Bryan Forbes's *The Stepford Wives*, 1975). Linked by tight relations of domination and de-pendence—rarely are they relations of complete equality—men count on their mutual obligations toward each other to consolidate the power of the patriarchy as their hegemonic social refuge. The man who does not comply with his homosocial obligations toward the patriarchy, who does not respect the vertical hierarchy of power, finds himself on the outside, banned and "desocialized."

In the social scheme of things, such as one finds modeled in well-known Marxist theories and those of social anthropology, the primordial function of woman is to confirm the relationship between men, and men exchange women, as Claude Lévi-Strauss has shown (for example, in *The Elementary Structure of Kinship*, 1949), as tokens of material and symbolic value, toward consecrating their position in the masculinist hierarchy of power: to join in matrimony is to solder the node of one's position in the patriarchal network. One man greets another through the body of a woman, and the responsibilities assumed vis-à-vis a woman establish the role that one fulfills with respect to other men. Likewise, to lose respect for someone else's woman—to make off with her, to rape her—is to violate the homosocial pact.

When the homosocial segues into the homosexual, the pact is also broken, since a transgressive proximity (the homosocial unites, but it also imposes distances) and the consequences of such a transgression begin with the repugnance of "real" men who know how to respect—who have resisted any opportunity or temptation to violate—the pact of proximity and distance. When a homoerotic relationship intrudes, it remains to be seen if it reproduces the hierarchy of power, even when it inverts it, or if an erotic surrender brings with it a fatal realignment in the homosocial microstructure on which it intrudes.

In a certain sense, one can see that the homosocial pact serves as an ideological grounding for almost all Latin American cultural production. It requires no great effort to construct an extensive inventory of paradigmatic examples drawn from Argentine culture (some of which I have mentioned in the preface to this study): in order to provide an adequate assessment of this issue, one simply does not know where to begin. Nevertheless, if my interest here lies with Carlos Galettini's 1993 film version of Oscar Viale's 1979 stage play *Convivencia* (Living Together), it is because some of Osvaldo Pellettieri's comments in his critical introduction to the text of the play make reference to the question of "homosexuality." The fact that Viale experimented in *Convivencia femenina* (1986) with the inversion of sociosexual paradigms cannot help but be suggestive of his insinuations of homoeroticism, no matter that it is not quite clear how well Viale and others understand that same-sex relations between men and their equivalent expression among women can never be a question of parallel lives, owing to the profound divergence between the social history of women and that of men.

Undoubtedly, one must recognize the legitimacy of interpretive practices that support specific creative efforts toward underscoring the homoerotic subtext of cultural production. Such a procedure not only has to do with the simple fact that the silence imposed on the expression of sexual preferences and practices in general and the homoerotic in particular forces us to find ways of saying what cannot/must not be said. All of this has also to do with the perception of what one can in fact say, thanks to the dynamics of compulsory heterosexuality, homophobia, and the effective intimidation and behavioral correction imposed by compulsory heterosexuality. What one can say constitutes a crass betrayal of the human body: if homoeroticism is "unnatural," so too is heterosexuality, and any attempt to hide the "polymorphic perversity" of the human subject and its embodied desire results in the return of the repressed that oozes through the ideological fissures of the text.[6] All of this is a good reason, beyond any deliberate reading, to take what a text says explicitly with a pinch of salt: there is a signifying excess in texts that leaves suspended in mid-air categorical reductionist readings.

It is for this reason that my point here is not to affirm (or reaffirm, in the case of comments by others) the hidden homoerotic text in *Convivencia*. It is of little consequence if in the end Viale or Galettini wanted or did not want to encourage a glance of homoerotic desire: I don't know if this is so, but one could venture to say that if such is the intent of the play and the film, they reveal scant familiarity with the parameters of such desire, since it is unable to go beyond a sorry homophobic version of same-sex desire between men and the relationship this desire can have with that of the feminine subject. Quite the contrary: one finds oneself compelled to say that, when seen from such a perspective, *Convivencia* as a parable of homosexuality is pretty much a heterosexist version of such things: Adolfo, always in a bad mood, has little good to say about anyone because Enrique ignores him. Such a ridiculous view of sexual relations has little artistic dignity to recommend it.

What I would prefer to stress about *Convivencia* here has more to do with the dynamic of homosocialism and the forms in which such a dynamic maintains a large measure of its authority by repudiating the transformation of the hierarchical relationship of homosociality into the leveling relationship of homoeroticism (I will not go into the circumstances in which homoeroticism loses equality; suffice it to say that this is most likely to occur when homoerotic relationships reduplicate heterosexist ones in unanalyzed reinscriptions of male and female, masculine and feminine, active and passive).[7] The tension between the homosocial

Woman as
unanalyzable middle

and the homoerotic explains why the institutions of the patriarchy view
homoeroticism with such panic, and the more formal the institution is
(the Church, the Army, the Board of Directors), the greater the ban on
homoeroticism is. (I also hold in abeyance here an examination of those
societies that permit a blending of the homosocial and the homoerotic.
With regard to the Catholic Church see Jordan; on one dimension of the
U.S. Army see Bérubé; on the Argentine armed forces see Viñas.)

With respect to *Convivencia,* what Galettini allegorizes filmically is the
hierarchical structure of homosocialism and, more specifically, the threat
to this hierarchy that derives from the loss of balance in the patriarchal
relationship, which only puts at risk its stability and smooth functioning. Adolfo and Enrique, much more than "just" lovers, real or potential
or latent (despite the constant flirting of the film with faggy details and
the presence, as Enrique, of the Spanish actor Luis Sacristán, who has
exceptional career experience in playing in "gay-marked" films, perhaps
his most fortunate being as the eponymous protagonist of Pedro Olea's
magnificent *Un hombre llamado "Flor de Otoño,"* 1978), constitute a buddy
pair that works in Western culture as something like a ground zero of
homosocial relations.

The close relationship between the two men (and it is important to
hold in mind that we are talking here about a detail of the patriarchy:
a close relationship between two women involves very different social
parameters) constitutes the basic nucleus of society. They are the ground
of social constitution, the cardinal points on whose basis society defines
and maintains itself, and the necessary condition for society to function adequately and profitably. To strike out against this structure is
to threaten the stability of patriarchal well-being. Moreover, the con-

flicts in the relationship between two men—between the two men of this film—are alarming to the degree to which they exemplify a social problem of expansive implications. At the same time, dealing with such conflicts with the goal of exposing them, in a particular interpretation of the social order, can serve to underscore the strange nature—the queerness—of patriarchal structures as well as show clearly how they function to destroy relations and how they serve to maintain a masculinist power that has little to do with the psychological and emotional needs of the individual.

It is in these terms that I would propose that what is on display in *Convivencia* involves, quite beyond the norms of "getting along" that the patriarchy prescribes, the sinister forms in which the latter operates to ensure the lack of friendship, communication, and affection in their best forms (which might—why not?—include homoerotic desire in any one of its multifaceted manifestations). The relationship between Adolfo and Enrique seems to be a longstanding one, since for more than ten years they have shared the mansion where the action takes place, on the island in the Tigre Delta of the Río de la Plata upstream from Buenos Aires. The island (one of many in the Delta) is a lazy weekend hideaway, and the pact between the two men is that outsiders are not welcome, as this is a privileged space in which the friendship between Enrique and Adolfo is put to the test: in this sense, the Tigre refuge is a microcosm of masculine society in the sense that outsiders are only allowed in if they collaborate in maintaining the agreed-upon structures. To refuse to do so is to provoke the conflict mentioned above and to risk expulsion in the harshest terms possible, no matter what the consequences might be. It is of little importance if the outsiders are men or women, since although the conditions of their interaction with the dominant duo might vary as regards certain strategic details, the result is always the same: contribute to the relationship or be cast out.

The working out of this sociosemiotic arrangement is made obvious in two key instances in Galettini's film in terms that are as realistic as they are fantastic. In the end, as much as these details are important in terms of the sense of the film, sociosemiotically they lead to the same end product: the reaffirmation of the homosocial relationship between Adolfo and Enrique as something that can never be breached. It is a relationship based on the ill-humored blathering of Adolfo, who runs the ship in the game of power that takes up so much of their time, and Enrique's protestations: both are nothing more than the explicit substance of the strong bond they maintain in their unimpeachable homosocial dynamic.

The two instances are divided, significantly, between the sexual genders, first in fantastic and then in more concretely realistic terms. The arrival of Tulio in the realm reserved for the Enrique-Adolfo pair, an appearance that provokes profound tension in their relationship, ends in what is essentially an assassination when he is left to drown in the flood-swollen waters of the river. Since this happened in the past, Tulio's ghost reappears in the collective memory of the two men as something that they have never been able adequately to repress. And perhaps they will never be able to do so, since the violent way in which they got rid of him works also to cement the bond between the two of them. Much remains unexplained about Tulio's presence, which is all the more reason, beyond his continual reappearance as a memory that remains unburied, to describe his function in the work as an element of fantasy or, in more proper psychoanalytic terms, of repressed memory syndrome.

Much less ghostly is the presence of two women, Aurora and Tina—especially Aurora, who is the *porteño* macho's paradigmatic good-time girl. I would like to set aside as an irrelevant detail whether the goings-on between Enrique and Aurora "prove" his heterosexuality (although I cannot help but note that the nature of patriarchal sexuality ensures that a man can never confirm once and for all his status as a heterosexual); I would also suggest little concern for Adolfo feeling left out and ignored by Enrique while he is occupied with Aurora. What the film confirms as categorically relevant, after Tulio's resubmersion in the waters of the Tigre Delta and after Aurora leaves, disgusted, and Tina just fades away, is the seamless dialogue in which Enrique and Adolfo take up again the sort of conversation with which the work opens, a dialogue of "unintelligible voices." In this sense, the relationship between Enrique and Adolfo is in no way homoerotic, despite some rather clumsy insinuations of the film in this regard. Much more interesting, it seems to me, is the complexity with which *Convivencia* portrays the ups and downs that sustain the relations lived between men on a daily basis, all with the goal of endorsing the masculinist patriarchy. It is for this reason that when Enrique insists at the end of the film, "Aquí somos gente normal . . . Somos normales, sí señor . . . Aquí hay machos, para que sepa" [We are normal people here . . . We are normal, yes sir . . . We are machos around here, make no mistake], one has, at least from a nonpatriarchal point of view, good reason to be terrified.

Political
Intersections

CONDUCTA IMPROPIA (MAUVAISE CONDUITE/IMPROPER CONDUCT)

Released in 1984, Néstor Almendros and Or-
lando Jiménez-Leal's *Conducta impropia*[1] (I will use the title with which
it is known in the Spanish-speaking world and among Hispanic scholars) was one of the first major international documents to protest human
rights abuses in Castro's Cuba, which along with the issue of Cuban
political prisoners is an extremely touchy and tendentious subject (two
reliable albeit outdated sources are Amnesty International and Timerman). There had, of course, been a steady stream of attacks from various
right-wing sources, including, obviously, the hundreds of thousands of
Cubans who had left the island and in a large number of cases settled in
Miami, where they created an organized base of resistance and a well-
oiled (and well-financed) propaganda machine (two personal testimoni-
als that received considerable international press are those of Valladares
and Valls). But the majority of the international community, especially
writers, artists, intellectuals, and scholars, had supported the need for a
revolution in Cuba, the effects of the successful Castro operation, and
the social reforms it had put in place, with the consequence that Cuban
cultural production attracted considerable attention and made Cuba—
at least during the 1960s and 1970s—a central point of reference for
knowledge about Latin America.

Those who have historically supported the Castro revolution have

Camp unbecoming to
a revolutionary

accepted a truism of all revolutionary societies: there will be a certain
amount of social injustice because of the sheer scope of the operation and
the very tangible ineptness—and certainly, frequently, self-interest—of
so many of its agents. While injustice can never be really tolerated from
the point of view of the socially committed, one recognizes that it is necessary to work with a calculus of phenomena of injustice: is the injustice
of the revolution in some way substantially less than the injustices of
the *ancien régime* (whose horrors are what led, in large measure, to the
revolution in the first place)? And what are the chances that the new injustices will be corrected as the revolutionary operation establishes its
authority in a society and regularizes—i.e., hierarchizes and effectively
and efficiently supervises—its operations? The promise held out by a
truly socially revolutionary society is that, by its very nature, social (and
thus personal) injustices will not occur, and what will occur is only the
legitimate persecution and excision of those elements that are resistant
to and unreconstructed by the revolutionary process.

When Castro instituted the program of the UMAPs (Unidades Mili-
tares de Ayuda a la Producción) in 1964 to reeducate social dissidents, he
was working off of a number of major ideological postulates: the necessary organization of society (*unidades*); the appropriateness of appealing
to the privileged agents of social changes, the military, which was in-
strumental in bringing him to power and in providing structural support
to his regime; the imperative to organize society toward a common goal
of social assistance (*ayuda*); and the accompanying imperative that that
assistance involve "production" (which, in this case, meant agricultural
harvesting) in the face of radical economic threat to Cuba's economy
represented by the U.S. embargo and the need to establish a functioning

program of international trade (I believe this came as part of the realization by the government that industrialization was not going to prosper and that Cuba was ignoring its long-established base of international trade, which was agriculture), and therefore, the UMAP program was to be of assistance in reinvigorating the agricultural sector (for an account of the camps see Lumsden, *Machos*, 65–71, and Leiner, 28–33).

On the surface, the UMAP program was of a whole with the need to purge Cuban society of antirevolutionary elements, always of major concern to socialist revolutions as well as neofascist military coups. Moreover, the UMAP program reinforced a major semiotic axis of the Cuban revolution, which was to reconstruct the relationship between a dominant urban society (the seat of the bourgeoisie) and the neglected countryside (which was controlled by the absentee bourgeoisie from its base of power in La Habana and, by extension, in foreign centers of capital). If the campaigns, first of literacy, took city people into the country, it was an effort enhanced by the recruitment of urban youth also to participate in agriculture, especially the harvests (both of these processes are well represented in Humberto Solás's paradigmatic revolutionary film *Lucía*, 1968, specifically in the third of the three historical installments; see also the fifth story, directed by Héctor Veitía, in the collection of shorts *Mujer transparente*, 1991). The UMAP program was an extension of this ideological shift in the sense that it took individuals corrupted by the bourgeois city into the countryside, where contact with the land and honest agricultural labor would accelerate their reeducation—this in contrast to incarceration in the urban prisons, which often only served to duplicate the antirevolutionary structures of the city. Reinaldo Arenas's writing is particularly interesting in this regard: as a man whose origins lay in the abject poverty of the countryside, Arenas pursues the sexual dissidence of his homosexuality in the city only to experience the abuse of the UMAP camps and then to experience the abuse of urban prisons (see specifically the circuit described by his autobiography, *Antes que anochezca*, 1992, and the story based on his UMAP experiences, *Arturo, la estrella más brillante*, 1984; see Soto for an assessment of Arenas's writing, particularly from a queer perspective; Ocasio discusses Arenas's position in postrevolutionary Cuba).

Although his story was published much later, when the abuse of the camps had been firmly established and after the regime had backed away from them in their original configuration and by now has virtually recognized they were a mistake, Arenas's writing is a primary point of reference for discussing this program and the efforts at moral cleansing it

Reinaldo Arenas
interviewed in
Conducta impropia

represented; already in New York when *Conducta impropia* was made, Arenas was also one of the major Cuban cultural figures interviewed in Almendros's documentary[2] (along with Cubans Guillermo Cabrera Infante,[3] Armando Valladares, María Simo, and Heberto Padilla; American writer and left-wing gadfly Susan Sontag; and Juan Goytisolo, Spain's most prominent gay/queer writer).

The point, however, of Almendros's film is the extent to which the UMAP camps served as a lightning rod for the international community—most notably Nobel laureate Jean-Paul Sartre, the most prominent international left-wing intellectual of the day—to begin to question the legitimacy of those camps, the justice of the campaign of moral cleansing, and the extent to which Cuba was really moving toward being a healthy socialist society: of course, it also served for those opposed to Castro and socialist revolutions to underscore, with what they considered a broader base of support, the very possibility that a just society could be a consequence of socialist revolution (concerning the persecution of Cuban gays see Young). For some from the right, it simply meant that there was no difference between Castro and the alleged abuses of the many military dictatorships that by the 1960s and still at the time of the filming of *Conducta impropia* were present in Latin America, while for others, such as U.S. Ambassador to the United Nations Jean Kirkpatrick, with her infamous formulation of the difference between regimes under "totalitarian" (i.e., Fidel Castro in Cuba) and "authoritarian" (i.e., Augusto Pinochet in Chile) leaders, it meant that the societies produced by socialist revolution were unremittingly the worst in the world.

I do not wish to review all of the ins and outs of this matter from a social and historical point of view, but rather to focus on its significance in Cuba—and, therefore, for Almendros's film—as it affects the lesbian and gay community in that country. Much has now been written on lesbigay issues in Cuba, both from the point of view of the legendary homoerotic culture of Cuba, the tribulations of gays and lesbians under Castro during the draconian period of social realignment, and the resurgence of an extensive queer culture, along with homosexual prostitution, during the recent decade in which the Cuban government literally can no longer afford to concern itself with moral hygiene. From a filmic point of view, post–*Conducta impropia,* the reader is referred to Luis Felipe Bernaza and Margarita Gilpin's 1996 documentary *Mariposas en el andamio* about a neighborhood transvestite culture (see "Unsettling Return" by Emilio Bejel)[4] and to León Ichaso's *Azúcar amarga,* also from 1996 and a faux-Cuban (because it was filmed in Santo Domingo but packaged, one might say, disingenuously, as though it had been filmed in La Habana) and retro (it is done in black and white, thereby evoking the 1960s, although references to AIDS place the action much later) interpretation of the consequences of social dissidence in Castro's Cuba.

There are many ways in which *Conducta impropia* is important for Cuban studies, beginning with the extent to which it is even a Cuban film: Almendros was born in Spain and lived in Cuba as an adolescent and young man before leaving; codirector Orlando Jiménez Leal is a Cuban exile; their film is mostly in English and French (both Goytisolo and Arenas are interviewed in French) and some Spanish, with appropriate subtitles for the latter two languages (see D'Lugo on the problematics of the film in its stance toward the issue of Cubans and Cuban exiles). It is also important as a documentary, joining a system of similar films and narrative films with documentary-like allusions to social history (e.g., Solás's aforementioned *Lucía* and Tomás Gutiérrez Alea's *Memorias del subdesarrollo,* one of the first great international successes of postrevolutionary Cuban filmmaking). But it is primarily important here for the semiotic process of homology whereby homosexuality is used as the master trope for social dissidence. For this reason, I will continue to use throughout the term "homosexual," not only because it was not as generally repudiated at the time that the movie was made and continues to be less repudiated in Spanish than in English as a medico-legal term used by a heteronormative straight world to define—to manage in an authoritarian manner the definition of—the sexual Other or the Other perceived to be different on the basis of sex; I will also continue to use it because it is the term used (the polite term, as the many words in general Spanish and Cuban Spanish to denote the sexual Other are also used in the film) to identify the individuals who came primarily under the scrutiny of the operations of moral cleansing.

My use of the adverb "primarily" is an important strategic choice here. The scope I wish to give to this adverb is that it is the hub of a semiotic process whereby, through processes of metonymy, synecdoche, metaphor, iconicity—in short, perhaps too many processes to enumerate and sort out—homosexuality is perceived as the most confirming manifestation of social dissidence and therefore, in the Cuban context, of antirevolutionary behavior. One of the terrible ironies of modern history is that for the Left as much as for the Right, homosexuality has marked the irretrievably damning: if it is the sure sign of Otherness for the socialist revolution, the absolute antithesis of the New Man the revolution sought to construct, and the most terrifying embodiment of bourgeois decadence, for neofascist tyranny, to be homosexual was to be in direct defiance of the Christian heteronormative patriarchy—the homosexual was living proof of the degradation wrought by godless socialism (hence the Cold War synonymy between being queer and being communist; see Wilkerson for research on this topic; see also Darsey on the gay Left in the United States and internationally).

Although it may not be possible to separate out all of the semiotic processes going on in this privileging of "homosexual" as the point of departure for the construction of a field of social/cultural/legal abjectness, it is possible to refer to some of the paradigmatic positions of the term. In the first place, it is used as an all-purpose sign to model social dissidence and, hence, the socially unhygienic. Working from a cluster of manifest signs that were held to constitute both the necessary features of the homosexual and, individually, circumstantial indicators of it, the social subject, once identified as homosexual, could then be subject to the whole array of the consequences of his uncleanliness: bourgeois decadent, antirevolutionary, corrupting influence, social pariah, economic abuser. The dynamic of homophobia is such that those handing out the label of homosexual, whether formal agents of the heteronormative establishment or its self-appointed guardians (and one will recall that the social organization of a socialist system, with its groups of neighborhood vigilance, encourages every citizen to be an informer regarding the inappropriate behavior of everyone else),[5] are never called upon to define it or, of equal significance, to justify the conceptual chaining on which their denunciation is based: to call someone else a homosexual is an absolute right under the aegis of homophobia, and the inability of most of the accused to defend themselves is taken as confirming the correctness of the attribution in the first place.

That is to say, homophobia makes sure that it accuses those who are not in a position to defend themselves, hence the way in which gays protected by the regime could never be accused of being homosexual. This was the case with the relative impunity of the painter René Portocarrero and the singer Pablo Milanés; although the latter did have some problems in the UMAP days, he was able to present a clearly homoerotic song like "El pecado original" (Lumsden, *Machos,* 128, 209–210). And it insists that the inability of the accused to defend themselves is a certain indication of their unmanliness—that is, their homosexuality.[6] Homophobia here is based, unquestionably and prior to any discursive revision of the homosexual as something other than the effeminate weakling, on a recognition of the *maricón,* the presumed woman-wannabe who is recognizable on the basis of dress, bodily display, mannerism, language, and interpersonal traits, that is, as a man who is somehow less than a man (for a survey of concepts relating to the effeminate man, the sissy, see Bergling).

Clearly, men of homoerotic interests who do not manifest any of these signs cannot be identified as homosexual, although one can never underestimate the ingenuity of homophobia to enrich the basis of identifying signs, to refine the degree to which they may become recognizable, or to generalize from the slightest shred of evidence to a full-spectrum assessment that the analysis is in the presence of the monstrous moral deviant. The many individuals interviewed in Almendros's documentary make it abundantly clear that the work of the homophobe—here in the guise of the vigilant revolutionary—is never done: some of these men (far fewer women are interviewed) are self-identified queers (a term which I use here to cover an enormous range of sexual dissidence, from a very effeminate transvestite performer to the epicene writer Virgilio Piñera to the hypermasculine Reinaldo Arenas), while some are only guilty by association (Heberto Padilla, for example, who is in no way presented as belonging to gay culture but whose poetry is dissident enough to get him lumped in with the queers as morally lacking).

In the second place, homosexual as an attribute becomes a self-fulfilling prophecy: if one is "not really a homosexual" or if one is not manifestly a homosexual, he (again, far less frequently, she, at least on the basis of this documentary) is treated as one. Poet Armando Valladares, who was early on something like a poster child of the Cuban repression of dissident writers (see Valladares), speaks of how the system essentially turned one adolescent youth into a homosexual through arbitrary labeling, sexual abuse, and permanent registration in his police file. Another interviewee speaks of how camp guards and authorities sexually used UMAP residents—that is, they presumed them to be available, as *maricones* commonly are seen to be in the larger heterosexist society, for sexual service. This is a circumstance that Arenas represents fictionally in *Arturo, la estrella más brillante* (see Foster, *Gay and Lesbian Themes*, 66–72).

In this sense, the UMAP system and the larger issues of moral cleansing that it represents go beyond merely identifying who the queers are: it necessarily creates queers in order to confirm the significant presence of the social Other so as to confirm the power of the norm to identify the Other, to eradicate the Other, and to demonstrate the triumph of the authoritarian establishment over the Other. The fact that this work is never done, because to do so would mean losing the excluded Other required to confirm the prevailing norm, is what accounts from the outset for the requirement that the analyzing enterprise (in this case, homophobia because of the paradigmatic role of the homosexual) constantly renew its strategies of identification: less so in order for the enemy to elude detection and more so because of the need always to have available a contrasting Other so that the normalizing system does not collapse. Since one of the terribly ironic double binds of heteronormativity is that one can never prove that s/he is straight but that one can potentially always find something to prove that s/he is queer, homophobia functions with unabated efficiency.

Finally, the chain of equivalencies that homophobia puts in action is an expanding matter: one thing leads to another (one is reminded of a song in Meredith Wilson's play *The Music Man*, 1958, that concludes "and that rhymes with 'trouble'"), beginning with the innocuous but always ending with the homosexual. One could be, in addition to a self-confessed or self-confirming homosexual (a reference is made to "la vuelta al salón"—just walk around the room and we can tell if you are queer by the way you hold your body), a Jehovah's witness or a writer, an intellectual, an artist with unconventional or nonconforming ideas, or one could in one way or another display the traits of the hippie (notoriously, by having longer than acceptable hair), and before you knew it, you were accused of being a homosexual, rounded up by the police, and shipped off to the UMAP camps (Guillermo Cabrera Infante, who is interviewed in *Conducta impropia*, describes in his 1979 autobiographical novel, *La Habana para un infante difunto,* how this process works when the protagonist is picked up at a concert for having overly long hair). Since any and all of these traits are "manifestly" examples of the inability to adhere to the model of the New Man (or, for that matter, in one of the neofascist dictatorships, to the model of the Good Christian), they must articulate by implication and extension an adherence to the binary opposite of the New Man (or the Good Christian), which is the homosexual, in whom is invested all of the threats to the social order. As I have already mentioned, the controlling motto of the UMAP camps was "El trabajo os hará hombres" (work will make you men), in itself pompous—that is, rhetorically disingenuous—because of the use of the *os* pronoun, which does not occur in any register of Cuban Spanish (it is only to be found in the "universal" Spanish of the authorized translation of the Bible and its parallel texts in the Roman Catholic mass).

It is as though this nonoccurring pronoun were used because it refers to individuals who must not occur in a properly constituted revolutionary Cuban society; the journalist José Mario cannot help but point out its Nazi intertextuality—the concentration camp motto "Arbeit macht frei" (In work lies freedom). Likewise, the motto rests on the undemonstrated proposition that work produces men (i.e., in the sense of categorically heterosexual social subjects), even though, and especially from a Marxist point of view, most of these men were engaged in work, even work that was not necessarily (as in the case of cabaret transvestites) of a decadent bourgeois quality. For example, Padilla was a diplomat.

On the one hand, *Conducta impropia* provides something like a registry of what it meant—and, once again, visibly means—to be gay in Cuba. On the other hand, it provides a dreary case study in how homophobia works, both when it is specifically directed against gays and when it functions to damn the lives of anyone by calling him or her homosexual; the latter, to be sure, only serves to increase homophobia, since many otherwise honest persons will profess to hate gays because to be alleged to be gay could destroy their livelihoods and even cost them their lives.

It is debatable whether homoeroticism is any more an essential ingredient of Cuban society than it is of any other, although writers like Arenas, with his famous allegation of having had sex with more than five thousand men, makes explicit points about how available all Cuban men are for homoerotic relations, even while promoting a macho masculinity, which includes homophobic violence against the very men with whom they are having sex (there is a particularly eloquent passage in Arenas's *Antes que anochezca,* 122, in this regard).[7] Certainly homosexuality was prominent as part of the nightlife in La Habana before the revolution (and was, as all public and commercial exploitation of sex, a major issue in the revolution). And homosexual prostitution is now very much in evidence in Cuba as part of the overall sex industry that supports the tourist trade so vital at this juncture to Cuba's economic survival (the essential homoeroticism of large segments of Latin American/Caribbean/Cuban culture runs through Quiroga's *Tropics of Desire*).

But one should be careful not to confuse the same-sex trade with homosexuality (despite Perlongher's insistence that his research in São Paulo showed homoerotic relations among taxi boys themselves), and sorting out what constitutes sexual spectacle (i.e., transvestite shows), what constitutes the sex industry, and what constitutes conformance to a gay or queer identity is not an easy task. *Mariposas en el andamio* tends to give the impression that there is a large gay community in Cuba that is independent of commercial sex and that that community is now in many ways being legitimized in late Castro Cuba, a point often made about the defense of "tolerance" that is supposed to be the sense of Tomás Gutiérrez Alea's *Fresa y chocolate* (1993), which is something like the first explicitly gay cultural production to come out of official Cuba (official because of the support it received from ICAIC, the Cuban film institute, and official because of the reputation of Gutiérrez Alea as one of the great cultural spokespersons for revolutionary culture).

Whatever the specifics of all of these issues, which belong to the domain of sociological and anthropological research, the impression left by *Conducta impropia* is that the Castro government felt that it was besieged by sexual deviants and that the sort of vigorous *depuración moral* (the official term in Spanish for the campaigns of moral hygiene) represented by the UMAP camps was necessary. These deviants who, as I have already noted, were considered to be a threat to the New Man ideology of the revolution were viewed as so many essentially apolitical holdovers from the bourgeois cesspools of Batista Cuba, as they were the generalized social detritus—for which sexual deviancy served as a master synecdoche—that could not be assimilated into the revolution, although it also obviously included those who fell away from the revolution, as was often the case with intellectuals or political activists (Guillermo Cabrera Infante, in the case of the former; Martha Frayde, in the case of the latter, both interviewed in Almendros's film). *Conducta impropia* makes two things quite apparent: (1) the wealth of public sexuality that the Castro regime in the early 1960s began to address specifically (public in the sense that there had to be something there to be read explicitly by the agents of the campaign of morality), and (2) the inventive synecdo-chal chaining whereby a whole range of alleged deviant social behavior becomes homologized with the master trope of sexual degeneracy.

The result is that Almendros's film is somewhat of a grab bag, but the phenomenon he is describing is like that. Ostensibly the documentary is about the persecution of social dissidents in Cuba, but it segues very rapidly toward the situation of "homosexuals" in any of the various definitions of the term utilized in the social contexts discussed in the film. Although the film returns repeatedly to the larger issue of social dissidence, once again it will slide back toward the topic of homosexuality. If this is not a conscious organizing principle of the director, it is nevertheless effective, for it demonstrates, with irritating eloquence, how the homophobia officially sponsored by the Castro revolution at that time was capable of drawing within its orbit of meaning, basing itself on the master synecdoche of sexual deviance, any manifestation of social or political dissidence. The closing words of the film, uttered by the writer René Ariza, are: "Ser distinto, ser extraño, tener una conducta impropia, es algo no sólo prohibido sino completamente reprimido y, además, puede costarte la prisión." [To be different, to be queer, to engage in bad conduct is something not only banned but totally repressed as well; moreover, it could land you in prison.][8]

THE DISAPPEARANCE OF GARCÍA LORCA

To attempt to represent any aspect of the life of Federico García Lorca (1898–1936) without some sort of reference to his queer sexuality is like discussing Sor Juan Inés de la Cruz without reference to her identity as a woman or Jorge Luis Borges without reference to his identity as an Argentine (on the gay dimensions of Lorca's works see Sahuquillo; Eisenberg, "García Lorca"). This is neither meant to say that individuals have a primary identity that must be always and consistently foregrounded in discussions of their work. Nor is it meant to claim that all of the identities associated with an individual, whether seen as randomly clustered or as a hierarchy, and whether relatively fixed or essentially mutable, must always be brought to the forefront in critical analyses.

It is true, however, that our culture does view certain identities as inalienably primary, particularly as regards nationality, native language, and gender, and that it would appear to be an act of willfulness to ignore such identity primes. And it is equally true, regrettably, that our culture views certain identities as manifestly trivial or, at best, considerably suspect, and this is nowhere more evident than in the area of what is called sexual preference, which—and herein lies the reason why such a category is basically a code word for potential discrimination—usually serves to alert the reader that what is about to be mentioned (if only to deny its relevance) is a deviation from what are understood to be the paradigms of compulsory heteronormativity. Even when "sexual preference" is not used to insinuate a discriminatory or condemnatory stance toward nonheteronormativity, it is nevertheless only used to indicate nonheteronormativity: one does not evoke the category of sexual preference and then go on to explain how the individual is committed to monogamous and reproductive heterosexuality. Much is said about our priorities of social identity when we speak of Manuel Puig as a gay or queer writer but do not, with the same weighting, speak of Carlos Fuentes as a straight writer.

Yet, one must speak of Puig in this way (see Puig's comments in his interview with Osorio on sexual identity). The reason for this is quite transparent: on the one hand, there is a clearly marked social importance attached to being queer rather than straight, whether that difference is received enthusiastically, bemusedly, or violently, and there is an unquestioned social commitment to the proposition that difference is unimportant, unworthy of being remarked, or profoundly heinous and therefore requiring aggressive silencing ("De eso no se habla"). Hence, Lorca could well have been killed for being gay and killed in such a way as to affirm the fact that his killers knew he was gay and were killing him for being gay (i.e., the assertion that the coup de grâce involved shooting him in the rectum), but until only relatively recently Lorca scholarship could continue to maintain that whether Lorca was gay or not had nothing to do with his poetry.[9] Which is something, I repeat, that would never be maintained with regard to the fact that Lorca was Spanish (or, more specifically, Andalusian) and that he wrote in Spanish. To begin to understand this matter, one must consider how the erotic identities of the poet/the poet's voice are no less materially present in a poetic production than is the language in which that production is written.

Certainly, there is now a significant body of cultural criticism that recognizes fully the fact that Lorca was gay and that his poetry is suffused with a "gay sensibility," however that sensibility is to be defined in terms of linguistic, rhetorical, stylistic, or thematic features. Moreover, Lorca, as something like a paradigm of the modern gay writer, has served as a point of reference for undertaking a thorough analysis of the presence of queer issues in Spanish writing, either in terms of overt homoerotic references or in terms of textual fissures (Derridian "spurs") that can serve as a point of departure for raising questions of gender identity and sexuality in Spanish literature. The unbreachable façade of the Francoist era, during which questions of erotic desire could not be considered and writers who may have attempted to broach them were systematically eliminated from serious critical consideration, is no longer true for the cultural coordinates of the Peninsula (although it may still be the case for Peninsular specialists outside Spain, as, for example, in the United States).

Silence is not precisely the question with Marcos Zurinaga's *Muerte en Granada* (1997; distributed in English as both *Death in Granada* and *The Disappearance of García Lorca,* filmed in English with Spanish subtitles). It is not categorically evident in the film that Lorca's death was a consequence of being gay—indeed, the film is studiedly unclear as to why Lorca was assassinated, although there are certainly a fair number of antigay epithets used with reference to him: after his disappearance, someone answers with reference to his whereabouts that "maybe he is with a boyfriend down in Brazil" (Lorca's remains have never been found). Zurinaga's script is based on the extensive research conducted by Ian Gibson, for whom it is clear that Lorca was killed by right-wing agents because of his public sexual identity, but Zurinaga's plot is ostensibly primarily interested in the question of the guilt of the father as discovered by the inquisitive son. Toward this end, Ricardo is a young writer whose Spanish family went into exile in Puerto Rico when he was about ten years old. In this way, Zurinaga continues his interest, established in *La gran fiesta* (1985; The Grand Ball), in concerning himself with the lives of Spanish immigrants in Puerto Rico, particularly those associated with large migrations that took place around the time of the Spanish Civil War (1936–1939) and the social and economic instability of the decades previous to it.

Although it appears throughout the film that Ricardo's mother made the decision to leave Spain because her husband had been brutalized by armed thugs (police? army? unspecified agents?), we learn, along with Ricardo, that his father returned home covered not in his blood, but in that of Lorca, whom he was the one to finish off at short range (the aforementioned coup de grâce is not alluded to either by words or images). It is never clear why Ricardo is so obsessed with the figure of Lorca and with discovering the exact reasons of his death. The film opens with Ricardo and his family seeing the inaugural production of *Yerma*

(1934). After the performance, Ricardo chats with Lorca and has him autograph a copy of the poet's famous *Romancero gitano* (1928; Gypsy Ballads), much to the disapproval of his father, who clearly wonders why his son is so taken with a man who is quite evidently publicly queer (it is this public queerness that in Jaime Manrique's estimation makes Lorca so important as an "eminent *maricón*"; for an analysis of Manrique's essay see Foster, "El gay como modelo cultural"). It is interesting to note that the *Romancero gitano* may be considered the beginning of a specifically homoerotically marked writing by Lorca. This collection of ballads, which are also characterized by the adherence to an Andalusian (i.e., "gypsy") identity, are also marked by an intense eroticism that, while not always specifically homoerotic, is so deeply sensual and so verbally explicit as to be queer to the extent that it deviates from the soberly functional sexuality that one would identify with Ricardo's parents and his bourgeois world.

Even a "heterosexual" narrative such as "La casada infiel" is queerly nonheteronormative in the sense that it legitimates the violation of the taboo of married monogamy, and it is all the more so if a poetic voice, one identified with a public *maricón* like Lorca, implicitly invites the suturing into the poem of gay readers in either of the two narrative positions, that of the narrator, a "man" who confesses his tryst with an unfaithful "woman." This is not the place to rehearse the implications of heterosexual narratives undertaken by publicly identified lesbian or gay writers, but the extent to which readers can see themselves identifying with characters in multiple and even apparently preposterous ways (is not the attempt to control the meaning of texts also inherently heteronormative?) is compounded when there is some sort of tension or clash between author and poetic voice. In this case, what may jar some readers is the utilization of a heterosexual voice (and one that is specifically endowed with masculine sexual privilege—i.e., is that of a conventional "macho") by a gay man. This sort of juxtaposition has been explored by critics with reference to Lorca's approximate contemporary and fellow playwright Tennessee Williams (see Savran's analysis of the queer dimensions of Williams). It is not so much a facile matter of insisting that the characters of "La casada infiel" are really stand-ins for gay protagonists (or to say that Blanche Dubois is really a gay man), but rather of thinking through what it means for heterosexual plots (which abound in Williams's plays as well as Lorca's, but less so in Lorca's narrative poetry) to be written by authors whose sociocultural coordinates are queer or specifically gay or lesbian: this is, after all, no different than the perception of feminist criticism that it is one thing for men to write about the institution of marriage and quite something else for a woman to do so.

The fact that the enforcement of heterosexual norms is at issue in a text like Zurinaga's film is made evident in the second major sequence of the film: Colonel Aguirre, the military authority in Granada, sees his son, Jorge, and his daughter, María Eugenia, enacting a scene from Lorca's play *Yerma* with Ricardo; it is the play that Ricardo saw with his parents and the occasion when he met Lorca and had him sign his copy of the *Romancero gitano* (concerning outraged reaction to *Yerma* see Gibson, *Federico García Lorca*, 2:333–338). Aguirre is enraged that his children would be participating in such deviant games; if theater is considered by many to be essentially sinful, the representation of the theater of a known *maricón*, even by presumably innocent children, is doubly queer. What this scene accomplishes is to portray the infiltration into the heteronormative confines of a proper and upstanding society of the allegedly deviant and perverse sensuality/sexuality of Lorca's art.

If Ricardo's businessman father reacts with silent grimaces of disapproval when he sees his son conversing so enthusiastically with Lorca, who responds to the boy's interest with perhaps too much friendliness, Colonel Aguirre is openly outraged to see his children and Ricardo acting so "queer." These two reactions put into effect a chain of actions such that Aguirre's son, Jorge, is killed by marauding thugs while he is in Ricardo's company (his young admirers have heard that Lorca has returned to Granada, and they set out to find him, despite the disturbances in the street), while elsewhere in town that night Aguirre is able to order Ricardo's father, Vicente Fernández, to pull the trigger of the gun that delivers the coup de grâce to Lorca. What the film images here is the self-attributed legitimacy of Aguirre and his coerced accomplice, Vicente Fernández, in enforcing the homophobic imperative to rid the world of queers in order to safeguard (and in this case to atone for an assault upon) the institutions of heteronormativity. In the fashion of the enforcement of homophobic imperatives, it is never necessary to make clear what the threat of the queer is in general or of a specific queer, nor is there any question, at least in the minds of the enforcers of heteronormativity, that the elimination of the queer and the queers is an imperious necessity for the protection of the society of said enforcers.

If the film is rather laconic in its presentation of who Lorca is and what he represents, this can be as much an appeal to the way in which it ought to be assumed the audience knows about the importance of Lorca

García Lorca's
queer body

and the mysteries surrounding the facts of his death as it is attributable to carelessness on the part of the filmmakers in never developing Lorca as more than a sketchy caricature of the flamboyant queer, who is, of course, going to be manifestly thrilled at the interest shown in his work by the handsome adolescent Ricardo. Yet, without excusing the defects of the film's rhetoric as regards the establishment of the Lorca character, it is possible to insist that for the dynamics of homophobia to click into action, there is little need for much beyond the bare minimum of markers of sexual identity—or sexual misidentity, as it would be viewed in this case: Andy García's sketchy enactment of Lorca's queerness, as much in the case of a representation that would react homophobically to it as in a representation that would be critical of a homophobic reaction, is adequate to the minimalist demands of homophobia, whereby one article of dress, one display of body language, one linguistic marker is sufficient enough to bring into play an entire and overdetermined cluster of signs that irrevocably and unmistakably imprint one as queer. As Zurinaga's film makes clear, it was, by the mid-1930s, well known that Lorca was queer (in which case one wonders what Vicente Fernández was thinking, taking his children to see a Lorca play in the first place), and it is very evident that he has come to the disapproving attention of agents of military and civil power.

Where the film's meaning is cloudy concerns to what degree Lorca's queerness is the issue in the narrative action of the film. Certainly, the main point of Zurinaga's film is the oedipal relationship between Ricardo and his father, a relationship that is marked by the violence with which Vicente reacts to the news that his son intends to return to Spain to discover the precise details of Lorca's death. As Ricardo subsequently finds out, his father's concern is legitimate, as Ricardo discovers that it was his own father who administered the coup de grâce to Lorca. This relationship is oedipal not in the classical formation of the father/son dyad, but in the sense that Ricardo discovers the sins of the fathers (his own, specifically, and those of his father's associates) and is essentially blinded forever by that discovery. At the close of the film, back again in Puerto Rico and now married to his childhood playmate María Eugenia and in the company of their own children at a family birthday gathering, Ricardo is unable to look at his father without profound and disturbing emotions, and Vicente is unable to be looked at by his son without similar feelings: the death of Lorca confirms the way in which the Spanish Civil War was a monstrous family feud whose cataclysmic events brought rifts that, decades later (the framing events of the film are dated 1962) and in even a faraway idyllic island refuge (Puerto Rico), cannot be healed.

But let us return to the question of what is the importance of Lorca's queerness to the film. Although some viewers might have been outraged at such a decision, Zurinaga could have chosen to make no reference to Lorca's queerness, but then again, he need not even have had to use the figure of Lorca in the first place to make his point about the fratricidal nature of the Spanish Civil War. The same sort of plot could have been developed around some completely fictitious character. Yet having chosen Lorca, Zurinaga chooses to incorporate into his representation his queerness, not only as a reasonable component of Lorca's identity, but quite specifically to put into motion the events that lead to Lorca's death (because he is, from the point of view of those who will succeed in creating Francoist Spain, a deviant social element who threatens the integrity of the family and, by extension, Spanish society) and to the son's discovery of the father's complicity (albeit imposed) in an act of political assassination that almost universally has come to be viewed from the perspective of anti-Francoism as an overwhelming sign of the tenor of the Spanish Civil War and the society that was instituted by its victors.

In this sense, Lorca's queerness is integral to the film, although it is never articulated clearly: Lorca's queerness is a synecdoche of the threat to a particular version of established social order, the one that triumphs under Francisco Franco's leadership. Moreover, Ricardo's dissident attitude—his desire to know the historical truth of Lorca's assassination and his repudiation of the direct and indirect agents of that event—is confirmed by his seduction of the daughter of the man who is the paradigm of that established social order, his childhood playmate and the daughter of (the now retired) Colonel Aguirre. As adolescents in Granada, María Eugenia shows Ricardo her father's trophy room, packed with Nazi and Nazi-type symbols, mementos, and memorabilia, which only serves to affirm the fascist nature of Francoism and its protagonists. Subsequently, when she is put under house arrest by her father to keep her from seeing Ricardo (whom Aguirre has had brutalized by his thugs), María trashes his inner sanctum. This is all pretty obvious stuff and acted out in pretty obvious ways, but it makes clear the lines of ideological identity.

Ricardo's marriage to María Eugenia and the night of sex he has with her in his hotel confirm, one assumes, his own heterosexuality. Yet the film would make no sense at all if Lorca did not cast an enormous and seductive aura over Ricardo's life. One would like to believe that heteronormativity's insistence that there is an unbreachable disjunction between heterosexual and homosexual—one is either categorically one or the other—is no longer a majority subscription by, one would hope, an audience sympathetic to Lorca's work. It is never made clear what Ricardo finds seductive about Lorca's work, what motivates him as a young preteen to be so enthusiastic about the *Romancero gitano* and to seek Lorca out at the opening performance of *Yerma*, or what motivates him as a young adult to wish to pursue the mystery of his death. Of course, Lorca had many admirers who did not self-identify as gay or who held no investment (consciously, at least) in queer culture, and the queer dimensions of Lorca's poetry can only account tenuously for his enormous popularity. This is so even if it is true that Lorca was appealing, if only subliminally, to the quintessential elements of "Queer Iberia," those elements that are less part of a modern gay subculture and more a part of a broad canvas of exceptions to heteronormativity: one layer of that canvas is often allegedly the Andalusian culture of deep Arabic inspiration that is, precisely, the backdrop of the wildly popular *Romancero gitano* (on the concept of Queer Iberia see Blackmore and Hutcheson).

Thus, what is elided from the film is what it is that motivates Ricardo in his enthusiasm for Lorca, an enthusiasm—virtually an obsession—that extends from his preteen years to adulthood. It is an enthusiasm that leads him and his friends to incorporate Lorca into their games, much to Colonel Aguirre's anger: his homophobia may be criminal, but there can be no denying the accuracy of his assessment as to how Lorca's cultural production is underlain by a very aggressive, blatant, and unrelenting celebration of the queer. Certainly, Ricardo's fascination with Lorca is mediated by a host of factors, in addition to whatever might be the queer resonances it inspires in him, much to the distaste of his father and the anger of Colonel Aguirre. As is often asserted, good poetry is good poetry, and there is no reason to have to justify why it inspires the enthusiasm of sensitive readers. Such a position, nevertheless, must be countered by ways in which not everyone is equally enchanted by Lorca, by the way in which for some the *Romancero gitano* is competent kitsch or, at least, not the best of Lorca's poetry (Lorca himself is said to have had reservations over its popular success).[10] Concomitantly, Ricardo undoubtedly has motives that are not specifically aesthetic: the need personally to understand the Spanish Civil War and the reasons for his family's departure from Spain for Puerto Rico, as well as the positioning of his own political convictions with regard to what his Spanish past means for him. These considerations become even more complicated when he discovers the facts of Lorca's death (of course, as the movie presents them, for they have not been validated historically), providing for an apparently never-to-be-resolved conflict with his father.

It is important to note that the political meaning of Lorca has, in many ways, continued to trump the poetic significance of his work, and much of the bibliography about Lorca outside of Spain (and now inside of Spain) has to do with his status as an icon of what the Spanish Republicans and their international supporters saw as the tremendous tragedy of the triumph of Franco and the draconian fascism he imposed on Spain for four decades. Such an iconic status had little to do with the quality of his poetry—or, it encouraged a valuation of his poetry for political rather than artistic reasons. It is also important to note that this iconic status suppressed all reference to Lorca's queerness, in keeping with the Left's own versions of homophobia in the 1930s and until well into the 1980s. This is obvious in the film in that, aside from the fragment of *Yerma,* his texts are absent from the film: neither he nor anyone else recites his poetry, and the uninitiated viewer has no idea of exactly why there was so much fuss over this man's writing.

In any event, one could say that Ricardo's enthusiasm for Lorca is partly artistic and partly personal and political. Nevertheless, whatever Ricardo's enthusiasms for Lorca are in terms of his self-awareness, the movie does not do a very good job of pinning them down, nor does it specify what other characters in the universe of the film understand to perhaps be his interests: at one point, Ricardo follows a man into the restroom to inquire about his knowledge of Lorca; the man looks him up and down as he stands at the urinal and asks, "Are you queer?" Thus, one must inevitably return to what meanings are attached to Lorca by the individuals responsible for his death, which are framed unmistakably in terms of Lorca's social threat as queer. In this regard, one is reminded of

Bill Condon's *Gods and Monsters* (1998): while Clayton Boone never has sex with James Whale, the man who directed the original Frankenstein films in the 1930s, the closing scene of the film makes it marvelously clear that, although now married and the father of a young son, Boone has assimilated a dimension of queer identity with Whale as he pantomimes in secret the director's most famous creation; Frankenstein's monster has become, of course, a legendary gay icon.

Perhaps where Zurinaga's film is ultimately a failure as a coherent filmic text is skipping any opportunity to relate Lorca's queer persona with Ricardo's enthusiasm for his poetry, something that would not make Ricardo the gay man whom the man in the restroom immediately supposes he must be. Rather, it would be the chance to explore the way in which Lorca's primary cultural meaning involves his many critical deconstructions of bourgeois Spain in the institution of marriage, in the oppression of erotic experience, in the conversion of the gypsy/Andalusian/*maricón* into a constellation of despised Others that served to hold in place a concept of a respectable Spanish society that found its most nightmarish expression under the Franco regime and the fascist values it represented. If this is the "profound Spain" that Ricardo wishes to understand (evoking Lorca's own concepts of the *cante jondo*), it cannot be done without addressing the queerness that was essential to Lorca's persona and that was the cause of his death, both historically, as far as we know, and fictionally, as concerns how the film portrays it (Aldrich, 241, notes that Lorca is one Mediterranean writer whom he does not treat, for reason of "linguistic limitations").

A final note: Zurinaga's film was originally released under the title of *Death in Granada*, but that title was subsequently changed to *The Disappearance of García Lorca*, which is how it is distributed in video and DVD. The change from the place of Lorca's death to a specific reference to Lorca is understandable, as it capitalizes on the renewed interest in Spain and internationally in Lorca on the occasion in 1998 of the centenary of his birth. The change from "death" to the more euphemistic "disappearance" is a bit mystifying, since Lorca's disappearance was never an issue: he was arrested and he was summarily executed; few have ever doubted, from 1939 to the present day, at whose hands he died. However, the use of "disappearance" evokes the image of the activities of right-wing death squads that operated in Argentina and elsewhere in Latin America in the 1960s and 1970s, activities that made "to disappear" a transitive verb meaning "to execute summarily" first in Spanish and now, because of international coverage, in English and other languages. To disappear social dissidents means to arrest, interrogate, torture, imprison, and kill opponents of (neo)fascist tyranny, as well as anyone who can be considered a supporter, directly or by implication, of those opponents in expanding waves of persecution. And in the context of the death squad legitimation of such almost universally mortal disappearances, a constituent facet is the specific targeting of gays/queers (along with women and Jews—and gypsies—in the social semiosis of the hated Other).

Thus, I would propose that by changing the title of the film from "death" to "disappearance," the distributors of the film wished to suggest how, almost forty years after Lorca's assassination (a term which, as Ian Gibson uses it, makes explicit a political interpretation of Lorca' death), the link between the right-wing murder of dissidents and the perceived social threat of queers is underscored. It is regrettable that, although his film is based on Gibson's many documents regarding Lorca's death, Zurinaga was unable to explore more eloquently this link and to relate it more concretely to what might have been the fascination Lorca held for Ricardo Fernández. By failing to do so, Zurinaga feeds just as much into the homophobia of Lorca criticism—both the studies penned by the old Left, which simply ignored Lorca as a gay man, and those signed by a liberal academic tradition for which sexual preference is not a relevant interpretive category—as he would have done if he had ignored altogether this dimension of the poet's biography.[11]

LA VIRGEN DE LOS SICARIOS

One of the clichés of the sexual revolution of the 1960s was "Eros or Death," by which was meant that to live without Eros—understood to include various combinations of love and sexuality, that is, a fully erotic life—if it was not conducive to literal death (i.e., an early death, as it became part of popular culture to consider the fate of those who were unpaired or, if paired, deprived of satisfactorily erotic life) meant at least an emotional starvation that was as good as death. This formula, which is customarily attributed to Herbert Marcuse because of his 1955 *Eros and Civilization: A Philosophical Inquiry into Freud,* echoes Freud's 1930 essay *Civilization and Its Discontents.* Both essays see in the promotion of civilization—i.e., the modernist project of civilization—a concomitant, virtually proportional, de-eroticization of human life. For Freud it meant recognizing that civilization was necessarily going to produce malcontents, who in turn would then not have any reason to support the project of civilization, resulting in suffering for them and a problem for society. For Marcuse, it meant being able to turn away from the stifling effects of civilization, to overcome the death threat inherent in civilization, and to reinvest in an erotic life that could allow one to live a fully human life, overcoming the deadly consequences of dehumanizing civilization.

Utopian concepts (in the radical sense of the word) like "Make love, not war" and "The Age of Aquarius" were part of an ideological chain that began with a repudiation of modern society and strove to reconfigure human intercourse in a way that was directly sexual: later, the formulation "Silence = Death" would be added, in the sense that the willful homophobic silence about sexual desire is the occasion for death, whether in the violent persecution of queers or, in what amounts to the same thing, in the silence about sexual acts and their risks that leads to the massive deaths of queer people. One derivation of this chain is the early gay movement in the United States and its international variants that saw in the unbridled promiscuity of abundant sexual experiences as much a full eroticization of the body as a repudiation of the antagonism to sexuality in general and to homoerotic sexuality integral specifically to patriarchal modernism. In short, the more one affirmed the erotic, the more one was fully human and therefore able to transcend the oppression of modern civilization — in a sense, to live free, if only sporadically, from what was viewed as the essential death grip of the latter. The bourgeois counsel in Latin America has always been (and, to be sure, only in the context of officially sanctioned heterosexual marriage) "Sexo, pero no mucho" (Sex, but not much of it), and the fully erotic life that is integral to gay culture is meant to be a contradiction of this principle of decency.[12]

One knows full well what happened to these romantic ideas under the pall of the nightmare of history. However, the simple fact is that while unbridled promiscuity can no longer be a universally accepted principle of gay male sexuality, there does remain a reservoir of avowal in gay male culture that there must be a freedom to pursue unconventional (i.e., nonheteronormative) sexualities, and that pursuit does in some measure dignify the sexual subject who is affirming the right to satisfy his own specific erotic needs.

Barbet Schroeder's *La Virgen de los Sicarios* (2000) works to a large extent with the postmodern versions of such views of liberating sexuality within the specific context of a late-capitalist and securely colonialized Latin American society. One can question the degree to which

Schroeder's film ought even to be classified as Latin American because of the director's Iranian origins and his basically European and U.S.-based film career. Yet the film is made in Spanish; it was filmed exclusively in Colombia with Colombian actors; it is based on the 1994 novel by Fernando Vallejo, who wrote the film script; and it focuses on the city of Medellín, one of Colombia's major drug centers and the setting for Vallejo's fiction in general. Moreover, Vallejo is the main character of the film (played by Germán Jaramillo), and the basic structure of the narrative is Vallejo's trenchantly nonstop caustic, ironic, and despairing commentary on his native Medellín. If in his earlier novels Vallejo commented on the hypocrisy of the founding myths of Medellín and its ruling bourgeoisie, in *Virgen* his focus is on the precipitous decline in the survivability of life in Medellín, where going out on the sidewalk is literally a life-threatening risk, as bullets fly right and left in the cross fire of the drug wars and their numerous ancillary derivations in the form of gang and personal rivalries with accounts to be settled.

The spectator quickly loses count of how many people are being killed in the course of this relatively short film (less than one hundred minutes), and one is tempted to wonder what it must have been like to enact death on the streets of a city for whose inhabitants the presence of the film crew must have looked like a high-tech presence of more of the daily same. Vallejo as protagonist witnesses killings in all degrees of proximity, killings by others, and killings by his two sequential lovers, both of whom have the disconcerting habit—a rather perverse expression of affection toward Vallejo—of quickly and lethally acting on any of his figurative allusions to getting rid of someone or even his passing expressions of displeasure with a person who is annoying him. Deadly violence is a continuum, not in the degree of its deadliness (everyone shoots to kill and usually no one misses), but in the motivations behind it: people are killed for revenge; people are killed for being annoying; people are killed as tokens of someone or something else; people are killed just in case; and no distinction is made between fact and fiction—it is essentially the same act to blow away a noisy neighbor as it is to assassinate a blowhard president by pumping a round into a television set.[13]

Vallejo's novels have consistently played with being inside and outside Medellín society, and his searing commentaries are as much directed against a society he is experiencing immediately—for example, strolling the streets and interacting with people—as it is a society he reflects upon in the detachment occasioned by his being away from Colombia. In the *Virgen* script, Vallejo has, he asserts, returned to Medellín to die. He has done all he needs to do in his life (written a couple of novels), and upon inheriting an apartment from a sister who was married to a mafia boss, he returns to his origins. This apartment, which he decorates with only a double bed and a glass-top table with four chairs, has large wraparound picture windows and a large balcony, an ideal watchtower with a sweeping view of a city spectacularly set in the Cauca River valley in the Central Range of the northern reaches of the Andes. As a wealthy colonial city and today as Colombia's second-largest city, Medellín has lovely architectural monuments, especially religious ones, which accounts in part for the title of the novel and the film.

Yet for Vallejo, the return to Medellín is the entry into an infernal underworld: no longer just the metaphorical hell of patriarchal hypocrisy that Vallejo evokes in his novels, Medellín is now literally hellish as a consequence of the society spawned by the so-called Medellín cartel. It is not just the drug trade, with all of the conventional hysteria surrounding the production, distribution, and consumption of drugs, but rather the late-capitalist dependency that trade has engendered in the form of a complex network of gangs and hit-men (the *sicarios;* cf. English *sicarius,* plural *sicarii*). The *sicarios* exercise a form of terrorism in the sense that they attack directly the citizenry, which already is victimized extensively by being caught in the cross fire of public shoot-outs and by being obliged to witness those shoot-outs. Among several insistent sounds of the film are the screams of bystanders as the bodies fall or, when the shooting is directed against the ubiquitous motorcycles of the young gang members, fly through the air. Dependency is present in the form of the consumerism spawned by drug money flowing through the economic system, which can neither account for nor control it; it is a consumerism that more likely than not prefers an American or American-like popular culture in stark contrast to the seigniorial culture of the monuments of the colonial period and the old native bourgeoisie: whether this is a social, political, cultural, and/or economic problem depends on one's ideology in these matters, but it certainly is a problem for Vallejo.

A recurring motif in the film is the music (mostly Colombian, admittedly) blaring out of stereo speakers in taxi cabs, which Vallejo interprets as a sign of the noise pollution that greets him at every turn. At one point, at his wits' end because of the maximum-volume music, he picks up the expensive sound system he has recently bought for one of his lovers and hurls it over the edge of his balcony; he then wryly asks if anyone below was killed by the equipment. Vallejo has no particular commitment to any social or cultural agenda, although like Gutiérrez Alea's camera in

Amulets of devotees
of the Virgin
of the Assassins

Fresa y chocolate that clearly captures the Cuban director's love affair with the city of Havana, Schroeder follows Vallejo's gaze as he comments on the city of Medellín, primarily to the first of his two lovers in the film, on the beauty of the city that has been marred by so much noise and bloodshed.

The Medellín to which Vallejo returns, then, is a Valley of Death, a fitting place for someone to go to die, although ironically Vallejo manages to keep out of the line of gunfire, not so much because he is lucky but because they, with their *balas rezadas* (bullets blessed in a ritual to honor the Virgen de los Sicarios), are so insistently accurate with their fire. This Medellín is most assuredly the image of civilization as death, not in the metaphoric way of Freud and Marcuse and the utopian formulations of the sexual revolution, but literally: the implicit point of the film that globalization—in this case centered on the drug trade so crucial to a Colombian economy that is merely fulfilling a bottomless pit of international demand for its major cash crop—brings with it not integration into a joyfully expanding capitalist fantasy but a dreadful social violence that rivals the worst images of lawlessness in human history. These are not the racist images by American popular culture of a dark Latin American continent (of which John Sayles's 1997 film *Men with Guns* is only a recent example) but rather, despite the non-Colombian director, an interpretation of Colombian reality driven very compellingly by the work of the Colombian writer Fernando Vallejo, to whose point of view Schroeder is remarkably faithful (regarding Vallejo's gay writing in general see DuPouy; Foster, *Gay and Lesbian Themes*, 124–128).

Schroeder's film opens with Vallejo's arrival at the "fancy" apartment of a professional-class gay man. The apartment is decorated with all of the tutti-frutti stereotypically associated with the middle-aged effeminate queer: a generalized Oscar Wilde–type decor, heavy brocades, massive homoerotic statues and paintings, intimate conversational nooks, but most of all, guests who are mostly middle-aged men of means and a bevy of young, handsome, virile street types. This world evokes the standard-issue Latin American (originally, Mediterranean) image of homoerotic life: older, often effeminate men of means who are willing and able to pay young men to engage in sexual acts as they demand (see Román on the non-Latino representation of gay Latino men; on the Mediterranean imaginary see Aldrich). Typically, these sexual acts involve penetration—in one of multiple ways—of the older men by the younger ones with the clear understanding that the latter will be paid for their services and that the sexual theatrics will in no way compromise their conditions as young machos—i.e., as completely masculine and thoroughly observant of the codes of heterosexist masculinity. In a sexual universe in which one's partners are feminized to the point of being understood to be surrogate women (which is the essential meaning of the morphosyntactic blend *maricón:* a male version of María, the all-purpose Hispanic female name), sexual relations with them are the same as though with women, and as is the case of a man's sexual prowess with a woman, it can only serve to assert, display, confirm his quintessential masculinity.

Undoubtedly in reality, things work out differently. The party that Vallejo attends may well be populated by older men who assume the penetrative role with young men and/or with older men, by young men who are penetrated by older men who would have a street value as *maricones,* and even by young men whose outward display of hypervirility is irreproachable—even though they may assume different same-sex roles with each other in private or as viewed as spectacle by other men, young or old, self-displayed as queer or straight. Schroeder's film does not even begin to hint at any variation from the conventional *Cage aux folles* scenario,[14] but the very fact that Vallejo is hardly a nellie, especially alongside his host, can begin to open the matter up to a more enriched consideration of gay life in Colombia and Latin America as figured by this film.

Vallejo's host welcomes him to the party and informs him that he has a present for him. He introduces Vallejo to Alexis, who looks to be not even twenty years old, notably beautiful beyond his Colombian version of a hip-hop exterior, and immediately attentive and compliant. Vallejo is introduced as a fellow *maricón* by his host, but he rejects this denomination, saying that his host is more the *maricón* but that perhaps Vallejo himself is, too, if sleeping with more than a thousand men counts. Of course, this is pretty common opening-gambit chitchat, but it functions to exercise a measure of seduction over Alexis that confirms the way in which Vallejo is somehow different in bearing than his host; the host is, despite the transparent prosperity of his apartment, a paradigmatic Latin American *maricón,* while there is somehow something different about Vallejo: he is a writer; he has lived abroad; he has, as he promptly says, come back to Medellín to die; he speaks in a language that exchanges stereotypic gay banter and bitchiness for a profoundly interesting analysis of his society. It is an analysis that skips from Medellín's history to the depredations of its late-capitalist economy, from the appreciation of profound cultural values (as seen in the churches he visits to escape from the overwhelming and omnipresent electronic noise of the city) to horrified commentaries on the unreflective violence that is manifest in virtually every block of his pilgrimage through the city of his youth.

Vallejo becomes a Virgil to his young lovers, who, although they may not be consciously thirsty for the knowledge and interpretation of social reality he offers them, are in some way enthralled by the way in which he has something different to say, something they have not heard already, something that contributes toward the development of the sort of self-awareness or self-consciousness that no one ever considered them capable of appreciating. In the end, it doesn't make much difference in the outcome of their lives: both of his young lovers in the film die shot down in the street. But the visual materiality of the film records the mixture of fascination and bewilderment of their reaction to what this man has to say.

For this reason, the film must image something other than a conventional gay relationship between older man and younger charge, between the modern-day version of the Greek duo of *erastes,* lover, and *eromenos,* beloved (see García Suárez on gay male prostitution in Colombia). After chatting with his "present," Vallejo is offered the use of the Sala de las Mariposas (the Butterfly Room). His new friend, Alexis, remarks that the room gives no evidence of butterflies (it is just more Oscar Wildean decorative excess), but his words are unconsciously ironic, since *mariposa* is one of the euphemisms in Spanish for "gay," and it is apparent that this room is specifically designed for sexual encounters between men. Yet several things happen in this sequence that displace conventional signs — or, better, reinforce some signs while questioning others. As one might expect, Vallejo, as the older man, is the one who is in charge, and he orders Alexis to strip. Alexis does, but in such a way that his gun falls to the floor. After a brief exchange as to why he is carrying a gun — Vallejo will soon learn that apparently every young man in Medellín now

packs a weapon—Alexis proceeds to cross the room with the gun covering his genitals; as he places it on the nightstand, the eye of the camera
briefly remarks on his evident endowments, although as he stretches out
on the bed, the position of his raised leg toward the camera denies any
further revelation or confirmation.

The film is, by comparison with other Latin American films and certainly by comparison with European films—even U.S. films—remarkably discreet. We do not see Vallejo himself preparing for the sexual act,
nor do we see anything even remotely resembling a sexual act, except for
the essential fact of two men, one of them now naked, being in a bedroom
together. The nightstand lamp gets turned off and the camera cuts forward before anything beyond these highly selective narrative markers
can be introduced. As is often the case with filmic discretion, it is assumed that the viewer can follow the dots, no matter how many of them
stretch from one end of the real-time event to the other. When the camera
resumes its business, both men have dressed again and Vallejo is offering Alexis money, which Alexis unhesitatingly accepts: Alexis has only
been a "present" in terms of introductions, and all three men—the host,
Vallejo, and Alexis—understand fully that Alexis will end up receiving
some monetary gratification from Vallejo, the exact amount of which is,
because of the power differential, left to Vallejo's discretion. Alexis needs
Vallejo more than Vallejo needs Alexis, since there is an unending supply
of needy young men in any society, which is only the masculine version
of the formula of female prostitution since time immemorial.

The important detail of this commercial exchange is not the amount
nor that Vallejo controls the amount nor that Alexis readily accepts what
he is offered: if it is not enough, there will always be some other older man
more willing to pay for his obvious beauty and endowments. Rather,
what is important is that Vallejo, as he hands Alexis the money, says that
it is for him, Alexis, to treat his girlfriend. Alexis diffidently says there is
no girlfriend, which opens the way for Vallejo to understand that Alexis
is perhaps not a casual pickup but rather the example of the emotionally
needy younger male who is genuinely interested in what the older man
has to offer beyond transitory sex. Thus, Vallejo's gesture of transaction
confirms the formula of the passive male paying the active male for sex.
If the willing Alexis were in practice the passive male, the narrative conventions would be unmistakably different: Alexis would either be the
transvestite prostitute paid for her services as any female prostitute, no
matter what penetrative role might take place between prostitute and
client, or he would be the passive male grateful for the attentions of the

macho; active and passive are used here with all of the problematics of sexual encounters that redefine themselves with each new set of human participants.

Yet Alexis eschews the opportunity to affirm his conventional masculinity, which depends on the presence, if even ghostly, of a woman. Sexual attention to a woman confirms the masculinity of the subject; sex with one woman trumps any and all quantity of active (and perhaps even, scandalously, passive) sex, with or without payment, with another man. In a sexual system in which heterosexuality can never be definitively proven, the illusion that "successful" sex with a woman — which may range from display of sexuality (i.e., public seduction) to procreation (the child as the proof token of performative masculinity) — is of unimpeachable, paramount importance. Alexis, by denying that there is any *novia* on the scene, confirms from a heterosexist perspective his own incomplete masculinity and, in a retrospective interpretive gesture, allows the reader to wonder if his first-to-the-bed supineness might mean in fact that he is penetrated — or at least willing to be penetrated — by Vallejo, even when the camera's eye goes blind as to what does transpire in the Sala de las Mariposas.

There are only two other scenes of explicit homoerotic sexuality, one in which Alexis and Vallejo kiss in a moment of tender rapture after Alexis has killed two men on a motorcycle out of revenge. Vallejo and Alexis mock a hysterical witness, a pregnant woman, and then kiss after Vallejo says that Alexis is the most beautiful thing life has ever given him. The other scene is the opening move in the sexual transaction between Vallejo and Wilmar, the young man who replaces Alexis after he is murdered in the street. Vallejo subsequently learns that it is Wilmar who shot Alexis, as revenge for Alexis murdering Wilmar's brother. In the end, it hardly seems to matter to Vallejo, as he learns to grasp the calculus of death that affects all of the beautiful young men of Medellín, images of himself as a young man, images of the young men of another generation that he loved (the "thousand" to which he makes reference in his first meeting with Alexis), without death being the necessary coda to that relationship.

One of the very traumatic points of Schroeder's film is that AIDS is not the concern of these young men and their lovers. Condoms and forms of safe sex, such as are of concern or, eloquently, of no concern in other Latin American societies (where campaigns to the effect that *SIDA* [the Spanish acronym for AIDS] ≠ *VIDA* — AIDS is the opposite of life — are part of public discourse in a way that has been impossible to

Vallejo contemplates
Alexis's gun, as barrier
to sexual desire

achieve in the United States), are nonexistent in Schroeder's film, since these young men are killed off by bullets before any virus can blemish them. It is at this point that the matter of Eros and Death comes into play. Significantly, and despite the very meagerly synecdochal display of homoerotic sex in three brief moments of the film, *Virgen* figures the disappearance of sexual attraction. To be sure, it is there in a latent way, as the flux of desire and dependence that allows Vallejo to keep two young men — one of them stunning, as ephebic beauty goes — within his orbit. But as sexually alluring as both young men are and as seductively intriguing as Vallejo is to each of them, the film shows scene after scene in the half-light of the bare bedroom in which Vallejo and his young lover lie rigidly side by side in bed, naked to the waist and covered below with a blanket. It is as though, like Tristan and Isolde, they were separated by the patriarchal sword of Mark, Isolde's legitimate husband. What to make of this frigid display of corporeal proximity?

I would suggest that one of the points Schroeder is getting at is the death of desire in the hideous context of violent social reality inhabited by Vallejo, first with Alexis and then with Wilmar. This is a long way from the Marcusian formulation of the conflict between Eros and Civilization, in the sense that the most touted descriptor of the social disintegration Colombia is experiencing is that of the breakdown of civilization. The tenor of Vallejo's remarks centers insistently on the current uncivilized nature of the once-seigniorial Medellín: bourgeois hypocrisy has now become one of Vallejo's minor concerns as he paces the streets of the city or peers from the watchtower of his apartment (Fernández L'Hoeste, in his discussion of the novel, speaks of the narrator as a Dantean guide through the inferno that is Medellín). Of course, another way of looking at the matter is that Medellín is the consequence of the inevitable logic of late capitalism, whereby its necessary insertion into a globalized economy through the capitalization and exploitation of the export crop it has to offer, drugs, has produced a grotesque parody of economic success that can only be sustained through high-tech violence: Alexis's greatest fantasy is to own an Uzi submachine gun.

At the end of the film, Vallejo has convinced Wilmar to leave Medellín with him, but Wilmar will not go until he has bought his mother a fancy refrigerator, one that includes an in-the-door ice cube maker. Vallejo, after paying for the purchase, sees Wilmar off in the delivery truck, and they agree to meet back at Vallejo's apartment to undertake their departure. Wilmar never makes it to his mother's house — he is gunned down in yet another revenge killing. Vallejo, concerned that Wilmar has not returned, receives a phone call that he can find him in the morgue, already sewn up from the autopsy on his body. The stainless steel morgue slab is only another high-tech component in the machinery of death that controls Medellín and, by extension, Colombia, and the camera makes certain that the spectator senses the vastness of this facility in fitting proportion to the number of bodies it must service on a daily basis.

The infernal quality of this death machine is confirmed by Vallejo's surreal fantasy that he is wandering in the vast catacombs of the city's cathedral. But the cathedral is decorated with an archway containing the words *Domus Dei Porta Coeli* (house of the Lord and doorway to heaven). As grotesque as the medieval Catholic symbology of death may be, it is underlain by a theology of human salvation and the promise of a paradisial transcendence of the soul. The reality of the society figured in this film has no similar theology, no theology whatsoever, to offer the bodies that pass through the gates of the ultramodern morgue.

The banalization of death and its destruction of the human will to live is best seen in Vallejo's reaction to learning that Wilmar is in fact the man who killed Alexis (there is something about Alexis being responsible for the death of Wilmar's brother, so it is a classic example of a revenge killing). Vallejo is at first tempted to kill Wilmar himself, the first time he really seems to give in to the temptation of violence except in one earlier scene in which he comes close to killing himself with Alexis's gun. But he resigns himself to the inevitability that everyone is connected to the killing of everyone else, and just as he inevitably accepts the killing of others by both his lovers, he also accepts that one has killed the other. Yet the point of the film is that all of this violence displaces Eros, and violence, rather than acting as an aphrodisiac (as it is claimed to be by some forms of heavy-sex theatrics in which pain and pleasure are two sides of the same coin), appears progressively to extinguish the opportunities for the erotic indulgences that, in accordance with the philosophy of the sexual revolution, are meant to restore a fuller existence to the human body.

Thus, the virtual disappearance of sex of any sort in *La Virgen de los Sicarios* is neither a direct consequence of the prudishness in such matters of Colombian filmmaking (after all, Schroeder is not likely striving first and foremost for the acceptance of his film in Colombia) nor even the consequence of some vow of chastity on the part of the *sicarios* in obeisance to an injunction by their Virgin to renounce the flesh, which one could well expect in the severest forms of traditional Catholicism, forms that authors from the religiously conservative Colombia like Gabriel García Márquez routinely parody. No, there is neither the observance of a religiously inspired sexual abstinence nor the compliance with rules of censorship. After all, same-sex acts are not illegal in Colombia, and even if there might be restrictions on their direct representation in film (restrictions which Schroeder is under no obligation to respect), sexual activity can always be suggested and represented obliquely, just as it is in the sequence in which the light goes out and the camera fades at the moment of Vallejo and Alexis's first encounter.

To the contrary, the subsequent narrative of *Virgen* makes it clear that sex is not taking place, or very little of it, despite the amount of sincere affection expressed. Wilmar undresses—but not completely—to receive Vallejo's kiss, standing, the first time they are together in Vallejo's bedroom, although we see no gesture on Vallejo's part to undress beyond removing his shirt, and again the camera fades before whatever sexual act is in store between them takes place; the camera only returns elliptically to show a blurred image of them showering together. Indeed, aside from lying side by side in bed without touching, the major intercourse that appears to take place between Vallejo and his male lover—whether Alexis or Wilmar—is Vallejo's running commentary as they traverse the streets of the city together. True, Vallejo addresses his lover as *niño* (child), a term of endearment that as much serves to underscore the generational difference between them as the nature of their sexual relationship (i.e., domineering and experienced older man, subservient and attentive younger man), and true, friends of Alexis and Wilmar they meet on the street make comments that show they understand the nature of the bond between each of the younger men of his older partner. But that is about as far as the display of homoerotic attraction is carried.

Now, one of the issues of a general sexual liberation and specifically of the conquest of gay rights is the display imperative, if not in public to a third-party audience, at least in private to each other, with the camera a witness to an audience through its omniscient invasiveness. This display imperative means engaging in an abundant range of gestures, acts, rituals, and practices that confirm not only the erotic liaison between individuals but the centrality those liaisons have in their lives. If a common Spanish saying is "sexo, pero no mucho," erotic display affirms excess, overdetermination, and experimentation. It is as necessary to affirm the erotic bond with one another as it is to display it publicly or semipublicly, and this display also serves as a form of mutual affirmation among those who say, "I am committed erotically to you, and I have no shame in so affirming before others."

There is precious little of this display in the film. Also Alexis's and Wilmar's friends know of the relationship between them and Vallejo and comment on it openly among themselves. Yet Vallejo and his lovers do nothing explicitly to provoke this commentary. To a certain extent, Vallejo's manner of speaking to these young men with the vocative *niño* undoubtedly alerts other men to their relationship, such as the drivers of the several cabs they take. But when Vallejo gets into altercations with taxi drivers over their habit of blasting music on speakers located right behind the heads of the passengers, the variations of *puto* and *maricón* that these cab drivers use is less an attempt to accurately describe a perceived relationship than it is simply to trot out the worst insults that can be hurled at one man by another in any aggressively heterosexist society like Colombia.

While there may be some reading of signs of homosexuality—as conventionally defined by the homophobia of aggressively heterosexist societies—the general dynamic is that one can define as a sexual Other (i.e., a queer) anyone who does not gibe with one's own signs of masculine identity—which in this case is an obvious preference for blaring popular music, just as it might be any of a myriad of other signs of heterosexist conformity. Moreover, once one has defined another as a sexual Other, one has the right to announce that definition loudly and emphatically—that is, publicly. This is something that one is willing to do on the assumption that the Other, by virtue of manifesting a deficient masculinity, will not be in a position to defend himself against by either refuting the definition attributed to him or by exacting retribution from the accuser for his declaration, be it right or wrong. Vallejo is horrified when Alexis and Wilmar are able to exact retribution by simply shooting the offending cab drivers or other accusers, but it is undoubtedly a reaction that is compounded by the realization that, on the basis of his experiences with violent homophobia, experiences likely shared with a great degree of unanimity with the fellow frequenters of the gay salon of the friend who originally introduces him to Alexis, *sicarios* who are queer no more tolerate homophobic epithets than would the machos who brandish them.

The only moment of unalloyed erotic display in *Virgen* occurs within the privacy of Vallejo's apartment. Alexis is drinking alcohol straight out of a bottle, and at one point he takes a long draught from the bottle, goes over to where Vallejo is seated, bends Vallejo's head back and slowly cascades the liquid from his mouth into Vallejo's. As a transference of a secondary bodily fluid (i.e., by being in his mouth, the alcohol has become, if only slightly, one of Alexis's own fluids), this act is a ritualized displacement of the transference of primary bodily fluids (blood, semen, urine) that is typically going to take place in the sex act.

Homoerotic sex acts, of course, are not substantially different from heterosexual ones, although their semiotics may be significantly different, beginning with the radically different gender baggage brought to a sexual encounter between a man and a woman as opposed to that which is brought to an encounter between two men or two women. As such, the display of homoerotic sexuality is significantly different than the display of heterosexual sexuality, even leaving aside the commonplace assumption that same-sex partners are likely to have more extensive and more intensive sexual experiences (the calculus of these matters is increased as the number of partners in any one act increases). Yet none of these is really pertinent to the relations between Vallejo and his two lovers.

Their communion is notably unerotic (at least in the film, though the novel would have us understand otherwise); their sexuality, in public and in private (at least as far as the film shows it) is notably uninteresting and infrequent; and they engage in little of the display that is supposed to be part of the territory of transgressive sexuality. Indeed, one of the points of homoeroticism for many is to use it to figure sexuality as triumphantly transgressive, in a process that denaturalizes Mommy-and-Daddy sexuality and repudiates the limitations of decency, sobriety, decorum, moderation, and the like that characterize hypocritical bourgeois heterosexuality. Moreover, it is never an issue whether Vallejo and his lovers (who are essentially interchangeable in physique, behavior, dress, looks, and other signs of identity) fit any identifiable category of same-sex couples. They do constitute a same-sex unit, but they appear not to be a "gay" couple in one of the various ways in which the gay rights movements have influenced Latin American society. They are most assuredly not the active macho and passive effeminate couple that is the essential meaning of homosexuality in Mediterranean societies, where the passive partner functions in extensive ways as a surrogate wife or considers himself/herself to be the same thing as a wife (i.e., the formula modeled in Manuel Puig's fiction). Nor are Vallejo and his lovers the sort of "act-up" queer partnership that now has some presence in Latin American metropolitan culture, a partnership for which the display aspects of transgressive sexuality may be an essential part of their unconventional relationship (cf. the male lovers in Jaime Humberto Hermosillo's 1985 film *Doña Herlinda y su hijo*).

From one point of view it is difficult to know if the rather bland homoeroticism displayed in *Virgen* is meant to be a significant departure from the more conventional Mediterranean model evident in the real-life novels by other Medellín novelists. But from another point of view, I would return to my proposition that the draining of sexuality, especially transgressive sexuality, of its presumed renovating vitalism and, indeed, the virtual retreat into an asexuality is in Schroeder's film a correlative of the Valley of Death to which Vallejo has returned: his announced intention to return to Medellín is far more literal than he could have originally imagined. As the film concludes, Vallejo returns to his empty apartment (itself an objective correlative of his retreat from life), and he sets about angrily to draw the drapes over the wraparound picture windows that afford such a spectacular view of the city. Whether or not he intends immediately to commit suicide or to do so indirectly by drinking himself to death or simply to descend into a reclusive state is unclear. But what is clear is that, with the death of the second lover since his return, he accepts the futility of human community and the inevitability of death, not as an unimpeachable human condition, but rather as all that is left of human experience in the Medellín of the *sicarios*.

Haz patria: ten hijos. [Build the nation: have children.]
OFFICIAL MEXICAN GOVERNMENT SLOGAN
DURING THE 1930S AND 1940S

*It is frequently assumed, not only within dominant
representation, but within certain kinds of psychoanalytic discourse, that there are only two possible subject
positions: that occupied on the one hand by heterosexual
men and homosexual women, and that occupied on the
other by heterosexual women and homosexual men.
Not only does this formulation afford a preposterously
monolithic reading of male homosexuality, but it depends upon a radically insufficient theory of subjectivity.*

Forging Queer Spaces

DOÑA HERLINDA Y SU HIJO

One long final sequence occurs in Jaime Hum-
berto Hermosillo's 1985 film, *Doña Herlinda y su hijo* (Doña Herlinda and
Her Son).[1] The sequence ends with the baptism of the infant child of the
main character, Rodolfo. Surrounded by his loving wife, adoring mother,
and closest friends, Rodolfo presents his son to the world to the strains
of a saccharine song in praise of motherhood. As she has done throughout the film, Rodolfo's mother, Doña Herlinda, presides with a look of
serene triumph, confident that she has successfully fulfilled her maternal
role of overseeing the reproduction of society. This serenely triumphant
look contains significant resonances. The look is an important tool of social control, and mothers often claim to have eyes in the back of their
heads as a caution to their children. The look of scrutiny is a radar sweep
that seeks to detect social deviance, and its sequel, the look of disapproval, seeks to rectify deviance detected. Doña Herlinda has indeed
looked into her son's life and detected his sexual deviance, but after her
mediating efforts and maternal machinations, her look communicates to
her son and to the world around them not disapproval but a beatitude
deriving from viewing the social code upheld—at least those aspects of
the social code that are available for public scrutiny.

One could argue that Doña Herlinda's demeanor is ironic in that it
masks that which can no longer be available for public scrutiny. I would
like to believe that such irony yields to bliss, the radiant smile of accom-

plishment, which in this case means the happiness of her family members. Doña Herlinda may have inherited the patriarchal mantle from her deceased husband, but Hermosillo means for us to understand that Doña Herlinda's social Otherness as a woman is the source of her effective queering of the patriarchy she is called upon to uphold.

As one might expect, Doña Herlinda's poise has a suitable masculine counterpart. Yet, as the viewer of this droll comedy knows by now, that counterpart is not Doña Herlinda's husband (a formulation that would, in any case, invert the male primacy in the masculinist world perpetuated by Rodolfo, the son). Rather, her counterpart, the individual who stands alongside Rodolfo's wife (but who in one portrait holds the baby), moving back and forth and keeping the festivities going, is Ramón, Rodolfo's male lover.

Prior to the film's concluding minutes, as Rodolfo's wife begins to experience final contractions of labor, the viewer is called upon to contemplate/cheer/abhor the explicit scene of Ramón and Rodolfo leisurely making love in the private space Doña Herlinda has created for them in a specially renovated wing of her house. Although Ramón is generally portrayed in the feminized role of the insertee, in this scene — and marking Hermosillo's earnest attempt to defy canonical conjugations of male homosexual bodies — it is Rodolfo, on the verge of assuming the patriarchal role of reproductive father, who is leisurely serviced by Ramón. In this context it is also important to note (in line with Hermosillo's general question about fixed sexual roles, including the role of the "total homosexual" uninterested in women) that in the only scene showing an expression of intimacy between Rodolfo and Olga, he lies back on the couch while she proceeds to seduce him.

This series of implausible acts, all carried out without any social or interpersonal tension, marks the problematical utopian space postulated by Hermosillo in the film. Transcending the tired clichés of tragic homosexual love (understood as same-sex eroticism dominated by a heterosexist medico-legal codification) that are found in early novels such as José Ceballos Maldonado's *Después de todo* (1968; After All) and Miguel Barbachano Ponce's *El diario de José Toledo* (The Diary of José Toledo, 1964; Barbachano Ponce is the producer of *Doña Herlinda*), or even the rather thinly configured gay identity of Luis Zapata's groundbreaking *Adonis García, el vampiro de la colonia Roma* (Adonis García, a Picaresque Novel, 1979), Hermosillo's film defies classification in terms of hegemonic homoerotic primes. Indeed, it transcends those formulations that, like José Rafael Calva's *Utopía gay* (Gay Utopia, 1983) — however interesting this text may be as a radical reinscription of reproductive marriage in Mexican society—can only have meaning if it is clear who the "man" is and who the "woman" (the one who ends up pregnant) is (see Foster, *Gay and Lesbian Themes*, 136–139). Hermosillo significantly modifies the Mexican representation of homoeroticism by confusing the issues of male/female identity, although it would be safe to say that Rodolfo is generally assigned the male role. For example, in one important scene, Ramón receives an "anniversary" gift from Rodolfo that includes a container of Nivea, presumably to be used as a lubricant to enhance his role as the insertee. Yet while Ramón plays the jealous lover on those occasions when, in order to maintain appearances, Rodolfo escorts women in public, he also plays the male counterpart to Doña Herlinda in her orchestration of patriarchal bliss in the baptismal denouement.

But the crucial axis of the film is Doña Herlinda herself. The crucial question is to what extent she is a token arbiter in the reduplication of patriarchal structures and to what extent she engages in their subversion. This subversion turns on the refusal to abide by the "epistemology of the closet" (Sedgwick, *Epistemology*), which involves the definition of homosexuality as a dark, dirty secret that sustains compulsory heterosexuality out of the constant threat of being revealed as the damning identifying mark of an individual.

Clearly, Doña Herlinda is fully capable of engineering the social space such that the closet is no longer a precarious site of public scrutiny. She invites Ramón to live in the same house with her son, while at the same time she maneuvers Rodolfo into an engagement with Olga. She also remodels her house so that Ramón can live in separate quarters, while Rodolfo and Olga, the apparently happily married professional couple, occupy with their son the main part of the house. And she balances with equanimity the relationship between Ramón and Olga, fully supporting the wife's desire to have her own career, which will involve a fellowship in Germany: while Ramón will be a companion to Rodolfo, Olga will be a loyal wife but not a dependent, subservient helpmate.

That lower-class, provincial Ramón will occupy this slot in the social structure in Olga's stead is one of the unexplored ideological issues of the film. When Ramón's parents come to visit their son in Guadalajara and find him living in Doña Herlinda's house, they are confused and even a bit suspicious. But the ever-attentive Doña Herlinda ends up winning them over, in a victory that is both a measure of her maternal efficiency and also a reflection of the uncertainties surrounding Ramón's social role. Thus Hermosillo glosses over class differences—those based on economic criteria (Doña Herlinda is a wealthy widow, while Ramón's parents are working-class provincials), profession (Rodolfo is a successful pediatrician, while Ramón is studying the French horn), and culture (Rodolfo is a big-city sophisticate, while Ramón has a relatively humble small-town background). The reason class is important here and that it is unfortunate that Hermosillo does not find a way to address it in the film is the long tradition of materially comfortable men attracting and being attracted to (generally) younger men of limited economic means. Such relations range from frank exploitation—the commercial arrangement (open or veiled) between the client/dependent man and his customer/independent man—to a modern version of the Greek model, whereby the older man is charged with the responsibility of educating the younger man sexually and emotionally. If it is true that the Greek model involved men of the same social class, in its modern version it turns precisely on class difference, where the professional older man serves as a guide to the younger working-class man; the latter is a common theme in modern culture and is colloquially alluded to as "rough trade," not so much because one assumes that sex received from a lower-middle-class man will be rough, but because he is "rough," unrefined, socially and culturally (cf. the immortal model in E. M. Forster's novel *Maurice*, written 1913–1914 but not published until 1971, and in James Ivory's film version of 1987). Hermosillo's film seems to assume the uncomplicated legitimacy of Rodolfo, as a professional man of a certain level of social experience, offering Ramón aid and direction in his life in return for a sexual liaison. Note, however, that Ramón is not completely "rough," as he is a trained musician.

The major emphasis in his film, however, concerns the question of public versus private space and the conflicts that cluster around the divergence between social obligations and private needs. Once again, Doña Herlinda is the pivotal figure. On the most explicit level, she is the one who undertakes to move her son and Ramón out of the sphere of public scrutiny into the privacy of the home. This assumes four stages. In the opening scene of the film, we see her son, Rodolfo, in front of the early-sixteenth-century Guadalajara cathedral, a monument to traditional Catholicism and a symbol of the rigid moral code of Mexico's second-largest city. For the viewer who is more of a Mexican film buff than I, this scene must have parodic intertextual connections with classic Mexican films and with the master narrative conjunction of mariachi music (which is typical in Guadalajara and which permeates *Doña Herlinda*), machismo (in the style of the great Mexican film idol Pedro

Armendáriz), and nationalist sentiment (iconized by the Guadalajara cathedral). Rodolfo's stance evokes Armendáriz's paradigmatic figure of the Mexican macho. Armendáriz is reputed to have countered Luis Buñuel's suggestion that he wear a short-sleeved shirt in a scene with the curt "eso es de maricones" (that's for queers); in this scene, Rodolfo is wearing short sleeves.

However, in an irony not lost on the cognoscenti, Rodolfo is also standing in one of the several interconnected squares in downtown Guadalajara that serve as the major cruising area of the city, and nearby side streets contain several of the city's quasi-gay bars, including the Bar Corona, which appears in the film. (Yet it should be noted that gay pairs in Guadalajara blend in rather indistinguishably with the traditional all-male clientele of most Mexican nontourist bars and that some of the city's bars more known for their legendary bohemian past blend this past with a specifically gay ambience.) In the opening scene Rodolfo is on his way to meet Ramón in his room at a boardinghouse that caters to out-of-town students. In a series of comic contretemps, it becomes evident that the boardinghouse cannot be a reliable trysting place since its public space, reminiscent of the public space of the plaza, is not conducive to intimacy in general and much less to gay intimacy. Everyone at the boardinghouse knows Rodolfo and is appropriately deferential to him given his social rank, but it is clear that he and Ramón cannot pursue their relationship there.

The second stage involves Ramón's move into the house of Rodolfo and his mother. As I have indicated, this move is engineered by Doña Herlinda. In an often-cited scene in the film (see Berg, 131), after the three have had dinner and the two men have retired to Rodolfo's bedroom to engage in intimacies now protected by the walls of the mother's home, Doña Herlinda settles down in her room to thumb through magazines, looking at pictures of bridal gowns. A third stage follows the marriage of Rodolfo and Olga. While the newlyweds inhabit their own apartment, Doña Herlinda and Ramón remain at home as though they were the proud parents of the couple. In one sequence they all assemble at the newlyweds' apartment to view the slides of their honeymoon in the United States and Hawaii. Afterward, Doña Herlinda explains to them how she is remodeling her house so that all of them—along with any children—can live together comfortably. The fourth stage involves the closing sequence described above, which juxtaposes the fullness of Ramón's and Rodolfo's protected erotic intimacies (in the film's most explicit sexual scene) with the fullness of Rodolfo and Olga's domes-

Joined across the
bridge of heterosexist
convention

tic tranquility, all presided over by the beaming Doña Herlinda, who as usual has little to say, her face gently fixed in a beatific but knowing smile.

Doña Herlinda is a pivotal figure in another sense as well. Olga is a key female figure in the film, signaling a modern sophisticate who is able to combine her career and motherhood—which she is able to do specifically because her husband has a male lover willing to assume parenting responsibilities. It would be inappropriate to lament Olga's being shoved to the margins as a wife: to do so would involve interpreting the film in terms of social coordinates other than those with which Hermosillo frames his narrative. Olga is fully aware of the arrangements Doña Herlinda has made. She has become good friends with Ramón and realizes that in the context of Doña Herlinda's world she will be able to fulfill herself both as a wife and as a professional; moreover, she will be able to accept the fellowship in Germany that has been offered to her, confident that she is abandoning neither her husband nor her child.

Doña Herlinda, therefore, does not overshadow or marginate Olga, and Olga's role could be understood as marginal only in terms of a heterosexist, socially reactionary standard. Rather, Doña Herlinda binds together the public and the private. As a wealthy widow, she is able to move comfortably in the public world, where she is called upon to exemplify maternal discretion. This she does on several occasions, the most notable one being at the beginning of the film when she mediates the initially tense situation between Rodolfo and his two "dates," Olga and Ramón, who have yet to forge their own alliance. But, most important, she exemplifies and ensures compliance with the social code of compulsory heterosexual, monogamous, reproductive marriage. Mexican society, perhaps more than U.S. society, admits the possibility of the conjunction of reproductive marriage and the transgression of the criterion of monogamous heterosexuality (whether through the traditional practice of men's extramarital affairs or through the varying degrees of homosociality and homoeroticism that can be associated with Mexican male bonding).

I do not wish to insinuate that male bonding in Mexico is the same as gay sexuality but rather that a continuum stretches from basic *compadrismo*[2] to the various manifestations of physical intimacy (what I have in mind here is something like a masculine version of Adrienne Rich's lesbian continuum). By contrast, in the United States the concept of buddyism is either viewed as a youthful phenomenon that one outgrows with marriage or as a characteristic of ethnic and other subaltern groups. This is especially so since the "reheterosexualization" of American society in the 1950s, which was in large measure a reaction to the strong male bonding romanticized in cultural productions like war films (see Silverman, especially chapter 2, "Historical Trauma and Male Subjectivity"). Nor do I mean to imply that Mexico is more "morally flexible" than the United States, at least as regards wandering husbands. But there appears to be a level of male-perspective cultural production that models such opportunities without the aura of condemnation that customarily surrounds such narratives in the United States.

Doña Herlinda exemplifies the private space of Mexican life. As a woman, her realm of power is her home, and therefore to a large degree whatever she does to enhance life within its walls is socially legitimate. Sexual intimacy is a private matter, which is why Mexican law and Latin American law in general have been historically less concerned with the nature of acts than with their distribution between public and private realms (this is detailed in Lumsden, *Homosexualidad*, 51 n., and confirmed by other commentators on the place of male homoeroticism in the Latin American social dynamic: see Acevedo; Trevisan; Murray; homoeroticism in Mexico is examined in Núñez Noriega and in Taylor). Transgression involves not the acts themselves but making private acts public, which is why the public display of heterosexual eroticism is as vigorously defended as homosexual display (both as acts of defiance against norms of public decency). This does not translate into any greater respect in Mexico for gay rights. But it means that the American concept of the long arm of the law reaching into the bedroom of consenting adults is an alien judicial principle in most Hispanic societies. Therefore, when Doña Herlinda creates within the confines of her own home a love nest for Ramón and Rodolfo, although she is flaunting a Catholic moral convention, she is also affirming the sanctity of the home and the privileging of her private domain. While the film might be decried as immoral by viewers who subscribe to institutional Catholicism, Doña Herlinda cannot be faulted for having "rescued" her son from the risks involved in the semipublic display of his sexuality in the boardinghouse, with its ill-fitting doors, and protecting this display behind the vine-covered walls of her home.

The questions have been raised as to whether *Doña Herlinda y su hijo* is an adequate example of gay liberation and whether it ends up reinscribing patriarchal values (Lozano, 30). I believe this question is an inappropriate formulation of the issues, because it implies the possibility of somehow transcending patriarchal values, whatever these may be. (That is, is reproductive sexuality in contemporary society necessarily patriarchal, or is modern medical technology enabling conception and pregnancy to circumvent patriarchalism and even heterosexuality?) Hermosillo's film might be viewed as utopian in that it supersedes the either/or disjunction—*either* heterosexual marriage for Rodolfo *or* the "gay lifestyle"—by modeling a conjunctive arrangement in which no one is victimized (except for the possible unresolved social subalternity of Ramón). Yet to the extent that the arrangement is possible in the real world, rather than being a social fantasy or a science-fiction proposal, *Doña Herlinda y su hijo* is hardly utopian. Embodying micropolitics at its best, Hermosillo's film constitutes a gesture of resistance that does not wait for the totally revolutionary restructuring of society in order to bring about the fulfillment of personal needs.

It is less a question of reinscribing the patriarchy than of living at cross-purposes to it, less a question of resigning oneself to accepting the impositions of society (Rodolfo does not seem displeased at becoming a father) than of taking advantage of the gaps or the contradictions in the system in order to construct dimensions of an alternate world (see the proposals of Jonathan Dollimore). In this case, the criterion of privacy, especially for the professional class, can displace fulfillment of the social code of compulsory heterosexuality. What audiences have likely identified with in Hermosillo's film (an identification that has been repeated in subsequent films such as María Novaro's *Danzón,* 1992) is the image of personal subversion in an alienating though not exactly hostile environment. For example, at least in the universe of *Doña Herlinda,* there is no organized persecution of Rodolfo and Ramón, no sense of threat or danger, only the discomfort of the semipublic location of their meetings. Developing the practice of seeking fissures in the social edifice allows for the subversive pursuit of personal needs without this pursuit becoming a utopian confrontation with the deeply sunk pillars of that social edifice.

Rather than a reinscription of the patriarchy (albeit a singularly defective one) or a utopian imaging of an impossibly polysexual world of alternative family arrangements, Hermosillo's film is, I would argue, an example of what Alexander Doty has described as the queer potential of popular-culture production. Doty develops the proposal that the queer is anything that challenges or subverts the straight, the compulsory heterosexual, through either an ironizing of its limited view of human potential or through the overt defiance of its conventions. The so-called gay sensibility and its lesbian counterpart are necessarily queer (although lesbians and gays may in some contexts endorse the straight), but queerness is something larger than gayness and lesbianism:

> I ultimately use [queerness] to question the cultural demarcations between the queer and the straight (made by both queers and straights) by pointing out the queerness of and in straight couples, as well as that of individuals and groups who have been told they inhabit the boundaries between the binaries of gender and sexuality: transsexuals, bisexuals, transvestites, and other binary outlaws. Therefore, when I use the terms "queer" or "queerness" as adjectives or nouns, I do so to suggest a range of nonstraight expression in, or in response to, mass culture. This range includes specifically gay, lesbian, and bisexual expressions; but it also includes all other potential (and potentially unclassifiable) nonstraight positions.
>
> This being the case, I like those uses of "queer" that make it more than just an umbrella term in the ways that "homosexual" and "gay" have been used to mean lesbian or gay or bisexual, because queerness can also be about the intersecting or combining of more than one specific form of nonstraight sexuality. (xv–xvi)

Doty goes on to analyze major popular-culture manifestations, finding that such productions are particularly privileged spaces for the elaboration of queer perspectives. Doty does not say whether this is the result of the need for mass culture to be constantly seeking new, usually superficially elaborated combinations as part of product consumerism or whether mass culture is only the most public face of a cultural production that is inherently queer because the straight mind has little need for practices that are premised on questioning the given. Such an understanding of the queer may end up by draining it of most of its transgressive value (indeed, many of the examples analyzed by Doty—such as *I Love Lucy* or *The Jack Benny Show*—have never been viewed as particularly transgressive). It may also serve to undermine the primacy of alternate sexualities viewed as alternate sexual practices and not just cute gender-bending. Nevertheless, Doty's formulations are valuable for defending the notion of queer as a global concept and not just a pejorative synonym of gay and for proposing that the queer be sought beyond the limited confines of the texts of those in the know.

John King describes *Doña Herlinda* as one of Hermosillo's gay divertissements. Although this description may not be intended as dismissive, it nevertheless gives the impression that the film only has meaning for a specifically gay audience. By contrast, I am proposing that Hermosillo's film be viewed as a significant reinterpretation of clan arrangements that are not utopian in any fantastic way but are instead legitimated by the full participation of the actors involved. Furthermore, I am suggesting that *Doña Herlinda* be viewed under the purview of Doty's concept of queer culture as a proposal for subverting the Mexican patriarchy through, significantly, the agency of Doña Herlinda herself, the one figure in the film most charged with defending the heterosexist system. Doña Herlinda "naturalizes" the perversion of the system as, perversely, a way of ensuring its reproduction (evident in the arrival of the newborn, whose baptism at the end of the film is a ritual of his entrance into that system). A good measure of the success of Hermosillo's film lies in the astuteness of his treatment of the borderlines between inscription and perversion (a "sweet subversion," according to Russo, 313), between legitimacy and transgression.

NO SE LO DIGAS A NADIE

Joaquín Camino's father tells him at one point in Francisco J. Lombardi's 1998 excellent adaptation of Jaime Bayly's rather mediocre 1994 novel that in Peru, "Se puede ser cualquier cosa, menos maricón." ["In Peru, you can be anything except a fag."] (Castro, "Gritemos," compares the novel and the film and sees them both as versions of a gay liberation stance.) In *No se lo digas a nadie* (Don't Tell Anyone) it is never explained why it is possible in that country to be a thief, a drug dealer, a murderer, a rapist, a child molester, a corrupt politician, or a dirty-dealing businessman but not queer. Moreover, no attempt is ever made to identify what is meant by the word, although this is not surprising, since, as one of the guiding principles of homophobia, those who use the word *maricón* negatively and disparagingly if not directly as a call to murderous violence are never called upon to define the term. Indeed, the two lacunae in the social discourse go hand in hand: there is no demand to identify what *maricón* actually means, and there is no demand to explain why one can be anything else except a *maricón*.

I will not rehearse here the effective reasons for failing to identify what the term *maricón* means, except to remind the reader that it neatly serves to cover anything that can be viewed as a questioning of or a challenge to patriarchal hegemony; of course, this only displaces the need to identify what is understood to be patriarchal hegemony, and the two propositions are held suspended in a tenuous dialectic in which neither gets defined, despite the power that dialectic exercises as a strategy of social control or as a pretext for deploying all manner of strategies of social control. One supposes that, as far as wondering why no explanation is forthcoming as to why the one thing that one cannot be in Peruvian society is a queer, there is the need for an absolute focal point of social abjection. Thus, it may be instructive to look to those Latin American or other societies in which being queer is no longer totally abject to search for what has replaced being queer as the realm of absolute total social proscription.

But more productive would be to observe two more verifiable social circumstances about Joaquín's father's assertion. The first involves the fact that only being a *maricón* is at issue, not being a *tortillera* (lesbian). While it is safe to assume that being lesbian in Peru is hardly more of a socially approved identity choice or sexual preference or way of being in the world than those of the gay male, the simple fact is that Señor Camino's affirmation is born of the notably failed attempt, via hallowed forms of homosociality, to fulfill his paternal responsibilities to ensure that his son is following the right path in life (note that his surname, *camino*, in Spanish means road or path). Presumably, if Camino or his wife were explaining the harsh facts of social life in Peru to their daughter, they might well say something similar about being a *tortillera*. But they do not because a daughter is not in question, and the film, following the lead of Bayly's novel, is resolutely masculinist, a fact that opens up a number of troubling ideological vistas for what appears to be an overall stance that is sympathetic to being gay.

The other sociological factor raised by this father's observation regarding the impossibility of being gay in Peru has to do with the fundamental ambiguity of the predicate *possible* between—in both English and Spanish—its deontic and its alethic scopes. The confusion between these two scopes results in the collapsing of semantic fields, thereby enabling one of the most potent strategies of homophobia: the assertion that because something is not permitted, it therefore either does not exist at all or is legitimately suppressed whenever it is discovered to pretend to exist. Deontologically, *possible* refers to the tangled web of what is permitted and what is not permitted or (to complete the semantic square) what is not allowed and what is not not allowed. Certainly, Joaquín's father is alluding to what is permissible—or, better, not to what is permitted, but what is not allowed: no one is allowed to be gay. One must understand from this the application of an entire apparatus, both that of the state and its institutions, and those institutions that while not officially state ones work in tandem with the state, to enforce this nonpermissibility. Consequently, much of the film has to do with examples of the way in which those who have the power to enforce the proscription on being gay—priests, parents, teachers, colleagues, friends, and lovers—read one's body in order to determine if a violation of the deontic meaning of *possible* is to be found. The implication is that if no such violation is discernible, fulfillment of the injunction obtains and society progresses free of the taint of homosexuality (again, whatever it precisely means) and from its threat to the patriarchy.

However, such a restricted frame of reference overlooks the alethic meaning of *possible,* the meaning relating to the truth of the assertion in which the predicate is used. In this sense, the scope of assertion concerns whether gays do or do not—that is, whether or not there is the likelihood that gays—exist in Peruvian society. Gays do, however, unquestionably exist in Peruvian society, for no matter how gayness is defined unless one subscribes to very narrow definitions of what it means to be gay or how one is gay, there is no more likelihood of the possibility of there being any truth in saying no gays exist in Peruvian society than there is to say no thieves exist in Peruvian society (with all due excuses for using a point of comparison that formulates a negative social condition, which is indulged in here because the speech universe of such assertions is, presumably, a unmitigatedly negative one).

If homoerotic desire and the accompanying identities, behavior, and acts that may attend the pursuit of such desire are an integral part of human sexuality (acknowledged or not, realized or not, and accompanied or not by what may popularly be known as "queer" sexuality), then Peru is no different from any other human society. This is so whether or not one subscribes to the inevitable homoerotic dimension of all human intercourse when viewed from any number of theoretical lenses ranging from a Christian theology based on the weaknesses of the flesh to Freudianism to contemporary studies on masculinity and the components of homosociality (i.e., the postulates underlying research in a collection like Warner's *Fear of a Queer Planet*). Although there is nothing especially perceptive or innovative in saying that the only "sins" virulently defined, rigorously proscribed, and violently punished are those that are most likely to be prevalent, the slippage between the deontic and alethic meanings of the predicate *possible* serves to occlude an understanding of how being allowed to be gay and in fact being gay (anyway) are two very different propositions.

It is an occlusion that serves to make it difficult if not impossible to contemplate how homoerotic desire is part of the human condition, how a rather startling number of social subjects are, since statistics began to be constructed, gay after all, and how social life for many may mean being gay to various degrees of active fulfillment of a homoerotic agenda while (occasionally not with complete success) keeping below the radar of the always fine-tuned homophobic apparatuses of detection. One might well argue that the function of such apparatuses, like the insistent confessor determined to ferret out one's most buried and denied sins (an activity that in its most strenuous application provided the dynamic of the Inquisition with its techniques and devices designed to extract a richly full confession), cannot allow itself to be frustrated by the absence of deviances to be denounced. There must always be some queer to smear: no one is beyond suspicion, and an obsessive self-enforced vigilance is a small price to pay for successfully evading the accusation of sexual iniquity.

Lombardi's film is, however, squarely centered on the aforementioned parenthetical "anyway": no matter what, one is gay anyway; no matter what, one has same-sex partners; no matter what, one adjusts one's accommodations with the heteronormative patriarchy in order to have same-sex partners. And no matter what, the business of society proceeds apace despite the violations to its integrity which—it is at least implied by the intensity of the homophobic screed—threaten its very survival in the form of disrupted procreation and disrupted family life. In other words, Lombardi's film is about the powerful force of hypocrisy that works in appallingly efficient tandem with homophobia to ensure that what is *possible* both defies social truth and permits that which is disallowed.

One dimension of Lombardi's film involves the representation of how Joaquín Camino's father undertakes to enforce heteronormative exper-

Claiming/displaying
the possibilities of
being queer

tise and how Joaquín develops ways to evade patriarchal injunctions
while nevertheless accepting assumption into the ranks of reproducers
of the patriarchy. That is, Joaquín defies the hypocrisy of heteronormativity while at the same time becoming yet one more spokesman for it. Although the film shows a brief interlude for Joaquín in Miami (to where
he flees in the belief that one of his lovers has died of a cocaine overdose
and he will be held in some way responsible for that death), he returns
to Lima when he finds out that Alfonso has not died. While in Miami, he
encounters a former girlfriend, Alejandra, at a discotheque; she encourages him to return to the university in Peru to complete his legal studies,
and she tells him Alfonso did not die after all. Joaquín and Alejandra become engaged, but later, at his graduation party in Peru, Joaquín runs
into another former lover, Gonzalo, and the film closes on the insinuation that despite Joaquín's marriage plans, he and Gonzalo will resume

their sexual relationship. This entire sequence of his return to Peru and resumption of the relationship with Gonzalo is a deviation from Bayly's novel (apparently with his acquiescence, since he and Giovanna Pollarolo receive credit for the script).

In this deviation, *No se lo digas a nadie,* reproducing in its own way the hypocrisy of the social text, makes it possible for Joaquín to contemplate the possibility of a satisfying same-sex relationship (actually, to renew and extend an earlier one), while at the same time becoming ostensibly integrated (to the enormous joy of his parents) into the patriarchal society he formerly had rebelled against and even opted out of by going to Miami, where he attempted to work as a male hustler. It is in this sense that Lombardi's film scores points about the hypocrisy of Peruvian (Latin American/Western) sociosexual code while also running the risk of reduplicating that very dimension by providing the viewer with "la historia más escandalosa de Lima" (the most scandalous story in Lima), as the International Movie Database characterizes it (in a blurb signed by Fredrik Olsson), and simultaneously comforting the viewer with final scenes in which it is evident that Joaquín will turn out fine after all, despite his alienation and anger accompanied by drinking, drugs, and hustling. More on this below.

Lombardi's film is intransigent in portraying the almost ludicrous attempts of the senior Camino to ensure his son's development as an appropriately masculinized member of society. Such a program includes the mandatory sequestering of the male child in an all-male world in which it is taken for granted that the setting and its guardians will collaborate to develop all of the charges confined to it along similar and forthrightly characterized paths of manly deportment. Western literature is filled with the evidence of how this does not work and how it serves to provide opportunities for homosocial bonding to develop into homoerotic attachment. Lombardi's *No se lo digas a nadie* inevitably has as a subtext his 1985 film version of Mario Vargas Llosa's 1963 novel *La ciudad y los perros,* in which the entire story takes place in the context of a military academy for teenage boys. The opening scene of the latter involves the hazing ceremonies characteristic of all-male institutions, which, as has often been demonstrated (cf. Mattoso for a Latin American interpretation of this matter), shade off into homoerotic rituals (or at least rituals with homoerotic possibilities). *No se lo digas* is less trenchant and involves a sleep-over for the boys in the Catholic school Joaquín attends. The forced cohabitation of sexually awakening bodies provides for the opportunity for the expression, no matter how tentative, of same-sex desire. I will also return to this opening scene in the discussion of the film's title.

However, the most painfully ludicrous demonstration of Camino's attempt to take seriously his fatherly obligations vis-à-vis his son's masculine identity comes in a long, three-part sequence early in the film that essentially is built around masculine initiation, youthful rebellion and escape, and the return to the fatherland.

In the first segment, the father attempts to engage his son in a boxing match "to make a man of him"; Joaquín makes a very poor showing, despite the father's very stern injunctions to engage in the give-and-take like a man.

In the second segment, Camino takes his son hunting. A lot goes on in this sequence, but its general sense is to provide the son once again with the opportunity to test himself in his father's presence and to prove he is a man; once again Joaquín fails. Yet he has begun to learn how to deal with his father, and he dissembles in two important ways. First, he goes on the hunt with the son of the *cholo* (indigenous peasant) caretaker at one of the father's *fincas* (rural properties). The *cholo*'s son, who is Joaquín's age, allows Joaquín to deceive his father by alleging that he killed the deer that his indigenous companion actually shot. It is not clear whether Camino believes his son because he is so anxious to be convinced that he is a real man, or whether he suspects the truth. (Why, then, did he not go on the hunt with his son? Perhaps he knew intuitively that his son would let him down again.) In any event, Camino is overjoyed at the evidence of his son's manly accomplishment. The point of this incident is the way in which Joaquín has begun to manipulate the truth in order to pass as appropriately masculine in his father's society — or at least in his father's presence.

Meanwhile, the younger *cholo* readily and without hesitation or prompting accepts his role as an accomplice in Joaquín's lie to his father — in a racially stratified society like Peru's, *cholos* and others who occupy their same place in society know that one of the keys to survival is through dissembling and in providing the more powerful owners of power with the truth they wish to hear. As for what really took place, it remains "allá entre blancos" (a matter between whites). The formula of hypocrisy as a strategy of self-defense is amply demonstrated here: *cholos* do not tell the truth to their social betters, children do not tell the truth to their parents, and queers do not tell the truth to the agents of the patriarchy.

The patriarchal
education of the son

The second dimension of this second sequence of Joaquín's education
as a real man involves the swim the two young men go for in a moun-
tain stream near where they go hunting. Although both remain in their
underpants, the two are soon engaged in a game of "I'll show you mine
if you'll show me yours." This incident of homosocial mutual confirmation, whereby one's masculinity is confirmed by displaying proudly (by
having to display proudly) the dominant phallic correlative, turns sour,
however, when Joaquín wishes to touch the other young man's penis.
He is rebuffed with the brusque assertion that "los hombres no se tocan"
(men don't touch each other). Why it is significant for men to see each
other but not touch each other (as though seeing and touching were divided by a line in which the first is not an erotic act, while the second is)
is necessarily left unclear: Joaquín's demand to know why they shouldn't
touch is left unanswered, because the imperatives of heteronormativity
are customarily unaccompanied by explanatory glosses. Surely, touching "must be" prohibited because touching is a first step toward execut-
ing a fully realized sexual act, but this can also be true of seeing.

The point is that, sheltered by his knowledge that the *cholo* is his social
inferior, Joaquín attempts to initiate a sexual act with the young man and
is rebuffed: it is unclear whether the indigenous youth rebuffs Joaquín
because of his own exclusive heterosexuality (this provides an opening
toward the issue of the sexual practices of Latin American indigenous
peoples, which, despite intensive Christianization, have no reason necessarily to parallel those of the dominant European culture) or because
of a sense of the potential problems that it could bring him (see the various essays by Stephen O. Murray on the subject of "indigenous homosexualities" in *Latin American Male Homosexualities*). In such a situation,
were the two of them discovered, it would likely be only the *cholo* who

Fleeing from the
homoerotic touch

would experience the wrath of both fathers, that of his own for compromising the family in the face of Joaquín's father and that of the latter because invariably the nonwhite would be seen as guilty of "corrupting" the white boy. The *cholo* violently rebuffs Joaquín's advances and threatens to tell his father, only to be attacked by Joaquín. But when the two older men arrive, the father of the *cholo* (without really knowing what has happened) brushes the incident aside, in order not to challenge the authority of the master's son. The point, in any case, is that the *cholo* youth learns that he must keep quiet and that Joaquín can appeal to the power differential in order to keep the former from snitching to either of the fathers, thereby providing Joaquín a lesson in hypocrisy more important than the lesson in manly sports that was the purpose of the hunting excursion.

Finally, this lesson in hypocrisy is sealed by the way in which Camino strikes a bicycling peasant with his van and then drives off, leaving the victim for dead, noting to his son that people like that are of no importance. The hunting excursion ends up being an extremely important lesson on three separate fronts for Joaquín, although none for the reasons intended by his father.

These first two sequences are important for Joaquín's lesson in self-preserving hypocrisy, but none has to do directly with sexuality. In fact, once again in line with underexplaining and taking for granted the internal logic of heteronormativity, no attempt is made to show why learning how to defend oneself with one's fists or being a successful hunter has anything to do with being properly sexed. (It is quite a different matter teaching queer boys — or queer girls — to defend themselves in order more effectively to deal with homophobic bullies, but that surely is not Camino's intent, given the context in which the lesson takes place.) What is at issue here is how the heteronormative discourse functions on the base of a number of interlocking premises that remain unproven and of which it is not even possible to demand proof, premises whose interrelationship is predicated on a relationship of dense metonymy such that each premise evokes and sustains the others and such that a failure or rejection of any one of them brings into question the fulfillment of any of the others.

In this fashion, being unable to engage in any of the manly sports—here, specifically, boxing and big-animal hunting—necessarily entails a failure in the realm of a fully functioning, reproductive heterosexuality: being unable to hunt means being unable to have proper sex with a woman, which means in turn being unable to contribute appropriately to the maintenance of the species through reproduction. A failure in any one of these metonymic tests necessarily presupposes a failure at any and all of the others, and it is this tight interlocking of circular entailments and presuppositions that provides the texture of density being invoked here. And while it is clear that there is some directionality in the various propositions (i.e., one usually learns to box and hunt before one learns to engender children; a girl usually learns to cook before having a baby), internal logic is ever-precarious, so that unless all of these truths about being a man are unquestionably/unquestioningly self-evident to the spectator, one wonders what any one of them has to do with the others. To be sure, cultural texts that endorse heteronormativity—such as the vast majority of Hollywood films and the vast majority of Latin American films made in the former's image—assume the logic of the dense tangle of masculine-confirming metonymies that *No se lo digas* refers to.

In the case of *No se lo digas*, which takes exception in ways that need to be fully explicated to hegemonic heteronormativity, the discourse of this heteronormativity is presented as a given also, but in ways designed to show the internal contradictions it betrays: logical connections are shown to be ludicrous juxtapositions, which is precisely why there seems to be so much, too much, going on in the hunting sequence, with Joaquín both appearing (at least to his father) to pass the test of masculinity while in reality he is studying for and passing the test of efficient hypocrisy that allows him to circumvent the logic of the discourse presumably being played out.

In the third segment, sexuality is more directly at issue, and while Joaquín's father unmistakably sees this experience (not as a test, since his son could not really fail it) as a whole with his son's prior education, it is in fact this one event that is manifestly significant in terms of Joaquín's sexuality. The experience consists of treating Joaquín to his inaugural visit to a brothel. After celebrating his high school graduation with a lunch *en famille,* Camino drops his wife off at church and then heads for the brothel with his son. Fortunately, custom in such matters does not allow the father to witness the son's activities in the prostitute's bed (undoubtedly he entertains himself with another member of the establishment's female workforce), and in one of the most honest parts of the film, we witness Joaquín's inability to function with the prostitute.

Although one can question whether, for a man, being able to function with a female prostitute is the mark of an adequate heterosexual and whether not being able to function with a female prostitute is the determining mark of a homosexual, this scene is honest in portraying nude bodies (with that of the star, Santiago Magill, apparently partially aroused sexually) setting about engaging in sex (unlike the rather bumbling clothed sex in the similarly arranged sexual initiation scene in María Luisa Bemberg's 1986 film *Miss Mary*). But what makes the scene in Lombardi's film eloquent is that when Joaquín is unable to function, despite several attempts with a very professional woman who does her best to put the young man at ease, the prostitute tells him that it doesn't matter and, more importantly, that there is nothing wrong with being gay if that is what the matter with him is. She goes on to tell him to have sex with a man. Her words are very touching in comforting Joaquín's concern at being there and his inability to perform satisfactorily, and the woman's sexual matter-of-factness contrasts dramatically with all of the strenuous efforts Joaquín's father has been making through the first part of the film to bring his son's performance as a man into line with the complexly overdetermined discourse of heteronormative masculinity.

Certainly, when the woman senses that she has little to do to earn her honorarium (which usually includes a nice tip in the case of having provided an initiation service for the son of a regular client), she must feel gratitude for the fact that the man is apparently gay. Likewise, when she insouciantly asserts afterward to the father that his son performed with exemplary manliness, she is only engaging in the self-preservation of the paid servant whose fault it is if things don't go well. After all, it is as much conventional wisdom that when a man fails to function with a woman, it is her fault for having failed to arouse him as it is conventional wisdom that when a man fails to function with a woman, it is because he is queer: the fact that these two propositions are directly contradictory is yet another demonstration of how the propositions of patriarchal heteronormativity are not required to add up. Even if this is not the direct point of Lombardi's handling of the final scene of the sequence, when Joaquín and the woman emerge from her chambers, it can be understood to be a corollary of what is manifestly going on here, which is that the father has unwittingly afforded his son yet another lesson in hypocrisy: it is enough for the woman to claim that her client has functioned properly to provide proof of his manhood without his actually having functioned properly.

A final sidelight here: Magill, the actor playing Joaquín, appears to be partially aroused in this sequence, which may or may not have been a ploy to highlight the masculinity of his body: in an obeisance to the conventions of Hollywood filmmaking (and especially its porn derivatives), no male agrees to display full frontal nudity unless his attributes fall beyond the horizon of potential ridicule. But I would like to propose another reading of Magill's apparent semiarousal, and this would be to stress the sexuality of his body in violation of the conventions whereby the queer man is always portrayed as an effeminate nerd for whom sexual practices involve a reduplication of what is believed (what is enforced to be) the female role in the sexual act. It is important not to lose sight of the legitimacy of those bodies in actual life that correspond to that stereotype, in that the stereotype is what is expected, and it is disturbingly effective when the stereotype is violated. Just as in the Mexican Jaime Humberto Hermosillo's 1985 *Doña Herlinda y su hijo*, in which the traditionally identified insertee becomes at a crucial moment in the film the inserter, thereby disrupting the stability of the heteronormative binary that is presumably carried over into gay sexuality, Joaquín's priapic depiction contradicts the stereotype of the gay individual as seen in a conventional and uncontestable representation like William Friedkin's 1970 classic, *The Boys in the Band*.

This sequence segues into the central portion of the film, which involves Joaquín's attempts to distance himself from his family and to pursue a series of adventures involving sex and drugs that cast him as a paradigmatic rebel without a cause in a Peruvian setting. Some of the film's sequences border on the trite, but it is important to keep in focus what they end up demonstrating, which is Joaquín's refusal to fulfill the patriarchal imperatives as set forth by his parents, whether the conventional bourgeois Catholicism of his mother or the strident heteronormative masculinity of his father. There is little need to enter into details here except to point out that Joaquín ends up on a course of self-destruction in which there is little left to him to satisfy his personal needs; a sequence

in which he flunks out of the university before going to Miami because
he turns in a blank examination booklet is an objective correlative of how
nothing else goes right for him.

Joaquín has a relationship with a woman that also serves to repudiate the assumption that heterosexuality and homosexuality constitute
an either/or proposition and that affirms implicitly the legitimacy of a
bisexual subjectivity. But it is evident that his sexual life begins to be significant for Joaquín when he has relations with two men, Alfonso and
Gonzalo. Both are conventionally masculine in what the spectator can
take to be either a continued rejection of the effeminate queer stereotype or a mainstream Hollywoodesque reinvestment in the need to reaffirm conventional masculine presence—even if it involves same-sex
erotic acts—in order to keep the film "serious." The relationship with
Gonzalo is ostensibly the most fulfilling, and this is borne out by the fact
that by the end of the film Gonzalo and Joaquín have become reunited
as accomplices in hypocritically subverting the patriarchy.

In their first liaison, before Joaquín goes to Miami, there is a blowup
in their relationship when Joaquín mistakenly believes that it can pursue a course similar to that of heterosexual romance, and he goes to
Gonzalo's fiancee's house to announce to her that he and Gonzalo are
having an affair, despite her engagement to Gonzalo. This is intolerable
conduct from Gonzalo's point of view; in the sexist terms of Peruvian
society, which the film rather too faithfully represents, it is intolerable
from the fiancee's point of view, but her anger is of little consequence.
Thus, Gonzalo confronts Joaquín, informs him in detail how stupidly
he has behaved, and tells him that their relationship is over. If Joaquín
is startled, it can only be because he still has a few lessons to learn as regards the most efficient use of the strategies of hypocrisy: his next lover,
Alfonso, has no intention of not getting married, and he has no intention of ceasing to have sex with other men. He has a very clear idea that
heterosexual marriage and its obligations are one thing, while sex on the
side with another man is quite something else again. Ironically, at the
end of the film, it is Joaquín who has now internalized this lesson, while
Gonzalo, after all, remains unmarried.

After breaking up with Gonzalo, Joaquín has sex—and drugs—with
Alfonso, but they go too far with the drugs. Alfonso passes out, and in
a panic Joaquín flees the country to avoid implication in what he believes to be Alfonso's death from the overdose. When he does return to
Peru, Joaquín finds out that Alfonso had married after he left. Alfonso
has children and holds a prominent executive position.

Joaquín's eventual accommodation to the multiple strategies of hypocrisy necessary to survive in Peruvian society and, in the end, to be a gay man in defiance of his father's assertion of the impossibility for this to occur, then seeing the newfound joy of his parents over his having returned to hearth and home, is portrayed in the film in perhaps too precipitous a fashion, given the distance he has traveled from the comfort of the patriarchal nest. When he rediscovers his former girlfriend Alejandra in Miami and she convinces him to return to Lima to eventually complete his university studies, the pull of her love is a bit incongruous, especially since in the closing scenes of the film, it is unclear what her role in Joaquín's life will be. Will she, like Olga in Hermosillo's *Doña Herlinda*, be comfortable with — and even favored by — marriage to a man who with her knowledge will have an erotic same-sex life in tandem with their relationship? Or can it be that Alejandra has no choice but to comply with roles for women, no matter how socially advanced those women may be, in which the homophobic conventions of the patriarchy can only be held in place by the studied disavowal of homoerotic events transpiring in the very profound cracks in its façade? Or, alternatively, is Lombardi's film so determined to make a point about the hypocrisy of Peruvian/Latin American sexual codes that it affords itself the sexist luxury of simply ignoring the fate of women, as though where they figure in all of this were simply unimportant?

The closing scene of the film would seem to confirm this third interpretive option in a stunning confirmation of homosocial hypocrisy, without leaving any room for the film or its director to assert a commitment to a revision of the sexism that contributes toward sustaining that hypocrisy. The film closes with a photo session that is part of the graduation party Joaquín's parents throw for him: since he had earlier flunked out, they are overjoyed at his apparently secure insertion now into patriarchal society. Yet, at that party, Gonzalo and Joaquín have found each other again, and Gonzalo very eloquently asserts that no matter what happens to them, married or unmarried to someone else (i.e., to women), they will have a life to lead together, by which Gonzalo clearly means a sexual life. When the Caminos and their guests pose for the celebratory photo, Joaquín and Gonzalo are looking directly and lovingly into each other's eyes, straight over Alejandra's head; she looks straight ahead as though oblivious to the relationship between the two men framing her.

Bayly never figured out how to end his novel, and it sort of drops off narratively into the abyss of Joaquín's triumphantly dissipated and irresponsible life in Miami. But Lombardi's film has a point to make about the compact codes of hypocrisy in the society being portrayed: the codes of hypocrisy function with greater efficiency and internal logic than do those of heteronormativity, which they serve to shore up precisely in its incoherence. Thus, when during his phase of deliberate rebellion Joaquín announces over the dinner table to his parents that he is gay and his father mounts the violence required on such occasions, striking his son and informing him that he prefers a mongoloid son to one who is gay (a more standard announcement in Latin America is to prefer that one's son be dead), it only serves to reinforce the grimness of how Joaquín in the end, rather than renouncing the sexually irregular life his announcement necessarily conjures up in his father's mind, only learns how effectively to cover it over by the smooth surface of hypocrisy.

In this sense, the title of the film, *No se lo digas a nadie*, really means "No se lo digas a mi padre" (Don't tell my father), which is exactly what Joaquín tells the *cholo* youth who rebuffs him on the hunting expedition with his father. The dominant imperative is not the proscription of doing, which is what ostensibly the rules of patriarchy are grounded on (cf. the negatively formulated injunctions that predominate in the Ten Commandments), but rather it is the proscription against telling about what one has done, which is the principal dynamic of hypocrisy.

Lombardi's film constitutes a positive validation of homoeroticism, but not without some ideological cost. In the first place, it reproduces the sexism of the hegemonic patriarchy. If it does not trivialize the story of women, at least it relegates them to decidedly incidental roles in the film, whether in the case of Joaquín's mother (who is limited to hysterical outbursts of Catholic profession), Gonzalo's fiancée (who is left to deal out of sight with her anger over Joaquín's revelation), or Joaquín's fiancée, whose feelings about Gonzalo and the renewal of the relationship between him and Joaquín are never taken into account. In the second place, the film engages in the lookism of Hollywood films and its extension into both Latin American filmmaking and gay filmmaking. All three male bodies in the film are conventionally masculine, and the man who is the most assertive in terms of his homoerotic rights, Gonzalo, is the most conventionally macho of the three. While this hypermasculinity may be legitimate in the effort to reject the effeminate stereotype integral to someone like the elder Camino's version of sexual deviation (as seen in what he views to be his son's effeminacy in handling the boxing gloves), it is purchased with the cost of seeming to naturalize homoerotic love: these men are conventionally masculine male figures in appearance, without the threatening, disruptive force of effeminacy.

Finally, the film is pessimistic in its apparent avowal that if homo-eroticism does exist in Peru and Latin America, despite the alethic force of Camino's avowal of its impossibility, it will never exist in any other space than the dark side of compulsory heterosexuality in the bleak terrain created by hypocrisy. This is rather a dreary social message: it's not that one could demand that Lombardi execute something like a Peruvian version of the Australian Stephen Elliott's 1994 *Priscilla, Queen of the Desert* (one of whose interesting dimensions is the ability to fistfight as a defense against homophobia), but as a critique of hypocrisy, *No se lo digas a nadie* concludes by reinforcing the allure of hypocrisy—if one can come to sexual terms with a superstud like Gonzalo or a semistud like Joaquín, then an investment in hypocrisy might not be such a bad deal after all.

EN EL PARAÍSO NO EXISTE EL DOLOR

Víctor Saca's 1995 film provides another variant on the topic of the protective space for a gay son of the knowing embrace of the mother's home. Like Doña Herlinda in Jaime Humberto Hermosillo's *Dona Herlinda y su hijo* (1985), Doña Carlota is also a comfortably well-off widow, and she lives alone with a jealous, by her own assessment, servant (Amalia) behind the gates of a rural refuge on the outskirts of Monterrey, Mexico. In Doña Carlota's case, however, she is willing to relinquish her emotional dependence on her son to accept a suitor's proposal, thereby releasing Manuel (although he does not yet know this) to pursue his own emotional needs.

Manuel is the surviving partner in an unspecified but highly successful commercial agency: his business partner, Juan, has died of AIDS.[3] Although it appears the two were not lovers, Manuel is concerned about having been contaminated by his partner's disease. While he seems to understand that this has not been the case, he spends a long night of self-discovery in which he comes close to having sex with a recent penitentiary inmate, a Mr. Jalisco, who is interested in him only in order to get across the border into the United States. Manuel succeeds in overpowering Mr. Jalisco and shoots him and Mr. Jalisco's uncle, who is also a physical threat to Manuel.

Manuel pursues his odyssey through the wastelands of Monterrey's nocturnal lower depths by getting involved with a female prostitute (who claims to know from the start he is not interested in women), and he saves himself again from violence by going along with a charade in which the prostitute's policeman protector believes Manuel is a hairdresser (and therefore gay), and he is obliged to give the officer a free hairstyling. After the prostitute—who has the intriguing cross-gendered name of Bruma (Fog) King—leads him out of the labyrinth of her hovel, Manuel returns to Juan's apartment, where he had left Marcos, Juan's cousin, in drunken tears over Juan's death. Marcos, who also had almost been a victim of the ex-con's come-on, proposes sex with Manuel; rather than express homophobic outrage at this request, Manuel only demurs for the time being: after all, he and Marcos met the ex-con at a gay bar where they go after they have fulfilled Juan's last request to scatter his cremated ashes in the desert outside the city. The ex-con then becomes violent and attempts to steal Juan's full-length fur coat (it would seem his intention is to hock it for money to get across the border): significantly, Marcos underscores that it was Juan's most treasured possession, one that he was never able to wear in public. All of these laments serve as oblique synecdoches to suggest Marcos's own gay identity and the possibility that he had a relationship, if only deeply emotional, with Juan.

Manuel, by contrast, avoids Juan's homosexuality (he disappears on a business deal just as Juan is dying), and he has little patience with Marcos's emotionality over Juan's death. Marcos pleads in vain for Manuel to listen to him, telling him that he desperately needs someone in whom to confide. After Manuel has returned to Juan's apartment, he invites Marcos to freshen up and to accompany him to his mother's place because it is her birthday. Marcos is delighted: "I've always liked Doña Carlota," he avows. When they arrive, they find that Doña Carlota has left them a note to the effect that she and Amalia have gone to mass, and it is at church, while Amalia is confessing her sins, that Doña Carlota tentatively accepts the marriage proposal of her poker partner.

When Manuel finds that his mother is not at home, he and Marcos adjourn to the garden. Manuel burns some of his documents and photographs (perhaps those that implicate him in a relationship with Juan: this is one of the many details left vague in the film). Then, as they enjoy a beer and watch a cartoon on the television set to the music of the *Traviata*, Manuel turns to Marcos and says, "I need to talk to you about last night." This statement is similar to the one Marcos had attempted to use to provoke a conversation of confidence and intimacy with Manuel, and the suggestion is that Manuel is now ready to drop his cold and indifferent demeanor, the one he carried throughout his odyssey through Monterrey's nocturnal sexual underworld, and to address Marcos as an equal—perhaps even as a sexual equal.

Saca's film skirts around questions of homoeroticism and the possibility of erotic relations between Manuel and Juan as well as between Marcos and Juan, and it concludes by skirting around the possibility of erotic relations between Manuel and Marcos. Yet the film is clear in repudiating heteronormativity, not only in the tender way in which the illness of Juan (we never see Juan's face, but in one scene we see his feet being massaged by Manuel) is presented, but in the matter-of-fact way in which various settings of gay Monterrey are presented. Monterrey, like Guadalajara, is reputed to have an extensive gay life, so much so that it is often called "Montegay" by gays themselves. These settings include the gay bar where the ex-con is introduced to them and directly attempts to have sex, in turn, with each of the men; another bar in which something like a Juan Gabriel look-alike contest is in progress (Juan Gabriel is one of Mexico's great popular culture gay icons; see Monsiváis, *Escenas*, 265–283; Geirola, "Juan Gabriel"); and finally a bar in which Manuel is approached by an apparently transvestite prostitute. Also, the treatment of AIDS in the film in a nonhysterical and nonmoralizing way suggests a gay-friendly proposition, and the final scene between the two men is positive, even if it is ambiguous: ambiguity may not always be appreciated, but it is to be welcomed as a substitute for categorical homophobia any day.

The *paraíso* referred to in the title is what most makes the film an adjunct of Hermosillo's *Doña Herlinda*. The title *En el paraíso no existe el dolor* (There Is No Suffering in Paradise) is a saying that is a consoling counterpart to the traditional Catholic (and therefore very Mexican) belief that life is a vale of tears and no one escapes suffering in this world. In Saca's film it is also a reference to the refuge of Doña Carlota's home, a veritable Garden of Eden redux, in the shade of whose trees, with the brook babbling in the background and the lushness of her green thumb everywhere in evidence, an understanding between Manuel and Marcos now seems to be possible. The return to the maternal nest is not just the escape from the hostile world as dramatically modeled by Manuel's midnight experiences: it is the accession to a privileged space in which, as demonstrated to Manuel by his mother's love, intimate human emotion is possible. Moreover, it appears that Doña Carlota will ensure that that possibility is confirmed, not only by letting go of Manuel by allowing another man into her life and accepting that man's suggestion that Manuel now has his own life, but also in the way in which her realm provides an assurance of protection.

One of the most interesting scenes in the film is of her killing a serpent that intrudes in her garden and threatens her chicken. Just as Manuel is about to be "devoured" by the ex-con, the camera jumps to an image of the snake devouring a chick; but as Manuel rescues himself from the ex-con, we see Doña Carlota beating the snake to death with a club (Manuel shoots the ex-con to death) and then skinning the snake and slicing its meat into bite-sized chunks, to be eaten one a day as a health elixir. Just as Doña Herlinda's home can only be entered by the outside world on her own terms, thanks to the privilege of upper-class private space in Mexico, so too can Doña Carlota offer a paradise that is the obverse of the hellish Monterrey nightscape of bars and sex-cruising.

This vision may be utopian and does nothing for the lot in general of sex workers and sexual outcasts in Mexican society. Yet it does portray through the popular medium of film a positive image of same-sex attraction that is useful for opening the way for its treatment in other social settings. Manuel is just as privileged socially as Rodolfo is in *Doña Herlinda* (and Marcos is privileged much more than Rodolfo's partner Ramón), and this is problematical for the viewer who might wish for greater social equality. But in acknowledging this fact, it is important not to lose sight of the very importance of any positive imagining of the legitimacy of homoerotic attraction in any sector of Latin American popular culture. Mexican soap opera (from whose ranks various of the stars of this film are drawn) is relentlessly classist. Yet there is the very real effect that if popular-culture audiences can appreciate the legitimacy in sectors of social privilege of what they have been taught is socially unacceptable, perhaps they can begin to see its legitimacy in their own lives, even if they do not enjoy quite the privileged spaces at the disposal of Manuel, Marcos, and Rodolfo, spaces to which Ramón, because of his homoeroticism, is able to accede.

Although *En el paraíso no existe el dolor* avoids any direct involvement with homoerotic desire, it is certainly suggested in the film through the phallic imagery of guns that figure prominently in many places in the narrative: it is part of the exchange between Manuel and Mr. Jalisco and the vehicle for Mr. Jalisco's aggression toward Manuel, masked by a homoerotic come-on. A gun is necessarily part of Manuel's exchange with the policeman protector of Bruma King, and Manuel agrees to style the macho's hair, playing the role of the presumed homosexual hairdresser in order to displace the violence the policeman insinuates with his gun. And finally, a gun is the one memento of Juan that Manuel wishes to preserve. Interestingly, it is Juan's gun that is used to eliminate Mr. Jalisco, allowing Manuel to survive this episode of the violence of the nighttime street scene.

By the same token, it is the fact that he is carrying the gun—and that he has committed two murders with it—that drives him deeper into the Monterrey night, evading the police patrol out checking marginal bars for armed patrons. Bruma King leads him out the back way to her hideaway, which is where he is accosted by the policeman. The officer ends up leaving him alone as a gesture of gratitude for the excellent haircut Manuel gives him. Thus the gun is associated with violence, as one might suppose.

But the gun also exercises a beneficent influence in that it is a token or fetish of Manuel's insufficiently specified relationship with Juan, a relationship that he now appears ready to redefine and refocus with Marcos. The mother's tranquil, Edenic garden is the counterimage of patriarchal violence of the streets beyond its gates, and it is ensconced in that refuge that Marcos and Manuel, reduplicating the love Manuel's mother is discovering elsewhere, will reconstruct their relationship. Although the film does not go so far as to insist that that love will be a frank and open homoerotic relationship in complete conformance with the narrative presuppositions of romantic love, part of the closing charm of the film is to leave the spectator with the challenge to provide an answer to the implied question of the two men's closing regard for each other: "Well, here we are; what do we do now?"

A INTRUSA

I do not know if there is a record regarding how long into a film before the opening credits appear, but if there is any interest in such a matter it would include Carlos Hugo Christensen's *A intrusa* (The Intruder; 1979), a film based on the short story "La intrusa" from Jorge Luis Borges's *El informe de Brodie* (1970). By the time the title and accompanying credits occur, fully twenty minutes of the film have played out, one-fifth of its total length. During these twenty minutes we see a series of scenes that affirm the bond between two brothers, Cristián (the older and more masculine-appearing of the two) and Eduardo (a strikingly handsome blond, almost an ephebus), against the backdrop of late-nineteenth-century homosocial frontier society. The film is set in the year 1879, the time of the conquest of the desert, when Argentine troops opened the frontier west of Buenos Aires up to mas-

sive settlement by dispersing—massacring to a large extent—what re-
mained of the native population. Borges's story is set in Turdera, in the
province of Buenos Aires, although Christensen's film moves northeast
to the Argentine-Brazilian border in the area of Uruguaiana (across the
Paraná River from the Corrientes Province city of Paso de los Libres),
a bilingual and bicultural area that allows the director to make use of
the Brazilian actors with whom he had worked since leaving his native
Argentina in the 1950s.

Whether Turdera or Uruguaiana, the Borges/Christensen setting is
clearly an Argentine version of the Wild West: brutal and uncompromis-
ingly, insistently, and unforgivingly masculine, a world in which violent
blood sports between men is a way of honing their skills for survival in
a natural setting that is even more hostile than the all-male society they
sustain. It is a society in which men test each other directly through knife
and machete duels and indirectly through horse races, an Argentine-
Brazilian version of horseshoes, and cockfights. It is a society in which
sexuality involves visits to a primitive frontier brothel where commerce
with a woman is as much a display of masculinity to other men as it
is physical release with a woman: there is the prevailing belief that to
spend more than five minutes thinking about a woman is not a manly
thing, but rather the sign of a faggot. It is a society in which competition for survival includes competition for the material goods of life, including women. And since women, a scarce commodity on the frontier,
belong to the realm of material goods—literally bought and sold, with
the brothel madam a shrewd auctioneer—if there is any sign of affection
or solidarity between the inhabitants of this outpost of civilization, it is
something that occurs between men alone.

The opening twenty minutes of Christensen's film constitute what
amounts to a litany of homosocial bonding, the arrangements by which
men forge social pacts among themselves, measuring, assigning, and sustaining social status in conformance with a severe code of masculinist behavior. The film opens with a cockfight, one of the most aggressively masculine enterprises in Latin American culture, to the extent
that great examples of masculinist literature of the late nineteenth century and early twentieth century—e.g., Ricardo Güiraldes's paradigmatic 1926 Bildungsroman of pampas masculinity, *Don Segundo Sombra*
—have obligatory cockfight sequences, and Gabriel García Márquez's
1961 short novel *El coronel no tiene quien le escriba* is built entirely around
a fighting cock. In *A intrusa,* the cockfight is used to assert the superior
masculinity of the Nilsen brothers (of Danish descent) and to suggest

what one observer will later make explicit: to make an enemy of one of the Nilsen brothers is to have two enemies.

The triumphant masculinity affirmed by prevailing in the cockfight (and prevailing in the collection of the bet against a contender who appears reluctant to pay up) is confirmed by the inevitable visit to the brothel, where the overpowering combined masculinity of the two brothers, reasserted by their success with the cockfight, allows them to go to the head of the line of waiting men. When the madam complains that she doesn't like that sort of assertion of privilege, the men they have displaced affirm in unison that they have all just arrived, and the two brothers go off with the pick of the women; Eduardo leaves his winning cock in the hands of one of the still-waiting men.

It is with the third scene of this opening sequence that the special bond between the two brothers begins to assert itself. They return across the countryside under a mantel of night to their shack, which the camera shows is dominated by the family Bible propped up on a rustic table. After placing the cock in his indoor pen (he is clearly a part of the close domestic unit), the men strip and, naked, engage in a mock knife fight as though they were storybook Roman gladiators. Shivering, they then jump back into their long johns and, after moving the nightstand that separates their two beds, they push the beds together, jump into bed, and snuggle up in the now-common bedding to spend the night in each other's warm embrace. It is not necessary to know what the sleeping practices of the Argentine-Brazilian border in the nineteenth century were to know that this is a special arrangement between two brothers.[4] We know that throughout history men (and women) often protected themselves against the cold by sleeping body against body (bundling). This practice is supposed to have been common in premodern times, many of whose practices—including corporeal sobriety and privacy—remain here and there untouched by the overarching concerns of bodily hygiene instituted by the bourgeoisie which defines our sense of modern life. Yet the everyday disposition of the beds, with the table holding the candlestick separating the sleeping domain of each brother from the other's, makes it clear that sleeping in each other's arms is a special privilege that is not part of the daily routine of frontier men.

Finally, as though it were necessary to mediate this scene of suggestive homoeroticism between the two brothers with an assertion of their respected public masculinity, the following sequence involves a cattle roundup in which Eduardo's horse is wounded. Eduardo is forced to put his own horse out of its misery, and the owner of the herd gives him the opportunity to replace it with any horse of his choice. This interlude of masculine respect, indebtedness, and reward serves to confirm the strict code of manliness that controls the everyday affairs of these frontiersmen: there is a complex network of expectations and demands that serves alternately to exclude those who cannot comply and to afford prominence to those who can. There is nothing particularly notable in the details of this code, and it has been enacted in innumerable versions, with slight variations, in a huge inventory of Western culture (in this case, in its slightly starker survival-on-the-frontier outlines), and it is the very essence of cowboy movies, whether U.S. or Latin American — so much so that it is sufficient here to refer to the iconic function of the sequence rather than to any narrative particularity it might have.

The next sequence, however, has considerable narrative particularity, and it is as an overlay to this sequence that the opening credits of the film are finally introduced. As his brother approaches across the open plains, Eduardo waits for him with eager anticipation. He leans against the hitching post, and a smile of thrilled expectancy lights up his face: it is the sort of smile one directs toward an arriving lover, one that is far removed from the sober mien one expects among these men's men. But as his brother draws near, Eduardo's smile shifts from delight to anguish: there is someone riding behind Cristián, and it is a woman he has brought home to live with him. No explanation is given as to where he found the woman, and no exchange takes place between the men as to how the woman is to be accommodated in their close-knit domestic economy. Eduardo is clearly devastated, and that devastation carries through as the woman settles in and begins to discharge her responsibilities toward the man who has selected her (see Brant concerning the homoerotic dimensions of the Borges original; on homoeroticism and Borges in general see Altamiranda; see also Balderston).[5]

One point of the domestic arrangements is immediately clear: Juliana will occupy her own room, separated from that of the two men by a thick blanket covering the access doorway. And another point is that the two men will continue to sleep in the same room together, although there is no any longer any suggestion of their two beds being pushed together in order for them to enjoy the warmth of each other's bodies and whatever other comforts that shared intimacy might bring with it. Juliana is from the outset clearly Cristián's sexual partner, and the first of several enactments of sex make it clear that the older brother intends to make full use of Juliana's body. In the case of Cristián's first visit to Juliana's bed after

her arrival, two details are emphasized by the camera. One is the primacy of Cristián's body and the relative disappearance of the woman's
body. Christensen's film was made at the height of the Brazilian *pornochanchada*, a style of soft-porn sexual comedy that was a staple at a time
in which the hard line of censorship in neofascist Brazil (which passed
under military rule in 1964) replaced the trenchant social and political
analysis characteristic of the internationally touted Cinema Novo of the
1950s and 1960s with a sort of sexual campiness that was not likely to be
offensive to anyone in relatively permissive Brazilian society (see Xavier
on *pornochanchada*).

Yet there can be no question of the filmic portrayal of a highly dramatically framed sexuality, and for this reason, the camera really focuses
on the male body, with only a few muted moans from the participating woman. This portrayal, however, is not unproblematical. I first saw
the film in one of the private showings arranged by distributors that allowed movie house operators during the neofascist dictatorship of the
late 1970s and early 1980s in Argentina to decide if they wished to option
a title and then begin the process of obtaining permission from the authorities to show it, with or without cuts. It was obvious that the mere
display of the naked male body was unacceptable given the censorship
of the time, and that display is so insistent throughout the film that it
would have resulted in a meaningless text to have attempted to cut the offending images. Hence the film, to the best of my knowledge, was never
shown publicly in Argentina, and if it became available at all after the
return to democracy in 1983, it certainly would have had a very limited
distribution. Movie house operators were more interested in showing
U.S. and European films that were either banned during the seven years
of the dictatorship or were, like John Badham's 1977 *Saturday Night Fever,*
originally shown with mutilating cuts.

Christensen's film had no problems with Brazilian censorship, and it
went on to win prizes at the Gramado film festival, the country's most
important such event. Yet the film is highly transgressive, not in the representation of the sexual act, but in the lingering cartography of the male
body. While Christensen ensures that the often dark shadows of his film
mask the genitals of his leading men, their lanky bodies viewed from behind allow their buttocks in particular to function as a synecdoche of
their male sexuality. This is probably the first Latin American film in
which there is so insistent a scrutiny of the male buttocks and their en-
dowment as a sign of sexual energy. Since the motion of the buttocks is
directly proportional to the act of penetration, Cristián's heaving body

underscores insistently the degree to which he intends to use the woman he has brought home.

But when Cristián concludes the sexual act, adjusting his pants, he leaves Juliana's room to join Eduardo in their shared bedroom. The look Eduardo gives him is one of devastating languor, almost despair, and it is an extension of the second detail of the camera's concern during the sequence, which is to record the pain on Eduardo's face as he witnesses, if only through the thick blanket covering the doorway, his brother's defection from his side to make love to Juliana. There is a significant difference between the shared rituals of the whorehouse, where there can never be any important meaning to the women each pays for a brief physical encounter, particularly when one remembers that the function of the brothel is more to confirm masculine solidarity than to relate to women as women. By contrast, as roughly and distantly as Cristián treats Juliana, she is his woman, which he confirms by regaling her with feminine trinkets; this only increases Eduardo's jealousy toward the woman.

It is after Cristián returns to his bed alongside Eduardo that the camera closes the sequence by returning to the prominently displayed Bible, above which appear the imposed words of 2 Kings 1.26 evoked by Borges's text as an epithetic allusion but not actually quoted; Christensen's film provides the Portuguese-language version of this passage, which in English reads "I [David = Eduardo] grieve for thee, my brother Jonathan [Cristián]: exceedingly beautiful, and amiable to me above the love of women. As the mother loveth her only son, so did I love thee." The opening words of this passage, one of the great homoerotic statements of the Jewish Bible, so often evoked in terms of other less explicit passages to condemn same-sex affection, provide the title for one of Argentina's first gay novels, Carlos Arcidiácono's 1976 *Ay, de mí, Jonatán* (see Foster, *Gay and Lesbian Themes*, 107–110; Costa Picazo). The chronological proximity between Arcidiácono's novel and Christensen's film and the fact that the former was censored and the latter not even shown publicly in Argentina probably meant that few could have made the connection between the two texts, although seeing the film over two decades later and knowing the prominence of Arcidiácono's novel in an inventory of Latin American gay writing makes it difficult to miss the quote's immediate allusiveness to the depth of homoerotic love between Cristián and Eduardo.

What is the nature of this love? Clearly, it is a far remove from the stereotype of abject homosexuality that dominates the Latin American imaginary, a stereotype in which a markedly effeminate man sees himself as a woman (and in the confirming gesture of watchful homophobia is so confirmed) and, as a woman, undertakes to win the attentions of an appropriate masculine man; part of the narrative involves the treatment of the former by the latter with the disdain accorded devalued women in general in a masculinist society, providing thereby the soap-opera pathos that is an essential ingredient of this paradigmatic homosexual narrative. There are so many examples of this narrative in Latin American culture that it is sufficient to cite a classic text like Manuel Puig's 1976 *El beso de la mujer araña* to characterize the vast bulk of them. (Interestingly enough, it was an Argentine director also working in Brazil, Héctor Babenco, who made Puig's novel into a film, but this time the film version was in English, the 1985 *Kiss of the Spider Woman;* see the discussion of the representation of same-sex desire in Babenco's film in Foster, *Contemporary Argentine Cinema,* 123–135.)

Although there is a degree of abjectness in Eduardo's sense of abandonment by Cristián, the relationship between the two of them is based on a sexual equality of masculinity/machismo that has only recently come to be recognized as potentially a full-fledged homoerotic relationship as well. The Chicano author John Rechy develops the model of the superstud homosexual, as against the legacy of the effeminate man as the only sexual agent who could be called homosexual, in his writing, especially in *The Sexual Outlaw* (1977, revised 1984), and categorically noneffeminate male-male friendships in Latin American literature begin to be read as segueing into the homoerotic with Gustavo Geirola's two critical analyses of José Hernández's *Martín Fierro* (1872/1879, a literary work set in the Argentine pampas at the same time as Borges's story).

The first clear examples of noneffeminate homoeroticism in Latin American fiction are probably Luis Zapata's *Las aventuras, desventuras y sueños de Adonis García, el vampiro de la colonia Roma* (1979) and Darcy Penteado's *Nivaldo e Jerônimo* (1981), and the founding gay text of Latin American literature, Adolfo Caminha's *Bom Crioulo* (1895), is notable despite its chronological proximity to a text like Oscar Wilde's *The Picture of Dorian Gray* (1891) for not repeating effeminate stereotypes. I do not wish to imply that there is anything to lament in a homoerotic model involving "effeminacy" or any other such nonmasculinist construction; the point, rather, is to call attention to the stereotyping, homophobic or otherwise, of this one model as necessarily the foundation of all same-sex male relationships (see the analysis of these issues as they relate to Latin America by Manzor-Coats).

Eduardo's love for his brother is continuous with a hypermasculinity that allows for no confusion with the feminine, no mistaking him with occupying any position of sexual subjectivity approximating that of Juliana, and certainly no exception to the hard-won and hard-defended manliness that he enjoys as part of his public persona. Neither is there an inside/outside problematic as regards a disjunction between public space and private space, no need to cover up a way of (sexual) being in the latter that cannot intrude on the former: there is no closet in *A intrusa*, because none of the signs that one might wish to maintain in the closet—dress, manner, behavior, acts—occur (at least not yet in the narrative's chronology) in Christensen's film. It is only later when Cristián says to Eduardo, prior to disposing of Juliana once and for all, with reference to their shack, "Here, it is only about us" that the need for the closet might begin to emerge. But in order to get to that point, an extensive amount of negotiation, with considerable attendant violence, must be gotten through.

Cristián is at first at a loss as to how to deal with his brother's high-pitched (if stoically unarticulated) despair. Eduardo tries to bring a woman of his own home but suddenly thinks better of it, as he unceremoniously yanks her out the door to take her back to town. When Cristián has to leave for a few days to tend to some business (the brothers, like many gauchos, depend on selling hides for their livelihood), he tells Eduardo to feel free to make use of Juliana. There is never any doubt as to Eduardo's ability to perform with a woman: another distracting element of the effeminate stereotype is that such sexual subjects are unable to perform with women; the belying of this is a major plot element in *El lugar sin límites* analyzed elsewhere in this monograph. By having sex with Juliana, he is, in a very real sense, having sex with his brother, which may explain from one point of view the bravura of his performance. The scene in which Eduardo makes love to Juliana repeats the outlines of the earlier scene in which Cristián possesses the woman, complete with the same degree of concentration by the camera on his body and on the display of his buttocks.

But the sharing of Juliana becomes untenable, another element of tension between the two brothers and also the occasion of Eduardo seriously wounding another man in a knife fight. Eduardo becomes outraged at the man's mocking query as to whether Juliana, despite living with the two men, is still a virgin. This man's brother will be wounded in another fight by Cristián, standing in for Eduardo, who was wounded in the first fight (as Domingo Faustino Sarmiento notes in chapter 3 of his classic 1848 study of the gaucho, *Facundo,* the purpose of the knife fight among gauchos is to wound rather than to kill, presumably because of the humiliation occasioned by being a defeated survivor). This is the only time in the film in which there is anything close to a public accusation of irregular sexuality in the Cristián/Eduardo household. If this all sounds a bit schematic, it is because it is a point of semiotic efficiency in the film: there is something like an ars combinatoria between the two brothers and Juliana, and the two duels are extensions of it, all with the effect of underscoring the negotiations that are going on between the two brothers with respect to the presence of Juliana in their lives and the disruption of their personal bond that it has brought about.

These negotiations continue with the first attempt to get rid of Juliana: Cristián, with Eduardo in tow, bundles Juliana off to the brothel, where he sells her to the madam for three hundred pesos; in an interesting gesture, he magnanimously gives some of the money to Eduardo. After all, Eduardo possibly saved his brother's life when he killed a poisonous snake in the grass by chopping its head off with his machete while Juliana looked on. Eduardo's masculine symbol, the machete, eliminates a sign, the snake in the grass, associated with woman, an agent of evil who always and forever upsets the balance of a properly maintained world of masculine values, homosocial bonds, and, by extension, homoerotic affection.

Yet, the story does not end there. Each man sneaks off separately to visit Juliana at the brothel, a fact that does not mean that the bond has been broken between them and that each has separately and individually committed his affections to Juliana, with an ensuing masculinist duel for the woman's affections. Quite the contrary, as a grizzled gaucho at the brothel utters the dictum to the effect that any man who thinks about a woman for more than five minutes is a fairy. Both Cristián and Eduardo are thinking about Juliana a lot, not because they respectively want her, but because they seem to need to make a point to each other about each other, which affords a highly ironic resonance to the old man's comments, even if they are a long way from being fairies in any ostensibly effeminate sense of the word (*maricão* is the word the old gaucho uses, which is a frontier Brazilian adaptation of *maricón,* the paradigmatic Spanish word for "faggot" or "fairy"). Cristián, however, discovers Eduardo in line at the brothel, and coming to the practical conclusion that there is no reason to wear out the horses, undertakes to buy Juliana back from the madam.

The most important sequence of the film takes place after the two men have returned home with Juliana, who reinstalls herself in her own bedroom. In one of the most turgidly homoerotic scenes in Latin American film, Cristián and Eduardo both make love to Juliana at the same time. One cannot really speak of a sexual threesome, since it is questionable that Juliana is a full-fledged participant in the act. In one sense, her participation is an extension of the way in which she is a partner in lovemaking with one or another of the two men individually. That is, all she is required to do is to lie still or to move minimally as required by her partner. This is the only participation demanded of Juliana, although she allows her upper body to be lifted in an embrace, she engages in minimal caressing of the man, and she moans quietly. However, it is not completely clear that her moaning is sexual pleasure, since she does not engage in any other movement associated with enthusiastic sexual participation. Indeed, she is always seen lying almost rigidly, her legs closed even during the highest pitch of her partner's involvement.

This leaves the matter open to varied speculation: (1) It is the standard position for the female in rural lovemaking at that time; perhaps other positions would have been associated with licentious prostitutes (when the madam sells Juliana back to the Nilsen brothers, she demands a two-thirds profit in her investment, claiming that Juliana has learned a lot in the time she has spent in her house); (2) It serves narratively as a counterpoint to the intensity of the brothers' sexuality, thereby highlighting the sexual need of both Cristián and Eduardo (more on their sexual needs below); or (3) It serves cinematographically to enhance the display of the male body, since the thrashing legs of the woman would have interfered in the leisurely gaze at the men's bodies, their legs, their buttocks, their backs, their arms, all sculpted by the hard physical labor of the pampas (more also on Cristián's and Eduardo's bodies below).[6] One commonplace of feminist commentary on the sexual utilization of female bodies by men who have little or minimal emotional involvement with the women they are having sex with is that the woman's body serves as an instrument of masturbation, little more than an inert doll and not far removed from one's own hand (which is often anthropomorphically euphemized in Spanish as Doña Manuela).

When the two men have sex together with Juliana, her role does not significantly change; it is not even clear what sort of sex sharing they engage in with her, as there is only the briefest suggestion of a simultaneous vaginal/anal penetration of her body; since neither sexual fluids nor sexual climax could be portrayed in a serious Brazilian film of the period, it is not clear how the two men come to climax or even that they do. If they do, it is likely that it may have been more a question of frottage than penetration. Either possibility only serves to enhance the way in which the two male bodies necessarily come into contact with each other as part of the sexual act. As Juliana's body disappears beneath the combined weight of these two imposing gauchos, the camera makes clear that the act is about their shared sexuality, not merely their simultaneous relations with Juliana: no matter what is taking place, it is taking place in ways that mean more than Cristián and Eduardo sharing Juliana's body, since the bodies of both men become involved with each other. This is true no matter what the specific nature is of the sexual acts taking place.

If frottage is involved, it is difficult for each man to have a clearly delimited region of Juliana's body: as both roam freely over her body, they are roaming over zones where the other may have, must have been with his body, thereby sharing with each other's body the fluid traces left on Juliana's body of their separate bodies (sweat, precum, perhaps finally semen). If simultaneous penetration is involved, part of the inevitable sensation is the presence of the penis of the other, separated by the merest of membranes and striving toward each other in the rhythm of coitus: one man may stimulate the other as much as each is stimulated by the woman's body, and if the sex becomes interfemoral at any moment, the men are directly stimulating each other. Finally, as though the foregoing were not physical realities enough as concerns the erotic pulsations that cannot help but pass between two men having sex with the same woman, at various points in the scene, the men end up groping for each other's bodies and, finally, engaging in a fiercely shared kiss between the two of them; it is at this point that the body of Juliana disappears completely between the joined heads of the two men.

As though Christensen had to back away from the increasingly overt homoeroticism of this scene, which lasts almost five minutes on the screen, Juliana's body reappears, her crotch grasped by Eduardo. Now, this is not a particularly reasonable finale for two reasons, the most obvious one being the masculinist aversion to the discharges of the female body; another is that it implies an unmanly interest in the stimulation of the female body: for a frontier gaucho of their day, the simple presence of his body and then the act of penetration are supposed to be sufficient for a woman, with sexual foreplay and afterplay being unnecessary, unwise, perhaps even unhealthy manipulations of the female body, even more so when zones of contaminating fluids are involved.

I would read this closing gesture on Eduardo's part in a more narratively symbolic way. It is Eduardo who, although he is not unable to have sex with a woman, is primarily interested in his brother, and it is Eduardo who is jealous of Juliana's invasion of their privately shared domestic space. Consequently, the covering of Juliana's vagina at the end of their shared sexual act, which has required considerable involvement between the two men's bodies (within the limitations of the relatively decorous eye of the camera of serious filmmaking), is a gesture as though to signal to his brother that this must be a forbidden realm for Cristián; this brings with it the concomitant insinuation that the only sexual realm open to Cristián is his, Eduardo's, body.

It is after this shared sexual experience that Cristián affirms to Eduardo that their shack is for them alone. In his slough of jealousy, Eduardo has refused to comply with one of the customs of the pampas, to provide lodging to another gaucho passing through; the latter, unable to understand Eduardo's expressions of anger toward him, rides off after having shouted at Eduardo that he must be crazy. Cristián rides up at that moment, and his comment is in response to Eduardo's version of the exchange. The next day, Cristián kills Juliana and hides her body under a load of hides that they will take to the trading post. When he tells Eduardo what he has done, Eduardo dismounts and pulls the hides aside to reveal Juliana's body, on her back and staring up, the same position she had previously assumed in fulfilling her sexual obligations first toward Cristián, then toward Eduardo, and then toward the two together. As the camera pulls back, the screen is overwritten with the closing words of Borges's story: "Se abrazaron, casi llorando. Ahora los ataba otro vínculo: la mujer tristemente sacrificada y la obligación de olvidarla." ["Almost weeping, they embrace. Now they were linked by yet another bond: the woman grievously sacrificed, and the obligation to forget her"] (Borges, *Collected Fictions*, 351). Indeed, the best way of forgetting one lover is to fall into the arms of another, and the camera lingers on the long embrace between the two brothers under the splendid sunset of the pampas.

Borges's closing words are just as problematical as so much of what this enigmatic narrator wrote, and they leave all sorts of questions hanging: What has Juliana been sacrificed to/for? Why is this sacrifice a sad one? (One can be certain that Borges did not use words carelessly and would not have used a facile adverb in this line.) One assumes that in a culture that legitimates the killing of others for material or symbolic survival (i.e., the preservation of masculinity), one forgets one's victims, especially as there are likely to be so many. But why is there an "obligation" to forget this one? Surely not because the victim is a woman: in a society that undervalues women, one's losing opponents in the struggle of masculine supremacy are more likely to be remembered, since their valor reminds one of the legitimacy of his own masculinity.

Eduardo's homoerotic abjection may provide the key here, since it is only by undertaking definitively to forget the woman that almost divided their brotherly unit that that unit can be reaffirmed and strengthened in the domestic space that is now categorically theirs alone (as in Cristián's aforementioned assurance to Eduardo). Juliana has been sacrificed to the bond between them, first symbolically in disappearing beneath their bodies joined in her bed and now literally as they undertake to dispose once and for all of her body (which they were earlier unsuccessful in disposing of by selling her to the brothel madam). I do not mean to imply this all works out like clockwork in Christensen's film. Rather, I am pointing to a series of events and an enigmatic textual overlay: as only the second such overlay in the film, it cannot fail to evoke the first one, the clearly suggestive homoerotic one of David's amorous lamentation to Jonathan.

I want to close by referring to the bodies of Cristián and Eduardo and to their presumed sexuality. As I have stressed above, in no way does the film read them as "gay" in a contemporary sense nor as "effeminate" in the classic homophobic sense. I repeat: these are men's men, and they move freely in the world as such, completely accepted for their imposing masculinity. This masculinity is overdetermined by their bodies. Christensen's actors are drawn from the world of Brazilian television, which is not surprising: in Brazil, the same personnel routinely move between the theater, television, and filmmaking. But José de Abreu (Cristián) and Arlindo Barreto (Eduardo) have the bodies of contemporary Brazilian actors, sleek, unblemished, and muscled in the way that professional training, and not rough-and-tumble cattle herding, brings. Christensen's camera dwells on their bodies. It dwells primarily on their handsome faces, underscoring the intense flicker of emotions between them that foreshadows the intensity of their physical coming together over Juliana's body.

Barreto/Eduardo is almost dangerously beautiful for a primitive gaucho, especially in the Prell-like perfection of his blond Prince Valiant cut. These two actors, therefore, signal a homoerotic presence through, in the first instance, the display of bodies that evoke the erotic codes of modern urban soap operas—if, in no other way, through the gender ambiguity of male prettiness—and then, in a second instance, through the uncustomary attention provided by a camera that lingers over their nude bodies engaged in first conventional heterosexual sex and subsequently in role-confusing group sex. The fact that such a display of the nude male body—and even more so in such group sex—remains problematic in Brazilian (or Latin American or even U.S.) filmmaking over two decades after *A intrusa* was made only serves to confirm the decided queer relationship sealed by their embrace as they go into the sunset together at the end of the film.

Queer
Transcendence

PLATA QUEMADA

There is a moment, about a half-hour into Marcelo Piñeyro's *Plata quemada* (2000, based on Ricardo Piglia's 1997 novel of the same name), of really quite purely tragic dimensions. I use the word "tragic" advisedly, not in its overused sense of "pathetic" or "unfortunate," nor to capture the inevitable violence and death that stalk all human existence. Rather, I use it in the sense of classical Greek drama to capture that instant in which the individual defies if not the unforgiving gods, the inflexible rules that govern the harsh realities of social life. If surviving means learning those rules and abiding by them, the essence of foolhardiness, leading implacably to untoward consequences, is to believe that one can chose not to abide by such rules or simply fail to do so out of carelessness, arrogance, or misplaced (i.e., ineffective) rebelliousness. The truly tragic, in its classical formulation, emerges when the individual who is otherwise careful about adhering to the rules of social existence—perhaps less out of nobility of purpose and respect for established institutions and more out of a desire to survive through minimizing conflictual errors of behavior—suddenly, in conformance with some other standard of behavior or belief, deviates, often with manifest abruptness, from the dominant code of conduct. In reality, in daily life the individual deviates from or fails to comply adequately with the social code on many occasions, with more or less unpleasant consequences. But in the tragic formulation, it is a particularly notable deviation that unleashes the furious chain of events leading to the violent denouement associated with the dramatic depiction of the tragic dimensions of human existence.

In the foregoing, I have specifically inflected my characterization of the tragic to capture its machinations as they play out in Piñeyro's film because, although the tragic in any of its many specific focuses may drive a wide array of cultural productions, it is particularly prominent in this film as central to every event that takes place, from its sudden incursion in the action forward to the film's violent conclusion. Moreover, because the event of tragic proportions in question is specifically tied to a narrative of homoerotic desire that intersects the main narrative of the film — the fictional version of an actual event, a bank robbery in the Argentine provincial town of San Fernando in late September, 1965 — the question of precisely how a formulation of that desire and the dynamics of homophobia enter into the film is of enormous interest and importance for Piñeyro's interpretation of the real-life events on which his film is based (see the film script, Piñeyro and Figueras's *Plata quemada*, which includes Piñeyro's discussion of making this film).

In 1965, payrolls in Argentina were still being met by cash disbursements. The tragic event in question occurs when what is planned to be a fairly simple heist in a quiet provincial town of an armored van carrying payroll money from a bank falls apart in a blaze of gunfire delivered by the van's armed police guards. One of the basic rules of such criminal operations is that you do not interrupt flight in order to rescue the wounded. If necessary, you deliver to them a coup de grâce (to prevent information being extracted from them by the police), but they must be left behind because of the precious few minutes that make the difference between making a clean escape from the crime scene and being caught by the police (the same is true of guerrilla operations). Yet, when El Nene's partner Ángel is shot in the shoulder by a bank guard, El Nene insists on stopping the getaway car to rescue Ángel from the pavement and pull him into the car before departing the scene. The result is that, because of El Nene's refusal to abandon Ángel or to kill him before the police arrive, the band of robbers is now saddled with a seriously wounded man, a burden that will necessitate revising their escape plans and eventually enable the police to corner them in a take-no-hostages shootout in the apartment where they eventually end up to await the healing of Ángel's wound.

El Nene's insistence on rescuing Ángel is not a sudden manifestation of a putative honor among thieves or a perception that Ángel is so effective a crime operative that he should not be sacrificed in accordance with the usual rules for effecting a getaway. Rather, it is because El Nene and Ángel are lovers. The relationship between El Nene and Ángel exists in what can fairly be called a series of interlocking, unalleviated homophobic instances that attest to the overarching homophobia of Argentine society. It is a homophobia of long standing that has to do with many of the founding circumstances and principles of Argentine society (Sebreli, "Historia secreta"; Jáuregui), Argentina's own version of the project of modernity (which, as part of a medicalized model of society, involved an idealization of heterosexual subjects that excluded what came to be highly ideologically charged definitions of "sick" and nonreproductive homosexuals; Salessi), along with layers of added characterization of sexual deviation that came with the Peronist governments, especially during Perón's second administration and the increased vigilance of various categories of actual and perceived social dissidence: after the death of Evita, who was in many ways a paradigmatic fag hag (Foster, "Evita"; Jamandreu), there was no sympathy for queers in Perón's government, no matter how problematical they were as a consequence of her influential voice, and in subsequent grimly heterosexist military dictatorships. The period of the film, 1965, is one of a very precarious return to constitutional democracy following the overthrow of Perón's de facto dictatorship in 1955 and on the eve of the military takeover of June 1966 that inaugurates a period of specific persecutions of homosexuals as a whole, I would want to underscore, with a compact history of homophobia in Argentina.

During the tentative return to democratic institutions between 1955 and 1965, there are some tentative manifestations of homosexuality (I continue to use this standard, if discredited, term, for reasons that will become clear below), such as one thread in Julio Cortázar's 1960 novel, *Los premios*, published in Buenos Aires by Editorial Sudamericana. But, of course, I am speaking here of a cultural production that begins to manifest a long-standing and heretofore mostly deeply closeted homosexual life in Buenos Aires; the images of this homosexual life, nevertheless, have tended almost exclusively to be those of the transvestite, effeminate *ambiente* as described by Juan José Sebreli in his work and of the particular type of *vida homosexual* whose supposed passing he laments in the face of gay liberation and queer politics, in whatever version they have been reaching Argentina (for a survey of contemporary lesbigay life in Argentina see Gorbato).

Precisely what is at issue in Piñeyro's film—what makes it of interest to contemporary queer politics and what sets it apart as an interpretation of homoerotic desire that is problematically continuous with what was accounted to be the "homosexual life" of the period in which it takes place—is the unalloyed macho masculinity that sustains the images of homoeroticism in the film and that characterizes the subjective identities of both El Nene and Ángel. It is this quality of the film that both constitutes the basis in which it can vie for attention as an example of contemporary queer filmmaking, especially for a country that, except for examples that can be taken as accidentally or circumstantially of queer interest—that is, that can be subjected to a queer reading in spite of their ostensible heterosexist ideology—has very little to offer in the way of a specifically marked queer production (see my analyses of the two important gay or queer films made in Argentina immediately after the transition to constitutional democracy in the 1980s, Foster, "El homoerotismo y la lucha").

Several of the journalistic sources on Piñeyro's film revealingly quote him to the effect that "Si [El Nene y Ángel] te oyen decirles gays, estos personajes te trompean." [If they heard you call them gays, these characters would knock your block off.] Leaving aside the threat of macho homophobic violence and why for Piñeyro or his characters it might be an appropriate response under the conditions postulated, the affirmation implies a disjunctive scope for the terms "gays" and "fully masculine men" that El Nene and Ángel apparently conceive themselves to embody—and which the conventions of the film do in fact serve to underscore. What is notable about this comment is the line it draws in the sand between being gay and being something not to be confused with gay. Traditionally in Argentine society, *homosexual*[1] is a (relatively) more polite—or at least putatively scientifically neutral—term for *maricón* (faggot) in the sense of a social-semiotic complex that brings together propositions of effeminacy, cross-dressing, the desire to be a woman, the proposition of a woman trapped in a man's body, the primacy of presumedly passive anal sex,[2] the goal of a male-to-female sex change operation, and prostitution by men in public places in competition (and accompanied by a goal of being confused) with women.

Whether or not men who self-identify with homoerotic desire can or do accept any of these propositions is open to question, though both the professional literature (medical, juridical, and a marked proportion of cultural production—most internationally recognized for Argentine literature in Manuel Puig's writing, especially *El beso de la mujer araña*, 1976) and what can be called street-level general knowledge subscribe to them and, indeed, generally hold that these propositions function as a vastly synergetic dynamic to characterize a specific and quite often immediately recognizable social type (for an interesting analysis of the interplay between these two broad categories of sexual knowledge see Delany).

By the same token, *gay* in Argentina, and especially in metropolitan Buenos Aires, also has its own specific range of meaning in the social semiotics of sexuality. In many cases *gay* involves, as it does in the United States, an alternative designation to *homosexual,* with the features associated with the latter simply being "translated" wholesale into what is a newer, trendier, more modern (or postmodern) term, one that signals post-dictatorship (post-authoritarian?) Argentina's intention to participate in an international (particularly U.S.-centered) consciousness of individual human rights. Nevertheless, *gay,* beyond simply transferring to its lexical domain what previously had been covered by the term *homosexual,* embraces, as befits its American-European origin, a sense of movement politics, of specific identities, quite commonly the idea of, beyond the conventional medico-juridical proposition that *maricones* are women trapped in men's bodies, a proposition that maintains the heterosexist binary of categorical feminine and categorical masculine, of a sexuality that is neither specifically masculine nor specifically feminine.

This is more the excluded and therefore unanalyzed middle than it is the alternative medico-juridical proposition of a putative third sex (which itself is heterosexist, since the term applies to men but not usually to women whose sexuality other than in conformance with heterosexism frequently simply gets elided). This is so because it implies a certain measure of sexuality under construction, of an agenda open to experimentation and the critical questioning of the multiple levels of heterosexist formulations about both the standard binary roles and those pertaining to the "other," "the dissident," "the alternative." In this sense, *gay* shades off into *queer,* a term not yet as naturalized in Spanish as *gay* has become. It is sensed, more for reasons of orthography than phonology, as still being very much a foreign word. Where *queer* is not used, *gay* will be used to cover its semantic territory, either with an understanding that there is *gay* and then there is *gay,* or with the inevitable fusion of what the term *queer* would like to hold on to as its difference from *gay.* There are other, more naturalizable or naturalized terms in Spanish that have been proposed to be useful for expressing the singular meanings of *queer* (Alzate).

Evidently, none of this—neither *gay* (as Piñeyro clearly indicates) nor *queer*—has anything to do with El Nene or Ángel. Of course *gay/queer* could only be pertinent to them as seen as characters of the film *Plata quemada*, that is, as read from the perspective of social priorities and identities as captured, explicitly or by interpretive attribution, in a cultural product generated in the late 1990s: just as María Luisa Bemberg queers the subjectivity of Sor Juana Inés de la Cruz in her film *Yo la peor de todas* (1990) on the Mexican nun of the early seventeenth century, a period in which neither current sexual terminology nor current sociosexual semiotics existed, it would be difficult—really, quite inappropriate—even in a film made in relation to Argentina in the mid-1960s to speak of characters aligning themselves with late-twentieth-century ideological parameters. I think it would be appropriate to assert that Piñeyro's film becomes queer, *malgré lui,* because of the way in which it interprets El Nene and Ángel and their relationship to their comrades, the crime they have committed, and the police who eventually massacre them (more on this below), but this does not mean that Piñeyro would, or even could, view them as gay men or as queer as to how they sense their sexuality.

What, then, does that leave us with as a way to describe the sexuality that drives the relationship between El Nene and Ángel? Let us begin with the proposition that they are two men who fuck each other. To be sure, we have to take the voice-over narrator's word for this, since we never actually see them engaged in sexual intercourse: we only see them in various states of undress, originally cruising each other in the bathrooms of Constitución (the large train station on the south side of Buenos Aires that has long been notorious for its lower-class—or middle-class-meets-lower-class—tea-room sex) or sharing a bed in less than proper manly separation. The narrator makes the point that Ángel has problems about engaging in sex, but for reasons that have nothing to do with the repudiation of same-sex acts: Ángel subscribes to the old canard that sex drains away virile energy; Ángel also attends to dark inner realms that tend to incapacitate him for open human commerce. After Ángel is wounded and the men have to hole up rather than make a clean escape out of the country as they had originally planned, the two become increasingly alienated from each other until the final holocaust.[3]

El Nene tosses out that he learned to be a *puto* (faggot) while in jail, although it is not clear how either he or Piñeyro understands one being "made" gay/queer; no similar point is ever made of the development of Ángel's sexuality. While their individual reasons for avoiding following through on the same-sex desire that originally brought them together mean that the film has a convenient reason for never having to show — never having to face up to showing and to resolve the staging issues related to having to show — them engaged in anything like one would understand as "real" sex, it is clear that the freeze in their sexual activities has nothing to do with any repudiation of or lingering heterosexist/homophobic concern over same-sex acts. And, just as it allows Piñeyro to avoid having to stage same-sex activity for a still-squeamish Argentine/Latin American audience (a matter that Mexico's Jaime Humberto Hermosillo addressed quite openly, and delightfully outrageously, as early as 1985 in *Doña Herlinda y su hijo*), it also allows him to show that the bond between the two men transcends sexuality, to be inspired more by a deep personal commitment (= love?) between them, which is what leads El Nene to insist on rescuing the injured Ángel in the first place, thereby putting into motion the tragic denouement of the film's story.

One could argue that this is simply historical fact, although Piñeyro has made it clear in other regards that he is not adhering to simply historical fact, and it is important to note that, at least to judge by the evidence of the cultural production available, no Argentine director would find much interest in telling the story of a heterosexual couple that abandoned physical love in order to nurture the supposedly higher spiritual bond between them. I will have more to say below about the seemingly disingenuous way in which Piñeyro plays rather forthrightly the card of homoerotic desire between men while at the same time in the final analysis engaging in the heterosexist suppression captured by the phrase "De eso no se habla."

The most important point to be made about the relationship between El Nene and Ángel then becomes the fact, despite what the homophobic discourse of their society should have taught them,[4] that they do not see themselves as any less men, as any less masculine, as any less securely within the orbit of heterosexist privilege because of the circuit of desire that exists between them and the fact that they both have a past of sexual activity with other men. The film, certainly, could have made an issue out of "homosexuality" as a marked space of criminality, not just because the guardians of heterosexist society do see homosexuality as criminal (hence the presence of the medicalization of so-called deviant sexuality in the project of modernity to which Argentina subscribes beginning in the late nineteenth century; Salessi), but because, in the tradition mined by Jean Genet, homosexuality and antisocial criminality have in com-

mon the radical Otherness of the individual who chooses to subvert conventional morality on all fronts possible. Piñeyro does not opt for the link
between homosexuality and crime as entwined acts of social defiance.
In fact, I know of no Latin American film that has pursued the Genetian
understanding of this link, although there are certainly many examples
of "homosexuality in prison" films, and Piñeyro could well have begun
with El Nene's observation that he "became" a *puto* in prison.

Thus, what Piñeyro does opt for is the depiction of two men who have
sex together and who are, in terms of dominant social models, a couple.
True, they are identified as Los Mellizos, the twins, which seems to be
both a euphemism to avoid calling them a couple (after all, both know
how to defend themselves, know how to *trompear*, so some deference is in
order here), as well as a bit of irony: they are twins in the sense that they
enjoy an exclusive relationship with each other of the sort twins often
do. Yet, there is another dimension to this denomination, and that is the
way in which the term *los mellizos*, precisely because it avoids evoking a
violent reaction from El Nene and Ángel, refers to the way in which they
can only in some sort of problematical way be characterized as *maricones*,
since they hardly fulfill the profile of what in Argentina is typically associated with being a *maricón*. Of course, *maricón* is not exclusively used
to designate the passive partner in a homoerotic dyad nor the medico-
juridical definition of couples who are not surrogate images of man and
wife, at least in appearance. But the fact that there is no indication of
the inquisition nor the resolution in Piñeyro's film of what is at the top
of the list of heterosexist questions regarding same-sex couples—who is
the mama and who is the papa, who is passive and who is active—should
signal that this all-male team must be viewed as outside the scope of the
popular designations of homosexual relations.

This does not mean that the language of homophobia disappears from
the film, that no note is taken of how, despite the fact that there is no
evident physical sex going on and there is no manifestation of a binary
masculine-versus-feminine role assumption involved, these men are different. Both Fontana, the mastermind of the crime, and El Cuervo, the
getaway driver, make comments that underscore for them the deviant
relationship between El Nene and Ángel. El Cuervo flaunts his own
heterosexist masculinity by having sex with his female lover in a room
with the door open; they end up performing under El Nene's gaze, with
the camera focusing on El Nene's contemplation of El Cuervo's buttocks during the sex act. At the same time, there is the insinuation that
Vivi herself is involved in her own game with El Nene, as though say-

ing, "Look, I'm the real woman El Cuervo can have; he doesn't need to have sex with *putos* like you"—a proposition that ignores the reasons why putatively straight men with ample access to women do, after all, have sex with other men, both those they consider effeminate and those they consider equally straight (this is also a theme that Genet, among others, explores, for example in his novel *Querelle de Brest,* 1947).

Although El Cuervo has his back to El Nene, Vivi tells him that they are being watched by El Nene. El Cuervo at first reacts with anger at being spied upon by "ese puto," but he admits that, after all, he does have a great ass. This suggests that El Cuervo is not altogether uncomfortable, after all, in having sex *for* El Nene while having sex *with* his female lover—that is, his sexual exhibitionism could well be part of an erotic transaction with El Nene, such that his female lover would then be used as a pawn in the game El Cuervo is playing for El Nene's gaze. After his comment of self-adulation, El Cuervo does, in fact, initiate sex again with Vivi, although it is not clear to the spectator if El Nene (who at one point closes the door after Vivi has signaled to him that she knows he is there) is still watching. Whereas Fontana is openly disdainful of the sexuality of El Nene and Ángel, El Cuervo appears quite intrigued by it, and on several occasions he makes remarks or overtures of homophobic violence more to open display of the matter than to repudiate it. But this remains a barely explored motif in the film.

To summarize, then, El Nene and Ángel are lovers in multiple ways, and their relationship does provoke various degrees of repudiation in the universe of the film. But yet they are homosexuals, *putos* in a very special way, which is indeed one of the terms that serve at present to cover the meaning of English "queer" when it is not viewed as simply a synonym of "gay." Piñeyro reinforces this special status, first of all, by making use of actors, the Argentine Leonard Sbaraglia and the Spaniard Eduardo Noriega, who comply with stereotypic images of the hypermasculine and are publicly known to be "straight." To be sure, since the emergence of the gay clone in the 1970s (see especially the Chicano writer John Rechy's *Sexual Outlaw,* 1977, revised 1984), the hypermasculine image is part of the gay repertory of sexual icons, especially as one way of refuting (problematically) the street-wise association of male homosexuality with the effeminate man. Yet what needs to be stressed is that the hypermasculine clone is a gay icon, not a paradigm against which heterosexism recognizes the gay/queer male: indeed, it is not always clear to the heterosexist paradigm how the apparently hypermasculine male (i.e., the apparently straight male who defies the semiotics by which heterosexism claims *always* to be able to spot the homosexual) can partake of same-sex desire and acts. This was the base of the confused outcry over Christopher Reeve's exchange of kisses with Michael Caine in Sidney Lumet's 1982 *Deathtrap:* "Oh, no, not Superman" (evoking the conventional, hypermasculine role of Superman that Reeve had played), and the scandal of Hermosillo's *Doña Herlinda y su hijo* is not the homoerotic relationship of a married man with another man, but the fact that Rodolfo is being penetrated in their private refuge by Ramón precisely at the same time Rodolfo's wife begins to go into labor with the birth of their first child in the chambers she shares with her bisexual husband: if he has always been the active partner, he is now willing to play the passive role, totally confounding the heterosexist binary.

By the same token, neither of Hermosillo's characters is stereotypically effeminate, and, if not supermasculine, both comply with adequate masculinist norms. To be sure, this raises ideological questions regarding the privileging of the "adequately masculine" and the implied disparaging of the effeminate, and it underscores the limitations of commercial filmmaking (even with sophisticated artistic and social aspirations) of addressing street wisdom about homosexuality: still lacking are films in which there is an Ángel/El Nene relationship between two men inscribed as effeminate, as well as one in which the effeminate man plays the active role to the hypermasculine but passive partner (i.e., an inversion of the classic "homosexual" paradigm of Babenco's 1976 *El beso de la mujer araña;* see also José María Borgello's novel *Plaza de los Lirios,* 1985). This is part of what is more properly queer about the film: the mining of heterosexist confusions.

However, the key special consideration, so to speak, for at least El Nene's status as a self-identified *puto* is the heterosexual relationship he enters into with the whore Giselle during the thieves' refuge across the river from Buenos Aires in Montevideo. Whether Giselle, as an experienced whore, can "read" El Nene's sexual history or whether she even cares about it, her version of the whore with a heart of gold welcomes El Nene into her life and (in her own version of a fatal mistake) believes him when he says that he loves her and will take her away with him. This relationship can be read on two levels, neither of which is exclusive of the other. In one reading, El Nene, who as previously noted "became a *puto*" in prison and who is clearly frustrated with Ángel's retreat further and further each day into the black hole of his demons, has not opted to "become" straight. Needless to say, from a queer perspective, if becoming a *puto* is a specious proposition, becoming straight is even more so, and one wonders to what extent in the universe of Piñeyro's sexual ideology he could pursue very far the way in which the disjunctive relationship between *puto* and straight comes under erasure in the face of the possibility of a polymorphous sexuality in which the heterosexist binary is viewed as or is rendered an inoperant fiction such that heterosexual and homosexual are an invalidated disjunction. This hardly seems likely, as the film turns quite assertively heterosexist in two instances, the first of which has elements of violent homophobia.

The first instance involves intertwined images of an event involving Ángel and another involving El Nene: Ángel, drunk, wanders into a church and ends up emptying his pockets at the foot of the figure of Christ crucified; meanwhile, El Nene, as the camera cross-cuts between him and Ángel, proceeds apparently to perform oral sex on a conventionally effeminate man who comes on to him in a public bathroom. If El Nene has any residual self-identification as a *puto*, it emerges in the contradictions of this scene, a contradiction that also involves the way in which oral sex especially blurs the division, so important to heteronormativity, between the so-called passive and active roles. El Nene, while carefully articulating a highly representative inventory of the many homophobic terms in Spanish/Argentine that are synonymous with *puto*, frightens the other man by pointing his gun at his head. The man begins to sob, certainly fearing an imminent incident of gay-bashing murder. But it is as though El Nene's sexual arousal depended on the other man's acute fear and humiliation, because we then see him proceed to kneel before the other man and reach for his pants; the camera cross-cuts to El Nene washing his mouth with drink, suggesting he has performed oral sex on the other man. Thus, there is a threatening intersection of homophobic violence and the preamble of murder, followed by an act of putatively passive sex on El Nene's part—although he is certainly the very "active" instigator of the act. This sequence seems less an assertion of El Nene's sexual confusion or even of internalized homophobia. Rather it seems to be a form of sexual drama that represents his anger over Ángel's unavailability as a sexual partner, something that is confirmed by the cross-cut sequence of Ángel seeking some sort of expiation of his demons by emptying his pockets at the feet of Jesus.

The second instance involves the way in which the only fully represented physical sex that takes place during the film satisfies amply the conventions of heterosexist coupling, with all of the full frontal nudity allowed in post-dictatorship Argentina: the film received the most restrictive rating, not for the display of either El Nene and Giselle's sexual

Homoerotic display
in *Plata quemada*

acts or those of El Cuervo and his lover, but for the intimation, limited
to some kissing, of sexual acts between El Nene and Ángel. In this way,
the only time we really see El Nene naked and the only time in which we
see his genitals is when he is making love to Giselle, not with Ángel; El
Nene seems to have no problem functioning as an active male but, as I
have asserted, less because Piñeyro understands that there is no necessary disjunction (although one is often created, as much by gay men as
by the heterosexist paradigm) between being sexually active with either
a man or a woman and more because El Nene has somehow reverted to
heterosexual preferences.

Yet, there is another way of interpreting El Nene's relationship with
Giselle: El Nene's need to find a new refuge for him and Ángel. This possibility involves a profound act of cynicism on El Nene's part: he seduces
Giselle in order to gain access to her apartment, where he intends to
transfer Ángel and the money from the robbery. The public restroom
scene with another man signals to the spectator that Giselle is only a convenient vehicle toward this end and not really a "return" by El Nene to
heterosexuality. Rather than involve Giselle in this scheme, he in effect
expels her from her own apartment; in her anger over his rejection of her,
she informs the police of his whereabouts. In this sense, El Nene's entire
interlude with Giselle has been a put-on. It has been a put-on at Giselle's
expense because of his need to find a new refuge since the house (it appears to be a duplex) he and Ángel share with Fontana and El Cuervo
has become compromised. It is supposed to be empty, but their comings
and goings and the noise they make while in the house have attracted
attention: Montevideo has never had the same degree of anonymity afforded by Buenos Aires, and the overt behavior of the three men, whom
Fontana can barely control, coupled with El Nene's cabin fever, which

leads him to the amusement park where he meets Giselle, is virtually suicidal.

So, in the end El Nene's interlude with Giselle has not really been a return to heterosexuality, no matter how well he functions with Giselle — which is well enough to deceive her into believing he is in love with her. The El Nene/Giselle interlude is based on an efficient heterosexual eroticism that allows the director the opportunity to turn his film into a showcase for the degree of male/female skin that has become almost requisite for credible late-twentieth-century filmmaking. One would have no reservation whatever about this display of unstinting female and male nudity if it were not for the fact that the major proposition of the film — the wholly determining quality of El Nene and Ángel's tragic homoerotic relationship — has hardly anything more visually provocative than the two thieves kissing each other through face-covering bandanas. There is a structural imbalance here that is almost laughable; it becomes frankly ludicrous in the denouement of the film.

Which leads us to the need now to speak of the title of the film. *Plata quemada* (Burnt Money), as it is based on Ricardo Piglia's dirty-realism novel, which in turn is based on barely remembered newspaper and other archival accounts of the period (an underlying motif of both the novel and the film is the way in which the full details of this historic event have been covered up for almost forty years), is the story not so much about a bank robbery as it is about a massive police operation that resulted in the massacre of the protagonists of that heist. Although some viewers might wish that Piñeyro had concluded his film with a bit less of the texture of a Hollywood shoot-out, the simple historical fact is that the police operation by combined Uruguayan and Argentine forces was nothing short of a bloodbath.

Why this is so is the consequence of a simply expressed issue of police procedure: the police are interested neither in capturing the criminals as such nor in recovering the stolen money for its rightful owners but more in obtaining the money for themselves (six million pesos was approximately $25,000 to $30,000 in the prevailing exchange rate in 1965) and, in the process, avenge the death of fallen comrades, the guards shot in the heist. Now, as stolen money goes, this is not a large amount: one will recall that the armored van was on its way from the bank to the municipal offices of a provincial town with a payroll to be paid in cash, and this would never have been an impressive amount of money. Yet, although this was a small-beans operation, some $30,000 from what was to have been a simple textbook assault make up a not insubstantial amount of

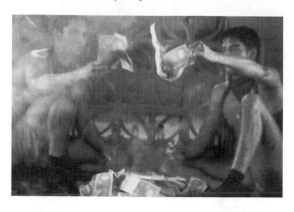

Burning money as
defiant homoerotic
bonding

money. This is an amount of money the police can easily cover up—after
liquidating the thieves.

There are, however, two major details that defy what for the police
will be their own simple textbook operation: El Nene and Ángel are well
aware that no matter what, the police have every intention of liquidating
them, and thus it is El Nene's intention that they die as much as possible in each other's arms;[5] and it is also El Nene's intention that the
police recover not a single peso of their loot. Thus, as the police close
in and the klieg lights are trained on Giselle's apartment and bull horns
scream at them while the bullets fly, the two men, in something like a
drunken stupor, incinerate all of the bills before the police finally burst
into the apartment; El Nene and Ángel do die in each other's arms, but
surrounded by the mounds of ashes of the "burnt money."

Now, one can indulge here in a neo-Freudianesque—or perhaps
Marcusianesque—disquisition on the antithesis between death-dealing
capitalism and liberating Eros: it is money, in the form of the bank heist,
that spoils the two men's personal love relationship. It appears that sex
was a problem for them as a consequence of Ángel's demons, as mentioned above, before the heist, but it is the tension of Ángel's wound and
their being holed up that almost drives them definitively apart. Yet by
contrast, it is the decision to face down the police ambush and to destroy
the real object of that ambush that brings them back into close physical
proximity: Ángel is gleeful for the first time virtually since the beginning of the film. There is no escape for them, not so much because they
are *putos*, although in the sort of Genetian context referred to above, this
might indeed be the case, or because, now as notorious homosexuals, any
return to prison could well mean officially sanctioned and even encouraged sexual abuse of the most violent nature. Rather, there is no escape

for them simply because one of the many variations on the Mediterranean practice of the *ley fuga* [6] means that they must be liquidated in order to obscure intentions by the police to confiscate the loot in the robbers' possession.

As the two men prepare to resist violent police assault to the very end while at the same time undertaking to destroy the money in their possession, they strip down, Rambo-style, for their trial by fire. It would be absurd to indulge in any fantasy about what would be appropriate attire for such a confrontation and what might constitute too much or too little in the way of clothing: these men opt for individualized boxer shorts. Let us say that El Nene wears version A of a boxer design, while Ángel wears version B. Given the relationship between the two men and the fact that they have in a sense come back home to each other (El Nene from Giselle's arms; Ángel from the realm of his demons), one could speculate that the naked warriors/Spartacus model might be appropriate to the circumstances. But no, not even form-fitting briefs, much less bikini-cut, but rather straight-arrow manly boxers are the order of the day.

If I sound like I'm getting carried away here, it is because of the uproarious consequences of Piñeyro's evident decision to shy away from what might be a definitive confirmation of the homoerotic circuit binding the two men — i.e., that they confront their tragic doom in the altogether. Piñeyro decides — and how can one determine whether it is conscious or simply an unexamined reflex of the conventions of commercial filmmaking? — to strategically clothe these Adonises. Their tragic quality,

Ángel and El Nene
reunited in death

enhanced by Everyman's fantasy (straight or gay) of being as hunky as these two heroes, is underscored by their stoic confrontation of the inevitable consequences of the mistake of violating the basic criminal code to dump the wounded. This directorial decision directs attention to the prolonged re-creation of the Hollywood shoot-'em-up finale, with no possibility that the spectator might spend more time focusing on the primary masculine attributes of the two men: if you didn't pay close enough attention to El Nene's body in Giselle's arms, you will not have the chance to see much of it as he wrings his own bloody end alongside his male lover.

Where the ludicrousness of this heterosexist punch-pulling staging really emerges is not in the sort of perverse, resistant reading I am sketching. Rather it comes from a blatant technical error on the part of the support crew: in the final sequence of the film, El Nene and Ángel are wearing each other's boxers. If one were yet even more perverse, it would be possible to entertain the possibility that, during some unreported lull in their death throes, the two men made love and, in their haste, happened to dress in each other's clothes (a confusion that could serve to reinforce the ambiguity over the heterosexist conundrum of who is the active partner and who is the passive one). But there is no textual evidence for this sort of explanation, and we are left with the bald probability that, in going from one day of filming to the other, the wardrobe person got each man into the other's drawers.

In this way, the technical details of getting the filming right (and films are notorious for this sort of flub, which mostly goes unnoticed in the rhythm of the film's delivery of changing scenes) underscore what is a major dimension of Piñeyro's film: the fact that he sets out to organize his film around the tragic flaw represented by love as it intrudes in and intersects with the code of conduct of criminal activity. It is to Piñeyro's enormous credit that that love is portrayed as homoerotic in a way that highlights what is only really alluded to in passing in Piglia's novel. And it is also to Piñeyro's enormous credit that he refuses to indulge in the clichés that hold that homoerotic desire is always doomed to wreck and destruction: love does lead to wreck and destruction here, not because it turns on same-sex desire, but only because it interferes with the severe codes of criminal getaways.

But yet, Piñeyro's credit is diminished by his apparent need to reinvest, if not in the worst and most tired clichés, at least in other clichés of sexual ideology relating to becoming/being homosexual and returning to/recovering heterosexuality. Accordingly, while the film engages in the forthright display of full-bodied physical sexuality when a heterosexual couple is involved (even when it appears to involve a cynical sexual performance on El Nene's part), the only alluded-to and talked-about sexuality that binds El Nene and Ángel, plus the noticeable chasteness in which as a couple they face police annihilation as tragic heroes, all serve to lessen the possibility of the spectator departing the viewing of this film as an uncompromising depiction of homoerotic desire and its intersection with some really very unpleasant truths about the circumstances of life that engender its tragic sense.

AFRODITA, EL JARDÍN DE LOS PERFUMES

Greek and Roman mythology may be the basis of much of Western narrative to the extent that it is not particularly interesting to point out that such-and-such a novel or play or drama or film is based on a certain classical story. Not coincidentally, the same sources are of interest from a lesbigay and queer point of view, as recent scholarship has shown and as the stories in even a very cursory reading reveal. If Ovid and Edith Hamilton are two milestones in pointing out the threat of these materials to bourgeois decency and its avatars, Queer Classical Studies is now a firmly entrenched enterprise (Williams; Ormand). But if a film like Jean Cocteau's *Orfée* (1950), a retelling of the Orpheus legend in such a way so as to bring out the homoeroticism of classical myths, a film project like Pablo César's *Afrodita, El jardín de los perfumes* (1998) is not so much interested in a particular tale as a queer model as it is in telling a particular story such that it first is queered and second may serve to suggest, in quite an impressionistic way, a queer message.

Third in a trilogy with *Equinoccio: el jardín de las rosas* (1990–1991, filmed in Tunisia) and *Unicornio: el jardín de las frutas* (1997, filmed in India), *Afrodita* was filmed in Mali. Although all three films received support from the national Argentine film institute and the Universidad del Cine, where César teaches, none of the three is referentially Argentine or Latin America. Indeed, as I shall point out, the severing of any allusionary basis to Argentine or Latin American sociopolitical reality is part of a distancing effect that sustains a poetic narration that in turn allows for a free rein for highly suggestive homoerotics.

Afrodita is more than the story of Aphrodite. In reality, it is somewhat of a mishmash of classical sources set in the Mali desert and filmed with local actors (preponderantly male, with women being barely present, a gesture of the repudiation of the gender binary and yet nevertheless emphasizing underdetermination in favor of a male dominance). What dialogue there is is spoken in a pseudoritualistic or pseudoclassical language against a backdrop of an eternally blowing desert wind. By saying that the narrative is a mishmash, I do not mean to imply that César gets his sources wrong or makes a narrative mess of them in the attempt to create a new narrative. Rather, in my characterization I simply wish to underscore how, although the main story of Aphrodite being birthed in the foam of the sea from the mutilated genitals of Uranus, which had been severed and cast there by his avenging son, is told in the first part of the narrative, and Afrodita's betrayal of Efesto (Hephaestus)[7] and her love for Ares is told in the second part. The third part of the film describes Afrodita's confrontation with the Immortal Gods assembled in judgment, her denunciation of them for the suffering of mankind, and her rescue from among them by the Argonauts, after which she mutilates her son Priapo (Priapus) by cutting off his arms as a way of preventing him from abetting in the reproduction of an unjust human race.

Afrodita, as the goddess of love, the mother of Eros, and in different forms the goddess of both a purer love and sensual lust, constitutes a crucial network of signifiers relative to various and contradictory ideologies gathered under the macrosememe LOVE, whose multiple inflections are paramount for both the construction of heteronormativity as well as queer desconstructions of it. Priapo, as the god of fertility, is central to heteronormativity, although his mutilation by his mother in César's film in a way other than by castration underscores the value of the phallic for homoeroticism, even when it is read in ways—principally through sexual practices—that deny its fertilizing function.

While Afrodita's betrayal of Efesto can be read from a feminist point of view as legitimating female sexual promiscuity in defiance of the law of patriarchal exclusivity (cf. the role of Mira Sorvino in Woody Allen's *Mighty Aphrodite,* 1995), in César's film it is queered because of the way in which Afrodita segues from being a woman into being a man. This is not the case of the biological dimorphism that is identified as hermaphroditism, which Michel Foucault studied as a trope of the queer because of its confounding of heterosexist binary and which Sedgwick ("How to Bring Your Kids Up Gay") revisits in terms of the imperative through modern science to always resolve this ambiguity as what heterosexism sees as female lack. Rather, it is the case of the body being perceived as either male or female according to the situational narrative of the lovers involved.

Although Afrodita is played throughout César's film by an apparently male body (genitals are never shown, just as lovemaking beyond looking, touching, caressing, and minimal kissing never takes place—these four acts constituting, alternatively, metonymies or synecdoches of the genital sexuality that must be understood to take place after the camera fades or cuts away), that body is equally interpreted as masculine and feminine according to the different sexual desires of the two men. Afrodita, as the object of Efesto's desire, is "feminized" where it is clear that her/his body is viewed as masculine by Ares. In both cases, a queering of the notions of the display body takes place.

As to the feminization of Afrodita's body—of the male body of the actor playing Afrodita—this occurs in two very different ways—narratively and culturally. Narratively, the camera focuses on Afrodita engaged in a cleansing ritual in which she is spied upon by Efesto (this is reminiscent of the sexualization of the body of Diana/Artemis through spying in another classical story of women as sexual signs), who subsequently engages in an adoration of her body. This adoration focuses insistently on the actor's buttocks, which is as much an evocation of the female buttocks as sexual fetish as it is the homoerotic resemanticization of the male buttocks: in heteronormativity, the male buttocks have no erotic value for other men and only occasionally for women (in some Hispanic societies, the male buttocks do constitute a specific heterosexual fetish for women). Since it would be difficult to confuse the actor's buttocks with a female configuration (I realize this is somewhat subjective, but here again lies the queer potential for the insistence on fetishizing this second-degree sex marker), there is a clear semiotic confusion—i.e., queering—generated by the female marker of Afrodita and the displayed masculinity of the actor's body as captured by the camera.

Moreover, from a culturally signed point of view, the actor's body is feminized: *Afro*dita's body is that of a North *Afri*can male, which is characteristically smooth and hairless, as are all of the bodies in this film. From the point of view of an Argentine director, this detail breaks with the normatizing imperative of the hirsute male body in a series of disjunctive male/female binaries via which the body of both sexes is overdetermined in a heterosexist paradigm of corporeal differentiation: specifically in this case, the male body must be marked by the presence of characteristic hair, while the female body must be marked by its removal. Argentine women who can afford to, which to be sure includes any actress, routinely remove axillary hair, in contrast to common practices of retaining it for religious, aesthetic, or social reasons. That is to say, from the perspective of what would be considered appropriately masculine in the heterosexist filmmaking against which César might be situating his film, his actors may all (or predominately) be male, but their bodies disrupt in significant ways those of paradigmatic Argentine male movie stars. Moreover, given the fetishizing of the "white" body in Argentine culture, a fetish that could also be disrupted by the indigenous body, the utilization of the inadequately masculine bodies of a racial Other (the black body, although present and even fetishized in other Latin American societies, is almost virtually absent in Argentine culture, especially in socially and culturally hegemonic Buenos Aires) to tell what are considered fundamental Western narratives is in itself sufficiently disruptive to imply a queer design on the part of the director.

Although César's film appears superficially to be a quirky retelling of a set of classical myths, it is in the third part of the film that a clearer queer agenda is articulated. Accused of adultery by Efesto, Afrodita is taken before the Immortals, where s/he expounds on the baseness of human society and defends the proposition that if she is a female to Efesto and a male to Ares, it is because sexuality is a matter of imagination; this sexual ambiguity is carried out in Afrodita's relations with Hermes and Dionisio (Dionysus). As Afrodita speaks, the assembled tribunal is seared by the sun, and as Afrodita stands over the fallen and calcined bodies of those who would judge her, the Argonauts arrive to carry her off. Although Afrodita bears children with Dionisio, her mutilation of Priapo is at the same time a refutation of heterosexual reproduction.

César's Afrodita is an ambiguous figure in portraying a female god in a male body, bearing children despite refuting the imperative to reproduce a human race that she sees as damned, and at least with Ares, being constructed as an object of homoerotic desire. By refuting the heterosexism that is essential to the sanitizing of classical mythology as it is recycled by patriarchal interpretations of sexuality, César's Afrodita points toward something like a timeless mutability of desire that reinforces contemporary queer postulates about the limitless erotic possibilities of the human body. César achieves this effect in part through utilizing a number of distancing devices that underscore the strangeness of his conception of Afrodita vis-à-vis prevailing versions: his version of Afrodita is as "strange" in terms of the prevailing versions of desire of compulsory heteronormativity as is the sexuality promoted by his film. This "exotic" texture of his film (a term used in an analysis by Marily Canoso included in the press dossier of the film) is enhanced by the radically foreign setting (at least for an Argentine film), the dominance on the sound track of the constant hum of the hot winds across the sand dunes, the use of a pseudolanguage, and, consequently, obligatory recourse to subtitles as the only way of making sense of the dialogue (César may have followed the lead of Paul Humfress and Derak Jarman's 1976 queer *Sebastiane*, in which the dialogues are spoken in Latin; since Latin is taught to few as a spoken language, this obliges the audience to resort virtually exclusively to the subtitles).

Afrodita is a limited film, not so much in its artistry—it was obviously made to counter the language of commercial filmmaking, and it is very competent and original in this regard—but in that it is essentially unavailable on the market and unknown to film registries (the Internet Movie Database, which has at least a sketchy entry for every other Latin American film I have dealt with in recent years, has no entry for this film and no entry for any of Pablo César's work, despite the fact that the Argentine Instituto Nacional de Cinematografía promoted his 1987 *La sagrada familia* internationally).

FRESA Y CHOCOLATE

No matter what other issues are raised with respect to Juan Gutiérrez Alea's film *Fresa y chocolate* (Strawberry and Chocolate, 1993), it is fundamental to hold in view a dominant question: Why do David and Diego never fuck? This matter is never directly addressed by the film, and consequently it is never answered. Moreover, so much of the critical commentary (characteristically in reviews of the film and its relationship to the sociohistorical parameters of postrevolutionary filmmaking in Cuba) focuses on the relationship between these two men as a paradigm in Cuban society for "tolerance" toward difference—sexual difference specifically, but individual difference in general—in the context of the struggle in Cuba to affirm institutional and personal values that do not impose as an imperative the need for the citizen/individual to conform to a rigid scheme of social behavior. Sexual hygiene was one of the original concerns of the postrevolutionary restructuring of Cuban society—more specifically and at least prostitution as a sign of capitalist exploitation, homosexuality as a sign of bourgeois decadence, and an inadequate standard of family life as a sign of an alienated commitment to the appropriate reproduction of the "new Cuban." Inevitably there emerged conflicting ideologies regarding sexuality before the revolution, sexuality as defended by various strands of the revolution, and sexuality as it might be defined against alternative paradigms arising from the interaction of postrevolutionary Cuban society with a very diverse set of allies. Some of the issues are raised elsewhere in this study with reference to the documentary *Conducta impropia*.

Although I will leave for others to chart in detail the influence of postmodernity in Cuba through its interactions with countries like Argentina, Mexico, Brazil, and Spain, the fact that *Fresa y chocolate* points toward the opening of a debate regarding the naturalization of same-sex relations in the mid-1990s in Cuba can only be an influence coming from these (and other) societies, all of which have seen enormous changes in the past ten to twenty years with regard to same-sex relations and institutional, collective, and personal attitudes toward them (on homosexuality in Cuba see Lumsden; Leiner; Behar; Quiroga; on the liberationist ideology of the film see Serna Servín; Bejel's "Strawberry"). It is an open question as to which, if any, of these societies (with the possible exception of Spain at the present moment) can really be called gay-friendly, and much less Cuba, although the imperative no longer to persecute a sex trade necessary to international tourism in Cuba today has brought with it the relaxation of postrevolutionary norms regarding other manifestations of sexuality: sexual hygiene simply cannot be a major issue in Cuban society at the beginning of this decade, and the publication in Cuba of Felipe de J. Pérez Cruz's defense of homosexuality is a notable occurrence (there are also two documentaries on gay Cuba, Kelly Anderson's *Looking for a Space: Lesbians and Gay Men in Cuba*, 1995, and Sonja De Vries's *Gay Cuba*, 1995; both directors are non-Cuban).

It is difficult to know whether this means that Cuba has entered a period of postmodern sexuality (the lesbigay, the queer), a period that allows for the recuperation of the ambiguous zone of homosociality segueing into homosexuality (both the long-standing Mediterranean code in which the *maricón* is a crucial figure and one in which same-sex relations also occur but without being able to be called homosexual in the use of that word as a sign of modernity) or a period of some significant overhaul of the two that marks this particular period of transition in Cuba. Merely to have raised the issue in *Fresa y chocolate* and to have it raised by Cuba's most venerated film director in a film that would attract international attention represents a significant cultural moment. In this sense, it is perhaps legitimate to speak of a film that promotes tolerance, since precisely the decade and a half between the action of the film—the period just prior to the 1980 Marielitos exodus and the mid 1990s is one in which Cuba had to see through a transition from the relative insularity of a fairly rigidly defined postrevolutionary society and the adjustments it has had to make to the disappearance of the Soviet system. Cuba is now supported by societies (the societies in which the film has circulated, in addition to the United States) that are characterized by economic and social liberalism that could hardly tolerate the persecution of sexual freedoms (the film acknowledges support from Mexican and Spanish film entities, as well as from Robert Redford, who has taken a special interest in Cuban filmmaking). I will have more to say about the importance of the particular period in which the film is set, as well as the significance of this historical distance.[8]

The issue of why David and Diego never fuck must be treated on two levels, that of the *enoncé* and that of the *énonciation:* that is, on the level of the story being told by Gutiérrez Alea's film and on the level of his telling. On both these levels, there are ideological problems that must be addressed. These problems have to do with the horizons of coherence with respect to sexual practices at the level of the circumstances in which the characters of the film are immersed, and they have to do with what the film conceives, through its strategic handling of the story of those lives, as the possibilities of relating same-sex relationships to the postrevolutionary *hombre nuevo,* a strategic phrase that appears in the title of the Senel Paz text on which the film is based, *El lobo, el bosque y el hombre nuevo* (1991).

On the level of the story being told, the film subscribes to a series of ideological assumptions—that is, it reduplicates them—that characterize fundamental assumptions regarding sexuality and the parameters of same-sex relations even while it is satirizing many of them, toward presumably forging a critique that might induce their revision by enveloping everything to a delightful degree in a broadly picaresque Cuban sense of humor. The film turns on the desire of Diego, a minor cultural bureaucrat, to seduce David, a serious university student, apparently firmly committed to the principles of the Juventud Comunista (Communist Youth). Diego has taken photographs of David in a production of Ibsen's *A Doll's House* (that marvelously heteronormative text, even if ironically and critically), and he hopes that offering David these photographs will draw him into a relationship (one suspects subsequently that these photographs never existed, since after all, David never obtains them from Diego). Moreover, Diego has made a bet with his friend Germán, a sculptor, that he will be successful in luring David home to have sex with him; Diego will display from the balcony of his apartment David's shirt as a confirmation that the mission has been accomplished.

Diego comes on to David at an outdoor table at the Coppelia ice cream parlor in downtown Havana. Germán watches from a nearby table. Since places at the tables are limited, Diego joins David, who is sitting alone at a table, and attempts to put his plan of seduction into action. An additional detail is the full display Diego makes on the table of books that are impossible to obtain in Cuba (i.e., in every sense banned) but that are extremely coveted reading, specifically Mario Vargas Llosa's *Conversación en La Catedral* (1969), one of the key texts of the so-called Boom of the Latin American novel of the 1960s and 1970s, of interest because of its treatment of a period of military dictatorship in Peru. David shows interest in the books, while he also appears anxious to recover the photographs, not because they are compromising but presumably because they are in the hands of a very openly homosexual man, a *maricón*.

In this way, the film recycles a set of Latin American stereotypes that eventually become problematical for the film. The most significant one is the disjunction between the straight man and the flamboyant homosexual. David, as played by Vladimir Cruz, is almost grimly straight. Although he has a boyish body, he is fully conscious of the heterosexist responsibility of being a man, with an intense and forthright gaze that brooks no doubt from the other as to his fulfillment of a prescribed inventory of features in appearance, bearing, and speech that conform to patriarchal norms. When first confronted by Diego, David is brusque to the point of rudeness, taking care to transmit to Diego the information that there should be no mistaking David's commitment to heterosexuality and his accompanying abhorrence of the sexual deviancy of the *maricón* and his transparent discourse of seduction: David stares boldly at Diego while his hand reaches into one pocket of his shirt, pointedly withdrawing his ID card whose cover identifies him as belonging to the Juventud Comunista and then putting it into the pocket on the other side of the shirt.

Under the circumstances, given the sexual hygiene that was integral to the Juventud, this is the equivalent of flashing a marriage band under the nose of one's seducer: in a heterosexual context, it means that one is not available; in a same-sex context, it is the suggestion of the brass knuckles awaiting the queer[9] tempter in the homophobic violence that is the only appropriate response to the insistent come-on. David, however, is still interested in the photographs Diego has, and thus he remains engaged in conversation with the latter while at the same time barely refraining from converting his request for the photos into a threatening demand. At the height of the persecution of undesirables and their confinement to the rehabilitation/forced labor UMAP camps barely a decade earlier, it would have been sufficient for David to denounce Diego as having attempted to touch him inappropriately for the police to have hauled Diego off, as Reinaldo Arenas explains in his autobiography *Antes que anochezca* and as is captured in Julian Schnabel's film version, *Before Night Falls* (2000). Perhaps this is still a possibility in 1979, when the action of the film takes place, but it is clearly not in the spirit of *Fresa y chocolate* to engage in the representation of homophobic violence, precisely because Gutiérrez Alea wishes to lead his audience toward a public ethos in which being homosexual is naturalized, as much as it is asserted, if only by implication, that revolutionary Cuba has outgrown concerns over public sexual morality that made possible the UMAP camps, aggressive policing practices, and the unquestioned/unquestionable right of the straight to denounce with impunity the queer.

Toward this end, *Fresa y chocolate*, on the level of the *énociation*, implicitly mocks David's attitudes, and the rhetoric of the film's language tends to convince the audience of the ridiculousness of his behavior: his phobic horror of Diego's come-on and the transparency of Diego's attempts to engage him seductively, the franticness with which he is on guard against the possibilities of further seduction when he does agree to go to Diego's apartment (including the way in which he is made the butt of Diego's joking reference, in the collective taxi upon arriving at his house, to David as "Papito" [Daddy] and another passenger picks up on the joke); his alarm when he finds homoerotic icons in Diego's apartment; the comic earnestness of his report on the experience to Miguel, one of his fellow university students back in the dorm, a young man whose own earnestness is also ridiculed in the film. Of particular interest is the way in which the film implies a critique of David's duplicitousness when he decides to pretend to be Diego's friend, at Miguel's suggestion, in order to get the goods on the subversive faggot (Manuel is apparently something of a monitor of other students' behavior). This is a particularly noteworthy detail of the film because it underscores the possibility of consciousness of two crucial facts. The first concerns how the repugnant nature of the disingenuousness of the practices whereby the straight set out to entrap the queer, out of the belief that queers are so repugnant, so vile, so injurious to public well-being that no attempt to identify and liquidate them can lie outside the pale of what is morally or ethically acceptable: given the horror of same-sex desire and its practices, no act of betrayal can be so grossly unjust as to be reproachable. Thus, when David subsequently warms to Diego's person, when a true bond of friendship (but never homoerotic love?) develops between them and when David defends his relationship with Diego to Miguel, the latter's repudiation of David's attitude and behavior reduplicates, in an even more hysterical pitch, David's original reaction to Diego.

The second matter at issue here for the film as text is countermanding the way in which queers are allegedly duplicitous in their conquest of straight men. The assumption appears to be that because straight men possess a sane and healthy sexuality, they can only be reached through subterfuge and deceit—they must be tricked into yielding up their healthy manhood to the corruption of the queer. This would seem to be borne out in *Fresa y chocolate* by Diego's attempts to trick David into going to his room (promising him the photographs and access to banned literature). He spills coffee on David's shirt in order to force him to remove it so it can be cleaned, thereby tricking him into revealing more of his manhood than sober heterosexuality would allow—David firmly insists that he be provided with something to cover himself with—and so that he can display the shirt from the balcony to Germán as a sign that he has successfully seduced David, which is, in turn, a bit of double deceit on Diego's part, since no seduction, as it is customarily understood, has taken place, although this remains to be seen as the film develops. However, these are fun and games by comparison to the betrayal of friendship that David agrees with Miguel to participate in so as to trap Diego and more effectively to denounce him to the authorities. Thus, David returns to Diego's apartment, ostensibly in search of the promised banned books and ostensibly to progressively thaw out in his icy distance from Diego.

The interpersonal dynamics of David's stringing Diego along requires David to accept Diego's offer of black market, U.S.-imported scotch;[10] the film jumps to David being treated for his hangover by the patriarchal Miguel and being warned as to the subterfuges of the enemy. What makes this jump cut a source for the ridiculousness of David's behavior is that, in passing, the only real action of homoerotic behavior of the entire film takes place at this juncture: the two men are in their underwear and, after holding David's head under the cold-water faucet, Miguel playfully slaps him on the buttocks, exclaiming at how nice and chubby his *culito* (ass) has become. Given the fact that Diego never touches David of his own accord, this bit of homosocial bonding, built around the ritual of the good buddy helping a guy through the rough spots of a bad hangover, cannot be missed as the film's further underscoring of the ridiculousness of the soberly straight line David attempts

David's self-discovery
in the "other" universe
of Diego's apartment

to sustain in conformance with Miguel's recommendations. Thus, on the level of the story being told, there is a direct appeal to the codes of heteronormativity and its conventional stance vis-à-vis recognized homosexuality, while at the same time the rhetorical strategies of the film question heteronormative assumptions and in fact openly ridicule some of them as they refer to the presumed conduct of gays and the legitimation of the reaction to them by those who identify themselves as straight.

There is, however, another framing of David's mentality that is even more slyly critical than the representation of his reaction to Diego's attempts to seduce him, and that is the way in which, even before Diego appears on the scene, the first ten minutes of the film are devoted to undermining the security of David's machismo (if not his masculinity). The film opens with David and his girlfriend Vivian having just arrived at a seedy hotel where lovers go to resolve the perennial problem of the lack of any other place to make love.

Although David is determined to have sex with Vivian and is further encouraged in his desire by the scene in the next room he spies on through a peephole he accidentally discovers while Vivian is in the bathroom, he is quickly confused by her wounded woman's "All you want is to have sex with me" speech. In a gesture of nobility, he jumps out of bed, reaches for his clothes, and promises to "respect" her until they are married and he can take her to a five-star hotel; the scene ends abruptly with the startled look on her face and the accompanying exclamation "¡Qué!" (Huh). This scene is designed to provoke the first outburst of laughter from the audience, because it is obvious that poor David completely loses himself in the sexual script he is expected to follow, with the result that he wastes his opportunity to assert his machismo and thereby to have sex with the very willing Vivian, who after all is only following the social script assigned to her not to be sexually aggressive but rather to be virginally reticent.

The camera cuts to Vivian's splendid wedding day, teasing with the audience as to the identity of her bridegroom. Of course, we see that it is not David, and with a haughty toss of the head in his direction (he is lingering in the background of the wedding party), she resolutely signs the civil registry. To add injury to insult, in this characterization of David's inadequacies as a paradigmatic Cuban macho, when they subsequently meet (David appears not to be able to get her out of his mind and hangs around her house), she offers to have sex with him. He is offended that, in a reversal of the macho scheme of things, she sees him only as a sex toy, and he stalks off angrily. It is with even greater reason that David is offended by Diego's advances after Vivian's wedding, because she has implicitly questioned his manhood, first with her pique at his inability to deliver—not for reasons of sexual inadequacy but out of a misplaced sense of bourgeois nobility—at the hotel and then by her decision to marry another man and throw the image of that decision in his face. Nevertheless, it is after spurning Vivian's offer of a sexual dalliance that David begins significantly to loosen up in his relationship with Diego, which slowly moves onto a plane of authentic friendship and affection. If David hangs around Vivian's house, it is perhaps because he needs her to confirm to himself that he is not gay: after all, one of the primary sociosexual functions of women in a (hetero)sexist society is to provide men with opportunities to affirm their manhood, not to women but to themselves and to their cohorts, through the use of women as a mirror for the male, in the endless and yet never conclusive demonstration that they are not queer.

Diego is equally a stereotype that constitutes a shorthand bundling together of diverse dimensions of the heteronormative definitions of the queer and what are assumed to be unproblematical understandings about the relationship of the queer to straight men. Diego is the paradigm of the flaming queen, whether it is in his mannerisms, his clothes (especially in private—precisely the aggressive police practices against queers focused on hair length and dress as primary signs of sexual deviancy), his voice/speech/language, his cultural choices and priorities (the defining passion for the operas of Maria Callas), and especially, in this case, his preference in food. The title of Gutiérrez Alea's film captures metaphorically the heterosexist binary as displayed by the choice of ice cream flavors at the Coppelia—men have chocolate and women strawberry; David is, of course, eating a bowl of chocolate ice cream, but when Diego sits down at David's table, he not only begins to savor his strawberry ice cream but to engage in an exuberant rap in its defense, going on about a succulent strawberry he has found in his bowl as though it were a ripe sexual fetish. Throughout this sequence, Diego manifests, in the very public space of the outdoor patio of the busy Coppelia, a stock array of characteristics associated with the homosexual male.

Diego's overdetermined behavior points in two directions. In the first place, it is a performance designed both to make it clear to David that he is cruising him, but it is also directed toward Germán, who is the specific audience of his friend's plan of seduction. Yet, Diego's behavior is so overdrawn at this point in which one knows little about either Diego or David that one wonders why the latter doesn't simply get up and leave when Diego launches into his routine. This leads to the possibility that Diego's performance is as much directed toward the audience as toward David and Germán: Gutiérrez Alea has Diego engage in a performance as an outrageous queen before the audience of the film as part of an opening gambit to appeal to the viewers' expectations regarding homosexuals and challenge their assumptions about the legitimacy of such a sexual persona.

In so doing, however, Gutiérrez Alea gives up a measure of semiotic capital while at the same time gaining in another quarter. He loses semiotic capital by very narrowly circumscribing the nature of the sexual persona identified with same-sex desire. By circumscribing the homoerotic to the outrageous queen (which in its specifically Cuban version is represented in Luis Felipe Bernaza and Margaret Gilpin's documentary *Mariposas en el andamio,* 1996), Gutiérrez Alea collaborates with a prime heteronormative practice. This is the belief to the effect that being a homosexual not only means assuming the so-called passive role in sex but in manifesting that fact—that is, that one is assigned to playing the passive role—by performing the part of the screaming queen as an overt display of one's "feminine position." Such a fissureless homology is less problematic in terms of the manifest performance, although it does reduce the targets of homophobia to only those who so perform, and assumes without the need for further evidence that by so performing, the individual necessarily engages in the not-always-visible acts that are the putative reason for the violence of homophobia. To be taken to be performing as the sexual deviant is the unquestioned equivalent of being taken to be, with a full range of horrendous attributes, the sexual deviant. Such a homology is more problematical in eliding the full range of the homoerotic as identity, feeling, desire, and practices: individuals who may pursue same-sex relations without performing as queens, unless they carelessly reveal themselves in other ways, remain free of a homophobic violence that focuses on that performance.

The *mépris* homology at issue here not only assumes such a bidirectional equivalence of queenly performance and sexual deviance (to be a queen means being a deviant; if one is a deviant, one will necessarily perform publicly as a queen) in what is supposed to really matter (the nonreproductive practice of acts against nature). It also forecloses any way of describing what heteronormativity might want to denounce as sexual deviance that does not involve performing publicly as a queen. This is the Rock Hudson paradox of the presumptions about ways of being nonheterosexual. To be sure, such a possibility of dramatic irony in *Fresa y chocolate* whereby Diego would end up really being more heterosexual than David is not a possibility, and indeed the film continues relentlessly to be driven by a conception of the mutual exclusivity of the categories of sexual desire even while striving for the naturalization of the *maricón* as a legitimate social subject of revolutionary Cuba. In their encounter prior to Diego's departure to accept an invitation from an unspecified foreign embassy—a decision he is forced to make because while David may now accept him, the revolutionary system cannot, and he is fired from his position as a cultural bureaucrat—David is radiant with the fulfillment of his sexual encounter with a woman, while Diego mimes the nausea that the thought of straight sex can only have for the totally committed *maricón* he prides himself on being.

Diego's miming on the level of the story being told is, certainly, another gesture by Gutiérrez Alea, in the film as cultural text, toward an audience that also holds such a belief about queer men, which in turn ought to provoke its own form of nausea in the straight male because of its overt rejection of the joys of sex with a woman and its implied preference for sex with another man: the representation of the relationship between Diego and David both opens and closes with appeals to the horizons of knowledge of the audience with regard to sexual preference.

Yet, if *Fresa y chocolate* invests in Diego a compact range of stereotypical queerness, it is important nevertheless to comment on the relative bodily presence between David and Diego. David at no time betrays any of the overt signs that would make him suspect from the point of view of the policing of sexual hygiene—that is, at no time is he in any danger of causing a blip in the radar screen of scopic homophobia; Diego strives for a perfect performance of the homosexual queen. Yet the simple fact is that Diego's body is manlier than David's. Jorge Perugorría has a muscular, pilose body that he shows to advantage; this body is particularly well utilized by Perugorría in films subsequent to *Fresa y chocolate* in which the hypermasculine display of his characters, synergized by his physique, is particularly evident (as though affirming that he, the actor, despite his role in *Fresa y chocolate* is definitively straight—a highly ironic possibility in terms of the aforementioned Rock Hudson paradox whereby the more insistent the display of heteronormative masculinity is, the greater the latitude is to suppose an ironic stance toward compulsory heterosexuality). Moreover, it should be noted that masculine bodily display is traditionally more legitimate in Cuba (and other Latin American societies, but not all: Argentina and Mexico, for example, would be exceptions) than in the United States.

The foregoing is a difficult generalization because of the many changes in American society directly relating to queer culture on the one hand and the greater informality of public dress in recent generations. However, the so-called gay clone image in American society coincides in many ways with a form of masculine display that is not necessarily marked in Cuban society, as can be seen from the well-displayed masculinity of Perugorría's character, for example, in his next film, Gutiérrez Alea's 1994 *Guantanamera* (in which the female lead is played by Mirta Ibarra, Diego's neighbor and spiritual sister, the sometimes suicidal black marketeer Nancy in *Fresa y chocolate*). I have written about the effective use of masculine bodily display with reference to the Brazilian Paulo Thiago's film *Jorge, um brasileiro,* 1988 (Foster, *Gender and Society,* 18–27). Jorge is also a straight character, invested iconically with all of the socially redeeming features associated with the heteronormative imperative whereby being straight means contributing to the reproduction of citizens for the State and reaffirming a series of manly virtues that sustain its proper functioning. The point is that Diego's hunky presence occupies the space also filled by the imposing straight man such as he presents in *Guantanamera,* where he is, in fact, a social redeemer, making that space suddenly ambiguous.

Moreover, Diego is really quite handsome, almost pretty, with dark, penetrating eyes, luxurious eyelashes, and smooth, well-kept skin, features that are traditionally suspect in an American male (historically in the United States, a man ought not be too good-looking),[11] but not in the complex of features prized by the Latin lady's man. Finally, what is most striking about Diego's physical beauty, aside from the ambiguity that it may provoke in a classification between straight and queer men, is that alongside David, Diego is the more imposing man. It is not that David is effeminate or slight (often also taken as a sign of effeminacy), but simply that Diego's muscular body overshadows David's often almost scrawny look. Vladimir Cruz's body, as seen in a recent Cuban film like Eduardo Chijona's 1999 *Un paraíso bajo las estrellas*, is much more filled out and muscular, without quite becoming the mesomorph Perugorría is, and this leads one to wonder if Cruz is deliberately made up in *Fresa y chocolate* to have a more emaciated look alongside Perugorría (Perugorría speaks of playing this "truly great role" in his interview with Kirk and Pardura Fuentes, 171; see also the interview with Birringer). Even if this is not so, the simple fact remains that Perugorría is quite hunky, which both underscores and undermines the queenliness of his character Diego. It underscores it because that queenliness is disconsonant with his hypermasculine presence, and it undermines it because it breaks the stereotype of this wispy gay man.

Consider, for example, what the effect would have been to have the part of Diego played by Joel Angelino (Angelino plays the part of Diego's sculptor friend Germán, over whose work Diego gets into trouble with his superiors in the cultural office where he works). The wispy redhead Angelino, with a soft body that is no match either for Perugorría's muscular frame or Cruz's hard one, would simply have fed so much into audience stereotypes of the gay man as to have invited complete dismissal. Thus, while Gutiérrez Alea reproduces stereotypes in order to question their validity, his characters articulate elements of homophobic violence at the level of the story being told in order to question at the level of the film's rhetoric the legitimacy of that violence (which, I repeat, remains essentially verbal in the film). At the same time, his film backs away from fully reproducing the stereotype by deploying an actor who is both a queen and a hunk, a contradiction that is clearly visible when reference is made to the completely stereotypic Germán.

There is another way in which there are ideological and rhetorical problems between the level of the *enoncé* and that of the *énonciation*. One of the major features of the film is David's virginity, which intersects his subscription to a severe heteronormality. It is not that the one is the consequence of the other (heteronormativity may not, in Latin America, exclude premarital sex as categorically as is argued to be preferable in the United States) but that, precisely, David has even better reason to be alarmed by Diego's advances: at the same time he fails with women, he is being pursued by men. On the level of the story being told, David is done the magnificent favor by Diego of arranging for David to have sex. This he accomplishes by persuading his neighbor Nancy to bed David (Nancy has good reason to be nice to David, as he donates blood once when she attempts suicide by slashing her wrists), and he carefully sets the whole scene up; Diego leaves them alone in his apartment, and Nancy and David make love in Diego's bed. David is subsequently euphoric and announces to Diego his intentions to marry Nancy. He makes this announcement at the same time he and Diego are saying their good-byes as Diego prepares to leave the country for his job with the foreign embassy.

Now, there are many curious issues raised by this plot that need to be viewed from the level of the film's rhetoric: David finally has a sexual adventure but with Nancy, and they make love in Diego's bed. What I would like to propose is that, while David does make love with Nancy and while it is (apparently) a totally satisfactory encounter with lasting consequences that can be summarized by the cover term "love," at the same time David has in a very real sense made love to Diego. It is important to note that the only real physical contact between the two men comes after David and Nancy have had sex: in Diego's now dismantled apartment, David is able to exchange a very warm, tender, and clinging embrace with Diego. Of course, it is a sign of the degree of friendship that has developed between them, and of course, it is a sincere gesture of farewell that David extends to Diego, who he knows is having after all to abandon a Cuba he identifies with so deeply (he had, at the outset of their relationship, assured David that he had no intention of abandoning Cuba, even playing for him Ignacio Cervantes's haunting piano dance "Adiós a Cuba"). And of course, hugging Diego is a sign of the degree to which David has accepted the naturalness of Diego's being gay. Of course, it is also true that David can now afford, so to speak, to hug Diego, since he likely feels that the tryst with Nancy has secured unquestionably his status as a heterosexual.

David underscores his acceptance of Diego when he switches their servings of ice cream in their farewell meeting at the Coppelia. He not only gives Diego the man's serving of chocolate, but he proceeds to dig into Diego's portion of strawberry ice cream in a way that replays Diego's miming of queenly discourse, down to savoring the plump fetish strawberry. None of this means that David, like Cary Grant's character in Howard Hawks's 1938 film *Bringing Up Baby*, "just went gay all of a sudden." But it does mean there is a sympathy between the two men—

Diego and David
embrace

and in public — that goes far beyond the mere matter of "accepting" the difference of the other. From this point of view, one could speculate on how David and Diego have sex together through Nancy in Diego's bed. It is a commonplace that one is never having sex just with the other person involved in the sexual act, but with all of the other persons who make up one's sexual history and one's sexual fantasies (a point clearly made by the opening scene of Paul Rudnick's play *Jeffrey,* 1994, and Christopher Ashley's 1995 movie version). And, moreover, it is a commonplace that women in a homophobic, homosocial, and sexist society (each adjective implies the other) are bridges in relationships that are really going on between men (this point is worked out in terms of repressed homosexuality in the Brazilian Bruno Barreto's 1981 *Beijo no asfalto,* in which the woman unknowingly stands between an erotic bond between her father and her husband; see Foster, *Gender and Society,* 129–138).

The proposition that, in the context of a hegemonic heterosexism, since men cannot fuck each other, they must displace their attraction to each other and express it through another means — often through the woman who brings them together and holds them in a hopefully lasting bond (such as the relationship between father-in-law and son-in-law in Barreto's film) — is amply explored in Cohan's study on the

long-standing relationship between the Bing Crosby and Bob Hope
characters in the road shows they made together. In these films, Dorothy
Lamour and other women constitute a bridge between two men —
a quasi-, pseudo-, not-really-for-real erotic duo whose interaction is
fluffed up in terms of broad jokes of sexual innuendo — and a guffaw
serves to replace, in the spectator, the moment of reflection as to what,
after all, could be going on between the two men. Marilyn Monroe's
character serves much the same function in the relationship between
Tony Curtis's and Jack Lemmon's characters in Billy Wilder's 1959
Some Like It Hot. Indeed, Sugar Cane is always complaining about how
with men, she always gets the fuzzy end of the lollipop (an image that
is basically nonsensical except, perhaps, as a lesbian metaphor), and
the woman Jack Lemmon plays, Daphne, is a bridge between him and
Joe E. Brown's Osgood Fielding III, who really doesn't care (because
"Nobody's perfect") that a man is really on the other side of the woman.
Indeed, what is really quite hilarious is that Cruz, as he is savoring the
strawberry of femininity, is told by Diego that the only thing wrong with
him is that he is not a *maricón.* David looks into Diego's eyes and says,
"Nadie es perfecto." What, for David, is on the other side of Diego's
queenly performance?

David gets into trouble with Miguel for defending Diego and ends up
getting verbally assaulted by his *compañero,* who accuses him of taking
flowers to his male lover (they are for Nancy). Miguel stomps off, yelling
that the two men are *maricones.* This goes far beyond the sort of "love the
sinner but not the sin" that is the conventional stance of liberal heterosexual tolerance toward the queer: one must express affection for the
queer, but there is a constant need to reinforce the message that anything
that can be taken as an opening toward the fulfillment of homoerotic
desire is strictly off limits. The need constantly to draw the line between
the two always assumes that there is a clear point in which the inaugura-
tion of the homoerotic program has begun to take place. But, certainly,
this cannot be so easily determined: Does it start with a kiss? Or is it
that unexpected moment of tender touching? Or is it the sudden lingering gaze of the sort that David blesses Diego with while uttering one
of the most famous phrases of contemporary gay culture? That Cruz,
whom one cannot expect to have much familiarity with the 1950s cultural icons of gay America, knows it in 1979, when American films could
hardly have been the order of the day, reinforces how Gutiérrez Alea is
playing with the blending of what is coherent on the level of the film's
story and what is coherent on the level of its rhetoric: Cruz speaks to the

level of the address of the film to a Cuban audience in the early 1990s, one that is more likely to have seen Wilder's film or, with the arrival in the 1980s of international gay culture in Cuba, to have heard the phrase, perhaps without even knowing what its origin is.

So, then, David and Diego do, in a way, fuck.[12] Cruz not only becomes Diego's deeply loyal friend, even suffering a confrontation with the relentlessly homophobic Miguel in an attempt to defend him. He also enters in a very significant way into Diego's world and, more importantly, into some understanding of what constitutes homoerotic desire, thereby understanding the suffering for individuals who not only see the fulfillment of their desire insistently denied (alongside which the postponement of David's first sexual adventure becomes trivial), but who in addition are brutally bloodied for it, both verbally and physically. David never ends up having sex with Diego in what is customarily understood to be having sex, although I would insist that the way in which they are together in the last third of the film does constitute a version of same-sex erotics, if only in a baby-steps way. Yet David performs his own sexuality for Diego.

In voyeuristic terms, the macho always boasts to other men of his conquests (often to other women, but more as a way of seducing them: heterosexuality must be constantly performed and reperformed), but it is done in the spirit of (re)conforming one's heteronormative masculinity to/for the benefit and approval of other heterosexuals, not as part of the consolidation of friendship with a gay man. Diego will disappear from David's world, at least from the perspective of the year 1979, but it is clear that he will remain in David's consciousness—and as something very much more than a gay friend David has learned to tolerate. Thus, in the end, Gutiérrez Alea, in a very halting way that is not free of some significant ideological problems (for example, where does all of this leave heart-of-gold Nancy?), allows David and Diego to attain a level of intimacy that is much more than that of "good buddies" while at the same time avoiding—but just barely—bringing them into the realm of the fully homoerotic engagement that is currently (and has been, since at least the 1980s) considered imperative for fully confirming the naturalization and legitimacy of same-sex love.

Notes

1. Néstor Almendros was born in Barcelona in 1930 and died in New York of AIDS complications in 1992; he had moved to Cuba as a young adult. After leaving Spain as a consequence of the banning of some of his films, he went on to become one of the most highly regarded contemporary cinematographers. With Jorge Ulloa, he also made *Nobody Listens* (1984), another documentary denouncing the abuse of human rights in Cuba.

2. I will tend to use "homosexuality" only as a bracketed term, as the descriptor of the medico-juridical assignment of deviance to same-sex erotic relations. Where such relations are endorsed as legitimate expressions of human sexual passion, I will use terms like "homoerotic," "gay," "lesbian," or "lesbigay" according to the context. Recognizing the substantial difference between women's history and men's history, I will avoid using "gay" as either an inclusive cover term or as a synonym for "lesbian."

3. Certainly, the American fraternity is an important institution for creating and maintaining homosocial bonds. In general, the American-style fraternity does not exist in Latin America, although athletic clubs in secondary schools and universities may cover some of the same territory. One significant exception is Brazil, where the *careca* is the pledge in university-level groups that bear a close resemblance to the American fraternity; both have common roots in the German fraternities. The major difference between the Brazilian fraternity and its American counterpart is that where the latter is organized on the margins of academic concerns, the Brazilian fraternities are organized by university discipline. See Glauco Mattoso's scholarly study *O calvário dos carecas*, which examines the fraternity system in Europe, the United States, and Brazil, underscoring the easy and—presumably—deliberate transition (for presumed purposes of bonding rituals) from homosociality to masked homoeroticism. Also of interest is Mattoso's comic book version (in collaboration with the graphic artist Marcatti), *As aventuras de Glaucomix*, which deals specifically with his personal experiences in the library sciences fraternity.

4. In addition to the films examined in this study, I have dealt in the following monographs with the respective films in parentheses explicitly as queer texts: *Contemporary Argentine Cinema* (*Adiós, Roberto; Kiss of the Spider Woman*, or *El beso de la mujer araña; Otra historia de amor*) and *Gender and Society in Contemporary Brazilian Cinema* (*Barela, escola de crimes; Beijo no asfalto; O boto; Vera*). The essay on *El Callejón de los Milagros*, included in *Contemporary Mexican Cinema and Mexico City*, deals partially with a queer strand in the film.

INTROIT: QUEER DIFFERENCE

1. See Foster, *Contemporary Argentine Cinema*, 14–26, on Bemberg's second major film, *Camila* (1985), and Foster, *Redemocratization*. On Bemberg's career see Fontana.

2. The distinction between carnival and circus is a tenuous one. By "circus" one usually understands live animal, clown, and trapeze acts; circuses (cf. the etymology of the word) are often understood to be traveling shows. The "carnival" is the side-show of the circus, or it may be a permanent installation as part of an amusement park, with displays of oddities, some type of "show," fortunetellers, and games of chance or skill.

3. There is an interesting sense in which Bemberg's last film can be read as a sort of self-homage: although Bemberg does not run off with the circus, she does abandon her comfortable middle-class life in order to dedicate herself to the very transgressive career of a woman film director.

4. One of my students, Daniel Enrique Pérez, has an interesting comment to make about Leonor's efforts to protect Charlotte from the outside world, to the effect that there is a continuity between San Juan de los Altares and the circus, only that the circus is an explicitly defined sideshow. However, Charlotte's "normal and decent" world in San Juan de los Altares includes the sinful priest, the Protestant German woman (Protestantism in the Argentine countryside, outside of certain immigrant colonies, is treated traditionally as tantamount to occultism), the mysterious Ludovico D'Andrea, the paralytic mayor, and the whorehouse flora and fauna; Gatto, 80, makes much the same point.

5. Alcón's character, Mojamé, is an apparent orphan who is Leonor's handyman and factotum. Although Charlotte wishes him to assume his identity as someone of Arabic descent and pronounce his name properly, he refuses to; however, at the end of the film, when he identifies himself as the narrator, he does so with a full Arabic identity: Mohamed Ben Alí.

HOMOSEXUALITY: IN AND OUT OF THE CLOSET

1. Reference can be made to Jorge Ibargüengoitia's quasidocumentary novel *Las muertas* (1986), which turns on lesbian rivalries leading to murder in a small-town Mexican brothel of the sort evoked in Ripstein's film.

2. Pérez Turrent, 108, relates *El lugar sin límites* to brothel-based Mexican films but recognizes its significant difference from treatments of female prostitutes, or *ficheras*.

3. The title appears on the screen in the opening credits with the *i* of *dois* in-

verted. This not only calls direct attention to what might be the referent of the word, but it also evokes male sexuality by virtue of creating an icon of the penis.

4. In Abreu's story on which the film is based, an answering machine is not involved but rather anonymous letters described by the narrator in the following terms:

> Quando janeiro começou, quase na época de tirarem férias —e tinham planejado, juntos, quem sabe Parati, Ouro Preto, Porto Seguro—, ficaram surpresos naquela manhã em que o chefe de seção os chamou, perto do meio-dia. Fazia muito calor. Suarento, o chefe foi direto ao assunto. Tinha recibido algumas cartas, anônimas. Recusou-se a mostrá-las. Pálidos, ouviram expressões como "relação anormal e ostensiva", "desavergonhada aberração", "comportamento doentio", "psicologia deformada", sempre assinadas por *Um Atento Guardião da Moral.* [When January began, almost at the time of their vacations—and they had planned on spending them together, who knows, in Parati, Ouro Preto, Porto Seguro—they were surprised that morning by a summons from the section chief, around noon. It was very hot. Sweating profusely, the chief went right to the point. He had received some letters, anonymous ones. He refused to show them. Paling, they heard phrases like "an abnormal relationship right in everyone's face," "a shameful aberration," "sick behavior," "warped psychology," all signed by "A Watchful Guardian of Morals."] (116)

5. The term "happy together" is used ironically as the title in English of a 1997 film by the Hong Kong director Kar-Wai Wong. Set in Buenos Aires, the two working-class protagonists from Hong Kong find anything but happiness in their homoerotic relationship, which only goes to prove that same-sex relations no more guarantee happiness than heterosexual ones.

6. Both Castro and Stavans discuss the sexual range, containable only with enormous difficulty, of the Hispanic male. Stavans even goes so far as to assert that the "Hispanic macho goes out of his way to keep up appearances, to exalt his virility, but he often fails. Sooner or later, his glorious masculinity will be shared in bed with another man" (156). See also Castro, "Crossing and Cruising," 55–56.

7. One of the best examples of a productive homosocialism in Latin American film, one in which the bond between two minds is not without its suggestions of homoeroticism but reaffirms reciprocally their human dignity, is the Brazilian Carlos Reichenbach's *Alma corsária* (1993). Another Brazilian film, Ruy Guerra's *Os cafajestes* (1962), is an excellent example from the Cinema Novo movement in which homosociality provides for a bond of thuggery and the exploitation of women and other social subalternities.

POLITICAL INTERSECTIONS

1. One of the producers of *Conducta impropia* is Barbet Schroeder, whose *La Virgen de los Sicarios* is examined elsewhere in this study.

2. Paul Julian Smith, in "Cuban Homosexualities," analyzes the references to each other in Arenas's and Almendros's autobiographies, *Antes que anochezca* (1992) and *Homme à la caméra* (1980), respectively.

3. Cabrera Infante dedicates his 1993 collection of essays *Mea culpa* to Almen-

dros; in his elegy to Almendros he writes: "It was Néstor who alerted the world, graphically, to what the sexual witch-hunt was like in Castro's Cuba. In his *Improper Conduct* the UMAP concentration camps for homosexuals that Castro built were revealed and almost seen through its protagonists" (410). Cabrera Infante's use of "protagonists" is noteworthy here, for if the UMAP system was meant to silence and to "disappear" alleged homosexuals in Cuba, the force of Almendros's documentary is to turn them into articulate and physically present protagonists of their own stories of oppression.

4. Two other film documentaries about gay life in Cuba are Sonja De Vries's *Gay Cuba* (1995) and Kelly Anderson's *Looking for a Space: Lesbians and Gay Men in Cuba* (1993).

5. One interviewee says the country was dominated by "una paranoia que sustentan todos — todo el mundo sospecha de todos" [a paranoia everyone defends — everyone suspects everyone else].

6. The proposition that there are those who are absolutely beyond reproach because they are too powerful to have their sexuality publicly questioned is subverted in the film by the poet-figure Jorge Ronet when he describes Castro as "una gran marquesa" (a grand marquise), an extravagant doyenne of drag — presumably a reference to the fetish of military fatigues (see also Desnoes on the fetish of Castro's beard) — orchestrating the whole affair. In the published script of the film Ronet narrates catching a glimpse of Castro:

> Una tarde que estábamos trabajando . . . [v]imos venir una caravana de jeeps . . . Como siempre, él nunca se acerca a la gente. Pasó con su jeep como una gran "marquesa", mirando así a los esclavos, ¿no? . . . El consideraba que nosotros éramos la escoria de la sociedad, porque a él le gusta ponerle carteles a la gente . . . y como tiene el espíritu de una gran marquesa . . . así pasó, como la gran marquesa que se cree que es . . . (*Ronet imita un gesto de desprecio.*) [One afternoon when we were working . . . we saw a caravan of jeeps approach . . . As always, he (Castro) never went up to people. He went by in his jeep like a grand marquise keeping watch on her slaves, right? . . . In his opinion we were the dregs of society, because he likes to label people . . . and since he has the soul of a grand marquise who thinks she is . . . (*Ronet imitates a gesture of disdain*).] (39)

7. Pier Paolo Passolini had the same attitude as Arenas with regard to male sexual "flexibility" in Italy; see, for example, his *Teorema* (1968).

8. It is important to heed Leiner's comments on *Conducta impropia* and to understand that for many young Cubans, the "UMAP is ancient history" (50). He goes on to state:

> The core of the film consists of interviews with twenty-eight Cuban exiles who testify primarily about the brutality of the UMAP camps and the kind of discrimination that encouraged many homosexuals to join the exodus from the port of Mariel to Miami in the spring of 1980. In this respect, these interviews are important as oral history protesting the institutionalization of homophobia. But there is something very static about the film as a whole. It focuses on an aspect of human rights in which significant improvement has taken place, yet the film tells us nothing

of these changes and implies that conditions of twenty to twenty-five years ago are the conditions of today. (52)

However, I assume the "today" of Leiner's comments refers to the year 1994, in which his book was published. The events described in *Conducta impropia*, which was released in 1984, are not at "twenty to twenty-five years" remove from the period of the UMAP camps.

9. Lorca was publicly outed by the conservative newspaper *ABC* when it published his *Sonetos del amor oscuro* in a supplement dated March 17, 1984. Although Lorca was long dead, this action by such a respected daily made it rather difficult to continue to refuse to acknowledge Lorca's homoeroticism.

10. Carl Cobb refers to the opinion of Lorca's contemporary Luis Cernuda, who was also gay, to the effect that the *Romancero gitano* "is often at the point of becoming too theatrical to be convincing" (64–65). I believe Cobb's overview of Lorca is the first extensive treatment in English of homoeroticism in Lorca, and he speaks at length of the *Romancero gitano*.

11. For example, a well-known book on the poet by Arturo Barea devotes a third of its text to "The Poet and Sex," but despite this recognition of the importance of erotic desire in Lorca's poetry, there is only the briefest mention of homoeroticism: "Yet there runs a pagan streak through Spanish eroticism . . . It emerges in the man's delight in the body of a woman or another man" (68). Otherwise, the treatment is completely silent on the subject, and no textual references of the sort that abound elsewhere are offered.

12. A lovely textual embodiment of the principle of "Sexo, pero no mucho" is to be found in Gabriel García Márquez's *Cien años de soledad* (1967). When Fernanda is about to be married to Aureliano Segundo Buendía, she consults with a priest as to the days on which she must not engage in sexual relations with her husband: "Descontando la Semana Santa, los domingos, las fiestas de guardar, los primeros viernes, los retiros, los sacrificios y los impedimentos cíclicos, su anuario útil quedaba reducido a 42 desperdigados en una maraña de cruces moradas [en el calendario]" (181).

13. Stanley Kauffmann, in his review of the film, makes a pointed comment that enhances one's perception of the level of this unmitigated violence: "In this new society, despite all the shootings, the police are never seen; there are no investigations, nothing; and though all the killings take place in the street, only once does a passerby react" (24).

14. The allusion is to Harvey Feierstein's 1983 homonymous Broadway play based on Jean Poiret's original French text (also of the same name). There is a 1978 film version of Poiret's text directed by Édonard Molinaro, with 1980 and 1985 sequels.

FORGING QUEER SPACES

1. This essay originally appeared as "Queering the Patriarchy in Hermosillo's *Doña Herlinda*" in Foster, *Sexual Textualities*, 64–72. An earlier version appeared in *Framing Latin American Cinema*, 235–245.

2. *Compadrismo* in Latin America is the special bond between two men; a similar bond between women is called *comadrismo*. Typically, men who are bonded by

compadrismo are the godfathers of each other's children and rely on each other for all forms of social support. In the case of women, their subaltern position provides the added dimension of a network of support against a totally masculinist society. In all cases, this special bond creates a privileged union in a hostile world, and in this sense it goes far beyond the Anglo American tradition of buddyism. However, *compadrismo*, in a weaker sense, may refer to the bond in a group of more than two men, in a sense closer to the American "buddy."

3. To the best of my knowledge, this is the only Latin American film in which AIDS is central to the plot. A false accusation of AIDS figures in Alfonso Cuarón's *Sólo con tu pareja* (Mexico, 1991). Latin America has yet to develop the sort of post-AIDS queer filmmaking described by Hood, although Saca's film, as an odyssey from the sexual jungle to a maternal paradise, is a good beginning.

4. Whether "real" sex takes place between the two men in this situation is somewhat beside the point. As Amy Taubin states with reference to Christopher Münch's 1963 documentary *The Hours and Times* about the relationship between John Lennon and Brian Epstein: "The film flies in the face of the hetero culture of *Rolling Stone* by suggesting that Lennon was capable of a homoerotic involvement. And it defies simplistic gay identity politics by representing a deep affinity between two men that is not defined by the sexual act. That the film doesn't specify what, if anything, happens when Lennon and Epstein share a bed, is exactly the point. Because, either way, it didn't change the relationship" (177).

5. Rebecca E. Biron discusses Borges's story on which Christensen's film is based, underscoring how it reinforces a violent pact of masculinity in order to repress homosexuality; the story in this sense stands in stark contrast to the film, where I am maintaining that the violent pact of masculinity serves to clear a space for an intense homoerotic bonding.

6. There is, to be sure, another possibility: to avoid the accusation of following the example of the *pornochanchada*, in which there is a necessarily egalitarian representation of sex, the erotic interest of these films lies in the heterosexual representation of female sexuality. Put differently, the representation of sexuality in the *pornochanchada*, by contrast to the demure sexuality of both men and women in classical Brazilian filmmaking (where innuendo, fades, euphemisms, and the like substitute for the direct representation of sex), has a certain pseudofeminist liberation about it: not only does sexuality begin to be displayed unflinchingly by the camera, but women are shown to be fully erotic participants in sexual acts and instigators beyond clichés regarding prostitutes or evil women who entrap men via sex.

QUEER TRANSCENDENCE

1. When I italicize what appear to be English-language terms, I am actually signaling my use of their Spanish-language cognates, and it should be borne in mind that the semantic scope may not always be exactly coterminous between the two languages.

2. I will be using "passive" and "active" here as though these were transparent and unproblematical terms: they are not, at least not as synonyms, respectively, of "penetrated" and "penetrator." However, I leave them unanalyzed here, strategically

accepting their street-wisdom sense, because actual sexual acts are only passingly at issue in Piñeyro's film.

3. At one point the narrative voice-over reports Ángel's inner monologue after he has rejected El Nene's attempt to engage in sex (I quote here from the printed script, while the actual words of the film vary slightly): "Sé que lo lastimo. Pero no puedo evitarlo. Yo también quiero. Pero no puede ser. No es por las voces. Ellas me dicen que sí, me dicen que no. Me gritan puto, marica, santo. Quieren confundirme. Pero yo sé qué hay que hacer. Por la leche. Hay que guardarla. La leche es santa. El Nene no entiende que lo estoy salvando. Si nos quedamos sin leche, nos quedamos sin Dios. La leche es santa." [I know I hurt him. But I can't help it. I'm also in love. But it just can't be. It's not because of the voices. They tell me it's all right, they tell me it isn't. They scream queer, faggot, saint at me. They want to confuse me. But I know what I have to do. On account of my semen. It's got to be hoarded. Semen is sacred. El Nene can't understand that I'm saving him. If we're left with no semen, we're left without God. Semen is sacred.] (Piñeyro and Figuera, 161)

4. Salvador Oropesa (in personal communication) has pointed out to me that on the basis of their names, "We cannot forget that El Nene and Ángel are a 'boy' and an 'angel'; they either do not have to justify (yet) their sexuality or they do not have one."

5. Moreover, Ángel articulates in the closing exchange between him and El Nene the view that their deaths are an escape from the untenable "here": "*(dulce, final)* . . . Ya casi estamos. En un par de minutos estaremos lejos de aquí" [*(sweet, final)* . . . We're almost there now. In a couple of minutes we'll be far away from here] (Piñeyro and Figueras, 251). From one point of view, this smacks of suicide as the abiding form of release from homophobic oppression, but in the context of the closing scene and the return of the two men to each other's arms, it becomes also an affirmation of the sort of romantic love that envisions perishing together.

6. "Stop or I'll shoot": the practice of faking the flight of prisoners in order "legitimately" to shoot them in the back, thus disposing of them once and for all.

7. More commonly known as Hefaistos in Spanish; I use Efesto, the form that appears in the subtitles to the film.

8. Smith notes that *Fresa y chocolate* is a response to Néstor Almendros's *Conducta impropia*, and Smith ("*Fresa y chocolate*") calls Gutiérrez Alea's film a "chamber piece" and unflatteringly subtitles his essay "Cinema as Guided Tour."

9. I am using "queer" throughout here as a synonym of the authoritarian term "homosexual" and the homophobic terms "fag," "faggot," *maricón*, ignoring, for purposes of the sociohistorical moment of the film, any need to distinguish between queer and gay. Although outside commentators have used "gay" with reference to same-sex relations and identity in Cuba, it is only recently that this international term has entered the speech of the island (for example, it now appears in Paz Pérez's 1998 dictionary of Cuban Spanish). It would certainly not be an available vocabulary item for any of the characters in the 1979 setting for the film. Thus, "queer" is understood to be here the proper English translation of the Cuban uses of words like *maricón* and *puto*.

10. Actually, the brand is Johnnie Walker red label, which is, of course, from Scotland. But it is identified as a "product of the enemy," confirming that it is contra-

band brought in from the United States, since Scotland has never been a political adversary of the Cuban revolution or the Castro government.

11. I must recognize that Spanish also reflects a belief to this effect, as seen in the saying "El hombre es como el oso: cuanto más feo, más hermoso" (A man is like a bear: the uglier he is, the handsomer he is). However, the point is that to be male and beautiful does not push the limits of heteronormative acceptability as much in Hispanic culture as it traditionally does in American culture. Likewise, note must be taken of the fact that Hollywood, while enshrining plain-looking American male icons—Van Johnson, Gary Stewart, Ronald Reagan, Rock Hudson—has also allowed for masculine beauty without confusing it necessarily with homosexuality, even if many of the notorious masculine beauties of Hollywood did have a queer dimension to their lives: Montgomery Clift, Cary Grant, Marlon Brando, César Romero. Romero, of course, worked for Hollywood as a Latin lover icon. See Meyer on Rock Hudson's body; see Hadleigh on various of the male Hollywood stars mentioned here.

12. I take note of the following: "In an interview that I conducted with [scriptwriter] Senel Paz about *Strawberry and Chocolate*, he spoke to this issue [of a sexual relationship between David and Diego], saying that if David had been a repressed homosexual (i.e., if Diego had managed to draw David out of a repressed homosexuality), the film would have been weakened because the intention was to portray a heterosexual character who had the capacity to understand a homosexual and his situation in Cuban society" (Bejel, "*Strawberry and Chocolate,*" 70). I do not deny the scriptwriter's and director's intention for the film nor the fact that the stated intention would be weakened by a sexual relationship between Diego and David; it's just that the surplus meanings of a text never allow for an unmitigated success in the execution of authorial intentions.

References

FILMOGRAPHY

Afrodita, el jardín de los perfumes. Dir. Pablo César. Script: Pablo César. Miguel César Producciones and Centre National de Production Cinématographique, 1998.

Aqueles dois. Dir. Sérgio Amon. Script: Sérgio Amon. Roda Films, 1985.

Conducta impropia. Dir. Néstor Almendros and Orlando Jiménez-Leal. Script: Néstor Almendros and Orlando Jiménez-Leal. Les Film du Losange, 1984.

Convivencia. Dir. Carlos Galettini. Script: Carlos Galettini and Luisa Irene Ickowicz. Negocios Cinematográficos de Convivencia, 1994.

De eso no se habla. Dir. María Luisa Bemberg. Script: María Luisa Bemberg, Jorge Goldenberg, Julio Llinas. María Luisa Bemberg, Oscar Kramer, and Aura Films, 1993.

The Disappearance of García Lorca. Dir. Marcos Zurinaga. Script: Neil Cohen, Juan Antonio Ramos, and Marcos Zurinaga. Antena 3 Enrique Cerezo Producciones Cinematográficas S.A., Esparza/Katz Productions, Le Studio Canal, and Miramar Films, 1997.

Doña Herlinda y su hijo. Dir. Jaime Humberto Hermosillo. Script: Jaime Humberto Hermosillo. Clasa Films Mundiales, 1985.

En el paraíso no existe el dolor. Dir. Víctor Saca. Script: Víctor Saca. Instituto Mexicano de Cinematografía, 1995.

Fresa y chocolate. Dir. Tomás Gutiérrez Alea and Juan Carlos Tabío. Script: Senel Paz. ICAIC, 1993.

A intrusa. Dir. Carlos Hugo Christensen. Script: Carlos Hugo Christensen. Carlos Hugo Christensen Produções Cinematográficas, 1980.

El lugar sin límites. Dir. Arturo Ripstein. Script: José Donoso and Arturo Ripstein. Conacine Dos, 1978.

No se lo digas a nadie. Dir. Francisco J. Lombardi. Script: Enrique Moncloa and Giovanna Pollarolo. Lola Films, 1998.

Plata quemada. Dir. Marcelo Piñeyro. Script: Marcelo Figueras and Marcelo Piñeyro. Lider Films, 2000.
La Virgen de los Sicarios. Dir. Barbet Schroeder. Script: Fernando Vallejo. Les Films du Losange, 2000.

BIBLIOGRAPHY

Abelove, Henry, Michèle Aina Barale, and David M. Halperin, eds. *The Lesbian and Gay Studies Reader.* New York: Routledge, 1993.
Abreu, Caio Fernando. "Aqueles dois (história de aparente mediocridade e repressão)." In *Mel e girassóis.* Porto Alegre: Mercado Aberto, 1988.
Acevedo, Zelmar. *Homosexualidad: hacia la destrucción de los mitos.* Buenos Aires: Ediciones del Ser, 1985.
Aldrich, Robert. *The Seduction of the Mediterranean: Writing, Art, and Homosexual Fantasy.* London: Routledge, 1993.
Almendros, Néstor, and Orlando Jiménez-Leal. *Conducta impropia.* Script. Madrid: Biblioteca Cubana Contemporánea, 1984.
Altamiranda, Daniel. "Borges, Jorge Luis." In *Latin American Writers on Gay and Lesbian Themes: A Bio-Critical Sourcebook,* ed. David William Foster. Westport, Conn.: Greenwood Press, 1991.
Alzate, Gastón. "N[ota] de t[raductor a Alexander Doty, 'Qué es lo que más produce el *queerness?*']." *Debate feminista* 8, no. 16 (1997): 98–99.
Amnesty International. *Cuba: Political Imprisonment, an Update.* Washington, D.C., 1988.
Aqueles dois. Online archive. http://www.casacinepoa.com.br/port/filme.asp/Codigo= 26.
Arenas, Reinaldo. *Antes que anochezca, autobiografía.* Barcelona: Tusquets Editores, 1992. Trans. Dolores M. Koch under the title *Before Night Falls* (New York: Viking, 1993).
———. *Arturo, la estrella más brillante.* Barcelona: Montesinos, 1984. Trans. Ann Tashi Slater and Andrew Hurley under the title "The Brightest Star," in *Old Rosa: A Novel in Two Stories* (New York: Grove Press, 1989).
Bach, Caleb. "María Luisa Bemberg Tells the Untold." *Américas* 46 (1944): 20–27.
Balderston, Daniel. "The Fecal Dialectic: Homosexual Panic and the Origin of Writing in Borges." In *¿Entiendes? Queer Readings, Hispanic Writings,* ed. Emilie J. Bergmann and Paul Julian Smith. Durham: Duke University Press, 1995.
Barea, Arturo. *Lorca: The Poet and His People.* Trans. Ilsa Barea. Reprint, New York: Grove Press, 1958.
Barletta, Leónidas. *Royal circo, novela.* Buenos Aires: Editorial Tor, 1927.
Bayly, Jaime. *No se lo digas a nadie.* 5th ed. Barcelona: Seix Barral, 1994.
Behar, Ruth. "Queer Times in Cuba." In *Bridges to Cuba. Puentes a Cuba,* ed. Ruth Behar. Ann Arbor: University of Michigan Press, 1995.
Bejel, Emilio. "*Strawberry and Chocolate:* Coming Out of the Cuban Closet." *South Atlantic Quarterly* 96, no. 1 (1997): 65–82. First published in Spanish as "*Fresa y chocolate* o la salida de la guarida: hacia una teoría del sujeto homosexual en Cuba," in *Casa de las Américas* 196 (1994): 10–22.
———. "The Unsettling Return of the Butterflies." *Chasqui, revista de literatura latinoamericana* 29, no. 2 (2000): 3–13.

Berg, Charles Ramirez. *Cinema of Solitude; A Critical Study of Mexican Films, 1967–1983.* Austin: University of Texas Press, 1992.

Bergling, Tim. *Sissyphobia: Gay Men and Effeminate Behavior.* New York: Southern Tier Editions, 2001.

Bergmann, Emilie. "Lesbian Desire in *Yo, la peor de todas.*" In *Hispanisms and Homosexualities,* ed. Sylvia Molloy and Robert McKee Irwin. Durham, N.C.: Duke University Press, 1998.

Bérubé, Allan. *Coming Out under Fire: The History of Gay Men and Women in World War Two.* New York: Free Press, 1990.

Biron, Rebecca E. *Murder and Masculinity; Violent Fictions of Twentieth-Century Latin America.* Nashville: Vanderbilt University Press, 2000.

Birringer, Johannes. "Homosexuality and the Revolution; An Interview with Jorge Perugorría." *Cineaste* 21, no. 1–2 (1995): 21–22.

Blackmore, Josiah, and Gregory S. Hutcheson, eds. *Queer Iberia: Sexualities, Cultures, and Crossings from the Middle Ages to the Renaissance.* Durham, N.C.: Duke University Press, 1999.

Bogdan, Robert. *Freak Show: Presenting Human Oddities for Amusement and Profit.* Chicago: University of Chicago Press, 1988.

Borges, Jorge Luis. *Collected Fictions.* Trans. Andrew Hurley. New York: Viking, 1998.

———. *El informe de Brodie.* Buenos Aires: Emecé Editores, 1970.

Borghello, José María. *Plaza de los Lirios.* Buenos Aires: Editorial Galerna, 1986.

Brant, Herbert J. "The Queer Use of Communal Women in Borges' 'El muerto' and 'La intrusa.'" *Hispanófila* 125 (1999): 37–50.

Brouws, Jeff, and Bruce Caron. *Inside the Live Reptile Tent: The Twilight World of the Carnival Midway.* San Francisco: Chronicle Books, 2001.

Butler, Judith. *Gender Trouble: Feminism and the Subversion of Identity.* New York: Routledge, 1990.

Cabrera Infante, Guillermo. *Mea Culpa.* Trans. Kenneth Hall with the author. London: Faber and Faber, 1994.

Castro, Pércio B. de, Jr. "Crossing and Cruising the Oceans: Contradictory Images and Prejudices from the Iberian Legacy in Hispanic Literature, Media, and Society." In *The Image of Europe in Literature, Media, and Society,* ed. Will Wright and Steven Kaplan. Pueblo: University of Southern Colorado, Society for the Interdisciplinary Study of Social Imagery, 2001.

———. "Gritemos a plenos pulmones y contémoselo a todos: revelando secretos en *No se lo digas a nadie* de Jayme Bayly y Francisco Lombardi." In *Cine-Lit 2000: Essays on Hispanic Film and Fiction,* ed. George Cabello-Castellet, Jaume Martí-Olivella, and Guy H. Wood. Corvallis: Oregon State University, 2001.

Cobb, Carl. *Federico García Lorca.* New York: Twayne Publishers, 1967.

Cohan, Steven. *Masked Men: Masculinity and the Movies in the Fifties.* Bloomington: Indiana University Press, 1997.

———. "Queering the Deal: On the Road with Hope and Crosby." In *Out Takes: Essays on Queer Theory and Film,* ed. Ellis Hanson. Durham, N.C.: Duke University Press, 1999.

Corvino, John. "Why Shouldn't Tommy and Jim Have Sex? A Defense of Homosexuality." In *Same Sex: Debating the Ethics, Science, and Culture of Homosexuality,* ed. John Corvino. Lanham, Md.: Rowman and Littlefield Publishers, 1997.

Costa Picazo, Rolando. "Arcidiácono, Carlos." In *Latin American Writers on Gay and Lesbian Themes: A Bio-Critical Sourcebook*, ed. David William Foster. Westport, Conn.: Greenwood Press, 1991.

Curtin, Kaier. *We Can Always Call Them Bulgarians: The Emergence of Lesbians and Gay Men on the American Stage*. Boston: Alyson Publications, 1987.

Daly, Mary. *Gyn/ecology: The Metaethics of Radical Feminism*. Boston: Beacon Press, 1978.

Darsey, James. "Gay Left." In *Gay Histories and Cultures: An Encyclopedia*, ed. George E. Haggerty. New York: Garland Publishers, 2000.

De Jongh, Nicholas. *Not in Front of the Audience: Homosexuality on Stage*. London: Routledge, 1992.

Delany, Samuel R. "Street Talk/Straight Talk." *différences* 5, no. 2 (1991): 21–38.

Desnoes, Edmundo. " 'Will You Ever Shave Your Beard?' " In *On Signs*, ed. Marshall Blonsky. Baltimore: Johns Hopkins University Press, 1985.

D'Lugo, Marvin. "From Exile to Ethnicity: Néstor Almendros and Orlando Jiménez-Leal's *Improper Conduct* (1984)." In *The Ethnic Eye: Latino Media Arts*. Minneapolis: University of Minnesota Press, 1996.

Dollimore, Jonathan. *Sexual Dissidence: Augustine to Wilde, Freud to Foucault*. Oxford: Clarendon Press, 1991.

Doty, Alexander. *Flaming Classics: Queering the Film Canon*. New York: Routledge, 2000.

———. *Making Things Perfectly Queer: Interpreting Mass Culture*. Minneapolis: University of Minnesota Press, 1993.

Dunn, Katherine. *Geek Love*. Reprint, New York: Warner Books, 1990.

DuPouy, Steven M. "Vallejo, Fernando." In *Latin American Writers on Gay and Lesbian Themes: A Bio-Critical Sourcebook*, ed. David William Foster. Westport, Conn.: Greenwood Press, 1991.

Dyer, Richard. *Now You See It: Studies on Lesbian and Gay Film*. New York: Routledge, 1990.

———. *White*. London: Routledge, 1997.

Edelman, Lee. *Homographesis: Essays in Gay Literary and Cultural Theory*. New York: Routledge, 1994.

Ehrenstein, David. *Open Secret: Gay Hollywood, 1928–1998*. New York: William Morrow, 1998.

Eisenberg, Dan. "Cervantes Saavedra, Miguel de." In *Spanish Writers on Gay and Lesbian Themes: A Bio-Critical Sourcebook*, ed. David William Foster. Westport, Conn.: Greenwood Press, 1999.

———. "García Lorca, Federico." In *Spanish Writers on Gay and Lesbian Themes: A Bio-Critical Sourcebook*, ed. David William Foster. Westport, Conn.: Greenwood Press, 1999.

Fernández L'Hoeste, Héctor D. "*La Virgen de los Sicarios* o las visiones dantescas de Fernando Vallejo." *Hispania* 83, no. 4 (2000): 757–767.

Finney, Charles G. *The Circus of Dr. Lao*. New York: Avon Books, 1974.

Fontana, Clara. *María Luisa Bemberg*. Buenos Aires: Centro Editor de América Latina/Instituto Nacional de Cinematografía, 1993.

Foster, David William. *Contemporary Argentine Cinema*. Columbia: University of Missouri Press, 1992.

————. *Contemporary Mexican Cinema and Mexico City.* Austin: University of Texas Press, 2001.

————. "Evita Perón, Juan José Sebreli, and Gender." In *Reading and Writing the Ambiente,* ed. Susana Chávez-Silverman and Librada Hernández. Madison: University of Wisconsin Press, 2000. First published in David William Foster, *Sexual Textualities: Essays on Queer/ing Latin American Writing* (Austin: University of Texas Press, 1997).

————. *Gay and Lesbian Themes in Latin American Writing.* Austin: University of Texas Press, 1991.

————. "El gay como modelo cultural: *Eminent Maricones* de Jaime Manrique." *Tema y variaciones de literatura* 17 (2001): 189–209.

————. *Gender and Society in Contemporary Brazilian Cinema.* Austin: University of Texas Press, 1999.

————. "El homoerotismo y la lucha por el espacio en Buenos Aires: dos muestras cinematográficas." *Tramas* 6 (1997): 13–42.

————. *Sexual Textualities: Essays on Queer/ing Latin American Writing.* Austin: University of Texas Press, 1997.

————, ed. *The Redemocratization of Argentine Culture, 1983 and Beyond: An International Research Symposium.* Tempe: Arizona State University, Center for Latin American Studies, 1989.

Foster, David William, and Roberto Reis. *Bodies and Biases: Sexualities in Hispanic Cultures and Literatures.* Minneapolis: University of Minnesota Press, 1996.

Foucault, Michel. Introduction to Herculine Barbin, *Herculine Barbin, Being the Recently Discovered Memoirs of a Nineteenth-Century French Hermaphrodite.* Trans. Richard McDougall. New York: Pantheon Books, 1980.

Freud, Sigmund. *Civilization and Its Discontents.* Trans. Joan Rivere. London: Hogarth Press, 1949.

Gambaro, Griselda. *Dios no nos quiere contentos.* Barcelona: Editorial Lumen, 1979.

Garber, Marjorie. *Vested Interests: Cross-Dressing and Cultural Anxiety.* New York: Routledge, 1992.

García Márquez, Gabriel. *Cien años de soledad.* Buenos Aires: Editorial Sudamericana, 1967.

García Suárez, Carlos Iván. "Los 'pirobos': nómadas en el mercado del deseo." *Revista nómadas* 10 (1999): 216–226.

Gatto, Katherine Gyekenyesi. "*De eso no se habla:* María Luisa Bemberg's Argentine Postmodern *Tour de Force.*" *Philological Papers* 45 (1999): 75–81.

Geirola, Gustavo. "Eroticism and Homoeroticism in *Martín Fierro.*" In *Bodies and Biases: Sexualities in Hispanic Cultures and Literatures,* ed. David William Foster and Roberto Reis. Minneapolis: University of Minnesota Press, 1996.

————. "Hernández, José." *Latin American Writers on Gay and Lesbian Themes: A Bio-Critical Sourcebook,* ed. David William Foster. Westport, Conn.: Greenwood Press, 1991.

————. "Juan Gabriel: cultura popular y sexo de los ángeles." *Latin American Music Review* 14, no. 2 (1993): 232–267.

Gibson, Ian. *The Assassination of Federico García Lorca.* Middlesex, England: Penguin Books, 1983.

————. *Federico García Lorca.* 2 vols. Barcelona: Grijalbo, 1985–1987.

González Rodríguez, Sergio. *Los bajos fondo: el antro, la bohemia y el café.* Mexico City: Cal y Arena, 1990.

Gorbato, Viviana. *Fruta prohibida: un recorrido revelador por lugares, costumbres, estilos, historias, testimonios y anécdotasde una sexualidad diferente: la cara oculta de la Argentina gay.* Buenos Aires: Editorial Atlántida, 1999.

Greimas, Algirdas Julien. *The Social Sciences: A Semiotic View.* Trans. Paul Perron and Frank H. Collins. Minneapolis: University of Minnesota Press, 1990.

Gresham, William Lindsey. *Nightmare Alley.* Garden City, N.Y.: Sun Dial Press, 1948.

Hadleigh, Boze. *Hollywood Gays.* New York: Barricade Books, 1996.

Halperin, David M. *Saint Foucault: Towards a Gay Hagiography.* New York: Oxford University Press, 1995.

Hood, Robert. "The Wilderness of AIDS: Sexual Identity and Cultural Politics in the New Queer Cinema." *Revista/Review Interamericana* 25, no. 1–4 (1995): 72–80.

Hotier, Hugues. "La Trangression au cirque." *Kodikas/Code: Ars Semiotica: An International Journal of Semiotics* 7, no. 1–2 (1984): 9–16.

Irwin, Robert McKee. "The Famous 41: The Scandalous Birth of Modern Mexican Homosexuality." *GLQ, A Journal of Lesbian and Gay Studies* 6, no. 3 (2000): 353–376.

Jamandreu, Paco. *Evita fuera del balcón.* Buenos Aires: Ediciones del Libro Abierto, 1981.

Jáuregui, Carlos Luis. *La homosexualidad en la Argentina.* Buenos Aires: Ediciones Tarso, 1987.

Jenckes, Katharine. "Identity, Image, and Sound in Three Films by María Luisa Bemberg." In *Cine-Lit III: Essays on Hispanic Film and Fiction,* ed. George Cabello Castellet, Jaume Martí-Olivella, and Guy H. Wood. Symposium series. Portland: Portland State University, 1997.

Johnson, Randy, Jim Secreto, and Teddy Varndell. *Freaks, Geeks, and Strange Girls: Sideshow Banners of the Great American Midway.* Honolulu: Hardy Marks Publications, 1996.

Jordan, Mark D. *The Silence of Sodom: Homosexuality of Modern Catholicism.* Chicago: University of Chicago Press, 2000.

Katz, Jonathan Ned. *The Invention of Heterosexuality.* Foreword by Gore Vidal and afterword by Lisa Duggan. New York: Dutton, 1995.

Kauffmann, Stanley. "Cruel Places." Review of *La Virgen de los Sicarios. New Republic* (October 1, 2001): 24.

King, John. *Mexican Reels: A History of Cinema in Latin America.* London: Verso, 1990.

King, John, Sheila Whitaker, and Rosa Bosch, eds. *An Argentine Passion: María Luisa Bemberg and Her Films.* London: Verso, 2000.

Kirk, John M., and Leonardo Padura Fuentes. *Culture and the Cuban Revolution: Conversations in Havana.* Gainesville: University Press of Florida, 2001.

Lechón Álvarez, Manuel. *La sala oscura: guía del cine gay español y latinoamericano.* Madrid: Nuer, 2001.

Leiner, Marin. *Sexual Politics in Cuba; Machismo, Homosexuality, and AIDS.* Boulder, Colo.: Westview Press, 1994.

Leland, Christopher Towne. "Güiraldes, Ricardo." In *Latin American Writers on Gay and Lesbian Themes: A Bio-Critical Sourcebook*, ed. David William Foster. Westport, Conn.: Greenwood Press, 1991.

Lévi-Strauss, Claude. *The Elementary Structures of Kinship*. Trans. James Harle Bell, John Richard von Sturmer, and Rodney Needham. London: Eyre and Spottiswoode, 1969.

Lozano Mascarúa, Alicia. "El cine de Jaime Humberto Hermosillo." *fem* 84 (1989): 28–30.

Lumsden, Ian. *Homosexualidad: sociedad y estado en México*. Mexico City: Solediciones and Toronto: Canadian Gay Archives, 1991.

———. *Machos, Maricones, and Gays: Cuba and Homosexuality*. Philadelphia: Temple University Press, 1996.

Maddison, Stephen. "All about Women: Pedro Almodóvar and the Heterosocial Dynamic." *Textual Practice* 14, no. 2 (2000): 265–284.

Manrique, Jaime. *Eminent Maricones: Arenas, Lorca, Puig, and Me*. Madison: University of Wisconsin Press, 1999.

Manzor-Coats, Lillian. "Introduction." In *Latin American Writers on Gay and Lesbian Themes: A Bio-Critical Sourcebook*, ed. David William Foster. Westport, Conn.: Greenwood Press, 1991.

Marcuse, Herbert. *Eros and Civilization: A Philosophical Inquiry into Freud*. Boston: Beacon Press, 1955.

Mattoso, Glauco. *O calvário dos carecas: história do trote estudantil*. São Paulo: EMW Editores, 1985.

Mattoso, Glauco, and Marcatti. *As aventuras de Glaucomix o pedólatra*. São Paulo: Quadrinhos Abriu, Quadrinhos Fechou, 1990.

McGuirk, Bernard J. "Est-ce bien de cela qu'on parle: en deçà et au-delà du surréel féminin en Argentine." In *La Femme s'entete: la part du féminin dans le surréalisme*, ed. Georgiana M. M. Colvile and Katharine Conley. Paris: Lachend and Ritter, 1998.

Meyer, Richard. "Rock Hudson's Body." In *Inside/Out; Lesbian Theories, Gay Theories*, ed. Diana Fuss. New York: Routledge, 1991.

Monsiváis, Carlos. *Escenas de pudor y liviandad*. Mexico City: Grijalbo, 1981.

———. "Ortodoxia y heterodoxia en las alcobas (hacia una crónica de costumbres y creencias sexuales en México)." *Debate feminista* 11 (1995): 183–210.

Mora, Sergio de la. "Fascinating Machismo: Toward an Unmasking of Heterosexual Masculinity in Arturo Ripstein's 'El lugar sin límites.'" *Journal of Film and Video* 44, no. 3–4 (1992–1993): 83–104.

Moreno, Antônio. *A personagem homosexual no cinema brasileiro*. Rio de Janeiro: Ministerio da Cultura/FUNARTE and Niterói, Brazil: EdUFF, 2001.

Murray, Steven O., ed. *Latin American Male Homosexualities*. Albuquerque: University of New Mexico Press, 1995.

———, ed. *Male Homosexuality in Central and South America*. San Francisco: Instituto Obregón and New York: GAU-NY, 1987.

Newfield, Christopher. "Democracy and Male Homoeroticism." *Yale Journal of Criticism* 6, no. 2 (1993): 29–62.

Newman, Kathleen. "'Convocar tanto mundo': Narrativising Authoritarianism and Globalization in *De eso no se habla*." In *An Argentine Passion: María Luisa Bemberg and Her Films*, ed. John King, Sheila Whitaker, and Rosa Bosch. London: Verso, 2000.

Noriega, Chon, and Steven Ricci, eds. "Retrospective: The Films of Arturo Ripstein and Jaime Humberto Hermosillo." *The Mexican Cinema Project*. Los Angeles: UCLA Film and Television Archive, 1994.

Núñez Noriega, Guillermo. *Sexo entre varones: poder y resistencia en el campo sexual*. 2d ed. Mexico City: Coordinación de Humanidades, Programa Universitario de Estudios de Género, Instituto de Investigaciones Sociales; Hermosillo: El Colegio de Sonora; Mexico City: Miguel Angel Porrua Grupo Editorial, 1999.

Ocasio, Rafael. "Gays and the Cuban Revolution: The Case of Reinaldo Arenas." *Latin American Perspectives* 29, no. 2 (March 2002): 78–98.

Ormand, Kirk. "Positions for Classicists, or Why Should Feminist Classicists Care about Queer Theory." Online at http://www.stoa.org/diotima/essays/orman96.shtml

Osorio, M. "Entrevista con Manuel Puig: 'Soy tan macho que las mujeres me parecen maricas.'" *Cuadernos para el diálogo* 231 (1977): 51–53.

Palaversich, Diana. "Caught in the Act: Social Stigma, Homosexual Panic and Violence in Latin American Writing." *Chasqui, revista de literatura latinoamericana* 28, no. 2 (1999): 60–75.

Paz, Senel. *El lobo, el bosque y el hombre nuevo*. Mexico City: Ediciones Era, 1991.

Paz Pérez, Carlos. *Diccionario cubano de habla popular y vulgar*. Madrid: Agualarga Editores, 1998.

———. *La sexualidad en el habla cubana*. Madrid: Agualarga Editores, 1998.

Pellettieri, Osvaldo. "El teatro de Oscar Viale (I)." In Oscar Viale, *Teatro*. Buenos Aires: Corregidor, 1987.

Pérez Cruz, Felipe de J. *Homosexualidad, homosexualismo y ética humanista*. Havana: Editorial de Ciencias Sociales, 1999.

Pérez Turrent, Tomás. "Crises and Renovations (1965–91)." In *Mexican Cinema*, ed. Paulo Antonio Paranaguá, trans. Ana M. López. London: British Film Institute and Mexico City: IMCINE, 1995.

Perlongher, Néstor. *La prostitución masculina*. Buenos Aires: Ediciones de la Urraca, 1993.

Piglia, Ricardo. *Plata quemada*. Buenos Aires: Editorial Planeta, 1997.

Piñeyro, Marcelo, and Marcelo Figueras. *Plata quemada, la película: guión cinematográfico, diario de rodaje*. Buenos Aires: Editorial Grupo Norma, 2000.

Prieur, Annick. *Mema's House, Mexico City: On Transvestites, Queers, and Machos*. Chicago: University of Chicago Press, 1997.

Pronger, Brian. *The Arena of Masculinity: Sports, Homosexuality, and the Meaning of Sex*. London: GMP Publishers, 1990.

Quinn, Sandra. *Pink Noir*. Ph.D. diss., Arizona State University, 2000.

Quiroga, José. *Tropics of Desire: Interventions from Queer Latino America*. New York: New York University Press, 2000.

Rechy, John. *The Sexual Outlaw: A Documentary*. 2d ed. New York: Grove Press, 1984.

Rich, Adrienne. "Compulsory Heterosexuality and Lesbian Existence." In *The Lesbian and Gay Studies Reader*, ed. Henry Abelove, Michèle Aina Barale, and David M. Halperin. New York: Routledge, 1993.

Román, David. "Tropical Fruit." In *Tropicalizations: Transcultural Representations of Latinidad*, ed. Frances R. Aparicio and Susana Chávez Silverman. Hanover, N.H.: Dartmouth College, University Press of New England, 1997.

Russo, Vito. *Celluloid Closet: Homosexuality in the Movies.* Rev. ed. New York: Harper and Row, 1987.

Sahuquillo, Angel. *Federico García Lorca y la cultura de la homosexualidad.* Alicante: Instituto de Cultura Juan Gil-Albert, Diputación de Alicante, 1991.

Salessi, Jorge. *Médicos maleantes y maricas: higiene, criminología y homosexualidad en la construcción de la nación Argentina (Buenos Aires: 1871–1914).* Rosario, Argentina: Beatriz Viterbo, 1995.

Santí, Enrico Mario. "*Fresa y chocolate:* The Rhetoric of Cuban Reconciliation." *Modern Language Notes* 113, no. 2 (1998): 407–425.

Savran, David. *Communists, Cowboys, and Queers: The Politics of Masculinity in the Work of Arthur Miller and Tennessee Williams.* Minneapolis: University of Minnesota Press, 1992.

Schifter, Jacobo. *Lila's House: Male Prostitution in Latin America.* New York: Harrington Park Press, Haworth Press, 1998.

Sebreli, Juan José. *La era del fútbol.* Buenos Aires: Editorial Sudamericana, 1998. First published as *Fútbol y masas* (Buenos Aires: Editorial Galerna, 1981).

———. "Historia secreta de los homosexuales en Buenos Aires." In *Escritos sobre escritos, ciudades bajo ciudades, 1950–1997.* Buenos Aires: Editorial Sudamericana, 1997.

Sedgwick, Eve Kosofsky. *Between Men: English Literature and Male Homosocial Desire.* New York: Columbia University Press, 1985.

———. *Epistemology of the Closet.* Berkeley: University of California Press, 1990.

———. "How to Bring Your Kids Up Gay: The War on Effeminate Boys." In *Tendencies.* Durham: Duke University Press, 1993.

Serna Servín, Juan Antonio. "An Ideological Study of the Film *Strawberry and Chocolate.*" *Anuario de cine y literatura en español* 3 (1997): 159–166.

Silverman, Kaja. *Male Subjectivity on the Margins of Discourse.* New York: Routledge, 1992.

Smith, Paul Julian. "Cuban Homosexualities: On the Beach with Néstor Almendros and Reinaldo Arenas." In *Hispanisms and Homosexualities,* ed. Sylvia Molloy and Robert McKee Irwin. Durham: Duke University Press, 1998. First published in Paul Julian Smith, *Vision Machines: Cinema, Literature, and Sexuality in Spain and Cuba, 1983–93.* London: Verso, 1996.

———. *Vision Machines: Cinema, Literature, and Sexuality in Spain and Cuba, 1983–93.* London: Verso, 1996.

Stavans, Ilan. "The Latin Phallus." In *Muy Macho: Latino Men Confront Their Manhood,* ed. Ray González. New York: Anchor Books, 1996.

Stock, Ann Marie, ed. *Framing Latin American Cinema: Contemporary Critical Perspectives.* Minneapolis: University of Minnesota Press, 1997.

Taubin, Amy. "Queer Male Cinema and Feminism." In *Women and Film: A Sight and Sound Reader,* ed. Pam Cook and Philip Dodd. Philadelphia: Temple University Press, 1993.

Taylor, Clark L. "Mexican Male Homosexual Interaction in Public Contents." In *Anthropology and Homosexual Behavior,* ed. Evelyn Blackwood. New York: Haworth Press, 1986.

Timerman, Jacobo. *Cuba: A Journey.* Trans. Toby Talbot. New York: A. A. Knopf, 1990.

Trevisan, João Silvério. *Perverts in Paradise.* Trans. Martin Foreman. London: GMP Publications, 1986.

Urbistondo, Vicente. "La metáfora Alejo/Dios en *El lugar sin límites.*" *Texto crítico 7*, no. 22–23 (1981): 280–291.

Valladares, Armando. *Contra toda esperanza.* Barcelona: Plaza and Janés, 1985.

Vallejo, Fernando. *La Virgen de los Sicarios.* Santafé de Bogotá, Colombia: Editorial Santillana, 1994.

Valls, Jorge. *Twenty Years and Forty Days: Life in a Castro Prison.* Washington, D.C.: Americas Watch, 1986.

Viñas, David. *Los hombres de a caballo.* Mexico City: Siglo XXI Editores, 1969.

Warner, Michael, ed. *Fear of a Queer Planet: Queer Politics and Social Theory.* Minneapolis: University of Minnesota Press, 1993.

Waugh, Thomas. *The Fruit Machine: Twenty Years of Writings on Queer Cinema.* Durham, N.C.: Duke University Press, 2000.

Wilkerson, William. "Communism and Homosexuality." In *Reader's Guide to Lesbian and Gay Studies,* ed. Timothy F. Murphy. Chicago: Fitzroy Dearborn Publishers, 2000.

Williams, Craig A. *Roman Homosexuality: Ideologies of Masculinity in Classical Antiquity.* New York: Oxford University Press, 1999.

Wittig, Monique. *The Straight Mind and Other Essays.* Foreword by Louise Turcotte. New York: Harvester Wheatsheaf, 1992.

Xavier, Ismail. "Pornochanchada." In vol. 3 of *Encyclopedia of Contemporary Latin American and Caribbean Cultures,* ed. Daniel Balderston, Mike Gonzalez, and Ana M. López. London: Routledge, 2000.

Young, Allen. *Gays under the Cuban Revolution.* Madrid: Editorial Playor, 1984.

Index

(*Note: Film titles are listed separately and by director*)